Cadbury's CREATIVE CHOCOLATE Cookbook

Cadbury's
CREATIVE
CHOCOLATE
Cookbook

Patricia Dunbar

Hamlyn

London · New York · Sydney · Toronto

Photography by Mike Vines and Richard London, The Photographic
Studio, Cadbury Schweppes, Bournville, Birmingham, except pages 74,
134 and 139 by Bob Challinor of Worcester.

The author and publishers would like to thank the following for kindly
supplying some of the accessories used in the colour photographs:
Kings Norton Cycles, Cotteridge, Birmingham for kindly supplying the
trains shown on page 58
Royal Doulton, page 26
A. Tullet & Sons, Northfield, Birmingham, page 227
Dartington Glass, pages 195 and 219
P. Lyons & Co, Stirchley, Birmingham, page 167

Acknowledgement
I owe a very large debt of gratitude to my team of home economists,
both past and present, and to Carole and Karen for typing it all – my
thanks to them all.

First published in 1978 and 1983 under the titles of
Cadbury's Chocolate Cookbook and *Cadbury's Novelty Cookbook*
by The Hamlyn Publishing Group Limited

Line drawings by Susan Neale and Roberta Colgate-Stone
Front Cover shows: Fingers Cottage, Braemar Men,
Cream Puffs and Cockle Shells

Back Cover Shows: Doboz Torte

This edition published 1984 by
The Hamlyn Publishing Group Limited
London · New York · Sydney · Toronto
Astronaut House, Feltham, Middlesex, England
© Copyright Cadbury Schweppes P.L.C. 1978, 1983 and 1984
© Copyright line illustrations The Hamlyn Publishing Group Limited
1978, 1983 and 1984

ISBN 0 600 32456 7

Filmset in 11 on 12pt Bembo by Tameside Filmsetting Ltd.
Printed and bound in Italy

Contents

The Story Of Chocolate

How it all started

In 1824 a young Quaker, John Cadbury, opened a shop in Birmingham mainly to sell tea and coffee. But he sold certain other things too, as he pointed out in his first advertisement in the Birmingham Gazette on March 1, 1824. 'J.C. is desirous of introducing to particular notice "Cocoa Nibs", prepared by himself, an article affording a most nutritious beverage for breakfast.'

His venture into cocoa was to have far-reaching effects. From a one-man business, the firm of Cadbury Schweppes has become one of the leading food, confectionery and beverage manufacturers in the UK.

Cadbury has revolutionised the eating habits of millions of people. And it all started in the cellar of that small Birmingham shop. Here John Cadbury experimented in the grinding of cocoa beans with a pestle and mortar and found that he could sell more cocoa and drinking chocolate made to his own Cadbury recipe than the unground 'nibs' mentioned in that original advertisement. He mastered the essentials of cocoa and chocolate making which he and his successors were to develop and perfect.

In 1822 only a total of 126 tons of cocoa beans were imported into Britain. Nowadays Cadbury is one of the world's major buyers of cocoa, purchasing over 60,000 tons a year.

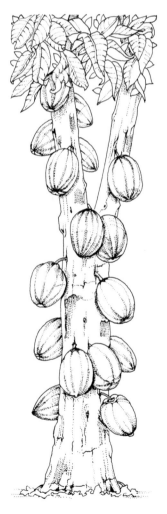

The cultivation of cocoa

Cocoa and chocolate are both derived from the cocoa bean, which grows in pods on the cocoa tree, or *Theobroma cacao*.

The cocoa tree originated in the Amazon forests and now grows as far apart as West Africa and Malaya. The trees can only be cultivated in conditions similar to those of its natural habitat. The climate must be neither too dry nor too cold and there must be shelter from the winds.

In 1879, the first cocoa beans were planted in the Gold Coast, now known as Ghana. Today, West Africa produces about 60% of the world's supply of cocoa, with 30% from South America. The remainder comes from several other countries.

Sometimes the young trees are grown from seeds planted by the cocoa farmer. More usually the seeds are grown in special nurseries and then transplanted in the cocoa farm. The

Cocoa pods, showing beans inside

trees start bearing fruit when they are four or five years old. In shape and size, they resemble an English apple tree but have broad, luxuriant leaves, and the fruit or pods grow from both the trunk and branches. Inside each pod are 20 to 40 seeds like plump almonds and covered by a sweet, white pulp. These seeds are the cocoa beans.

In West Africa, the pods are harvested during the last three months of the year. The pulp and seeds are scooped out and formed into a heap on a layer of large leaves. More leaves are used to cover the heap to keep off the rain and keep in the warmth. The fermentation which now takes place is a vital stage in the cocoa and chocolate making process, developing chocolate flavour as we know it and removing the astringency of the unfermented bean. The fermentation process takes five or six days and the contents of the heap must be turned from time to time as it proceeds. (Sometimes fermentation is carried out in a cascade of boxes and the beans are dropped from one box to another to attain this mixing.) During fermentation, alcohol and acidic, vinegar-like liquids are produced and drain away and the temperature rises to about 50°C/122°F. When fermentation is complete, the wet mass of beans is dried, usually by being spread out in the sun.

The dried and fermented beans are packed into bags containing about 63 kg. Samples are drawn for inspection and grading. Some beans are cut open and the colour determines whether fermentation has been carried out correctly—a well-fermented bean has a characteristic chocolate brown colour. Checks are also made for defects such as mould or damage by insects.

Sacks of beans are stored in dockside warehouses until required for shipment. All beans used by Cadbury in the United Kingdom are processed in one of the world's most modern cocoa processing plants situated at Chirk in North Wales.

Gathering the pods

Historical background

Cocoa was first introduced into England during the seventeenth century. But the Aztecs in Central America had been drinking chocolate hundreds of years before the Spanish explorer Cortez conquered Mexico in 1519. They called it 'chocolatl'. Cortez is said to have tasted his first drinking chocolate in a golden goblet in the palace of the Aztec Emperor, Montezuma. It must have been a rather bitter, pungent drink for the Spaniards improved the flavour by adding sugar and guarded the secret of its preparation for almost a century.

When it was finally introduced into the courts of Spain, Italy, Germany, France and England, chocolate remained an expensive luxury. When the first chocolate house opened in London in 1657, chocolate cost from 50 pence to 75 pence a pound in weight (when the pound sterling was worth far more than in the 1980s) and the high price was sustained for many years by heavy import duties.

It remained a luxury product until Gladstone's time when, in 1853, he lowered the duty to a uniform rate of one old penny per pound. In the early days, it was sold by auction in London. Producers sent samples to manufacturers who roasted and tested the beans and then bid for the variety they preferred. Auctions were known as 'sales by candle'. This was derived from the practice of having a lighted candle with pins stuck at intervals down its side on the auctioneer's desk. The last bid before the pin fell out secured the cocoa beans.

The manufacture of cocoa and chocolate

The cocoa we buy from the local shop is made from cocoa nibs roasted and ground, from which a portion of the cocoa butter has been removed. It takes a whole year's crop from one tree on a cocoa farm to make 454 grams/1 lb of cocoa. Chocolate is made by adding extra cocoa butter and sugar to ground cocoa nibs. In the manufacture of milk chocolate, milk is also added.

In at least two essentials, roasting and winnowing, modern methods of making cocoa and chocolate are similar to those followed by the Mexicans and Peruvians centuries ago.

Chocolate for eating was unknown until early Victorian times and the primitive recipes were only concerned with making a drink from cocoa beans. These were first roasted, generally in earthen pots, then winnowed in the wind to remove the shells. Afterwards they were ground either between two stones or with a stone rolling pin on a stone slab.

These homely methods have become far more sophisticated in the transition to large-scale production and there is no doubt that the finest drinking and eating chocolates of today are vastly superior to anything tasted either by the Victorians or the ancient Peruvians.

Cleaning and Roasting: When the cocoa beans arrive at the factory they are sorted and cleaned. The beans are then roasted in revolving drums. It is through this roasting that the bean takes on its characteristic flavour and aroma, and the shell becomes brittle. Roasting time is about an hour at an effective temperature of 135°C/275°F.

Kibbling and Winnowing: The roasted beans are then broken down into small fragments (kibbled) in preparation for winnowing. In the winnower, the brittle shell is blown away by an 'artificial wind', leaving behind the broken cotyledon of the beans, known in the industry as 'nibs'.

Extraction of cocoa butter: The nibs are ground between steel rollers until the friction and heat of milling gradually reduces it to a thick, chocolate-coloured liquid with the consistency of thick cream. The cocoa nib emerges as liquid, not powder, because it contains about 55% cocoa butter. The mixture is now called 'mass' and solidifies on cooling. This 'mass' is the basis of all chocolate and cocoa products, i.e. Bournville Cocoa, Drinking Chocolate and chocolate confectionery.

Cocoa is made by extracting some of the cocoa butter from it, otherwise it would be too rich to make a palatable drink. About half of the cocoa butter is pressed out leaving a solid block of cocoa. To produce fine high grade cocoa, this is ground and reground until it can be sieved through a fine gauze. Samples are tested in the quality control laboratory.

How chocolate is made

The 'mass' goes straight to the Bournville chocolate factory for the production of plain chocolate. It is different for Dairy Milk Chocolate. Here the 'mass' is sent to 'milk factories' at Marlbrook in the county of Hereford and Worcester and Frampton in Gloucestershire, where it is mixed with fresh full cream milk and sugar which has been condensed into a rich creamy liquid.

This chocolate flavoured condensed milk is then dried in vacuum ovens to give milk chocolate 'crumb' which is taken to the chocolate factories at Bournville and Somerdale.

The Chocolate Factory is the final stage where extra cocoa butter is added to help the processing for the moulding into the familiar bars. After being ground and mixed, both plain and milk chocolate undergo a final pummelling treatment known as 'conching' which gives Cadbury's chocolate its famous smoothness.

After 'conching', chocolate can either be moulded into blocks of, for example, Cadbury's Dairy Milk Chocolate or extra cocoa butter can be added to make it more fluid for use in covering chocolate biscuits or in confectionery.

Using Chocolate Products

Both Bournville Plain and Dairy Milk Chocolate depend to a large extent on cocoa butter for their flavour and characteristic eating qualities. The so-called 'cooking chocolates' usually do not meet the United Kingdom legal definition for cocoa and chocolate products, and therefore have to be suitably labelled. The cocoa butter has been replaced with other fats such as coconut and palm kernel oils, which alters the melting properties to the detriment of the flavour. Some cocoa powder is usually included in these 'cooking chocolates'. Other essences and edible fillers are often added as they are cheaper than the product of the natural cocoa bean.

Cocoa is the most economical chocolate flavour for use in cookery. When a high proportion of starch ingredients are used, such as flour and cornflour, it is generally better to sieve the cocoa in with the dry ingredients. Cocoa is also better when the mixture is to be thoroughly cooked, such as in cakes, biscuits, puddings and sauces. In other recipes, the starch cells should preferably be broken down before cooking. A practical way to do this is by the addition of enough boiling water to the cocoa to make a thick paste. This also enables the cocoa to be easily blended into a recipe.

Drinking Chocolate produces a milder flavour and is sweeter, containing a high proportion of sugar with the cocoa. When used in a recipe, the sugar quantities have to be adapted and generally lowered to counteract the extra sweetness. As the name implies, Drinking Chocolate is particularly suitable for milk drinks.

Cadbury's Flake is made from milk chocolate which is compressed so that thin layers roll against each other, forming flakes. These are then cut into lengths. Flakes are often served with ice cream but can be most useful for cake decorating and in other recipes. Buttons are made from milk chocolate.

Nutrition Chocolate confectionery is classed amongst the most valuable of foods. The high concentration of nutrients can easily be assimilated by the body and are consequently a most suitable food for those taking a great deal of exercise. 28 g/1 oz of plain chocolate provides about one-twelfth the daily requirement of iron in the diet.

Multiply the amount of Calories by 4.2 to obtain the approximate conversion to kilojoules.

Composition of Bournville Cocoa per 28 g/1 oz

Calories	130
Protein	5.4 g
Fats	6.0 g
Carbohydrates	13.8 g
Calcium	31.0 mg
Iron	2.9 mg
Sodium	265.0 mg

Composition of Bournville Plain Chocolate per 28 g/1 oz

Calories	145
Protein	1.1 g
Fats	8.3 g
Carbohydrates	17.3 g
Calcium	10.6 mg
Iron	0.7 mg
Sodium	6.2 mg

Cocoa and chocolate also contain other mineral salts, e.g. phosphorus and potassium, in amounts comparable with many other foods. The milk in milk chocolate adds valuable calcium.

The Developing Art of Entertaining

Throughout history, eating has been a social occasion and 'breaking bread' together a sign of friendship. Sumptuous meals, banquets and feasts, set off by imaginative and eye-catching centrepieces have long been held to celebrate all kinds of important events. The decoration of food to make it look more festive also dates from early times. In ancient Greece, a cook was regarded as an artist who had an important role in society.

The English came to excel in the sweet dishes which formed the dessert course and which were considered to be the most pleasurable part of the meal. English subtleties became renowned all over Europe and were the forerunners of the centrepieces with which the great English and French chefs decorated royal tables in the eighteenth and nineteenth centuries. Elaborate sweet dishes were sculpted or moulded into splendid shapes: lions, birds, crowns, coats of arms; even, as in a feast given by Cardinal Wolsey, the form of a chess board, complete with chessmen.

The cooks were amazingly inventive as it was their chance to please and amaze a great company. They used entirely edible materials – chiefly marchpane, a forerunner of marzipan, stiff fruit pastes and moulded sugar. Later still, chocolate was moulded or carved into wonderous shapes and even today these ingredients are regarded as special.

The Advent of Afternoon Tea

Afternoon tea became popular in Victorian times and this was when the grandest cakes that we know today really developed. The earliest English cakes were spiced and sweetened breads but they soon became more extravagant with icing and decorations. Traditional English rich fruit cakes were developed and became renowned throughout the world and are the basis of many celebration cakes. Birthday cakes, christening cakes, wedding cakes, Christmas cakes and a simnel cake at Easter are still popular. Every country seems to have its own festive specialities – the Christmas gingerbread house in Germany, Russian Mazurka cake or Polish Easter ring are examples.

Celebrations Today

Much of today's food appears quite frugal in comparison with the ostentation of our forefathers. Nevertheless, we still prepare grand meals when the occasion demands and very often the centrepiece is a cake or gâteau. This may be lovingly prepared for another member of the family or for a friend or a special celebration. Today, many people may only bake a special cake four or five times a year. All the more reason for it to be a really super one!

Entertaining with Ease

Some people seem to be natural party givers, able to cope with large numbers of guests on any occasion with seemingly minimum fuss. Others approach the prospect of social occasions, such as children's birthday parties, an inescapable event in every child's calendar, with fear and trepidation.

For both categories, forward planning and a little common sense will help to make all social occasions enjoyable to both guests and hosts. So here are some hints for a successful party whatever the occasion.

● Plan well in advance – the type of party, number of guests, theme (if applicable), food to be served and entertainment to be organised. Try to make as many things as possible in advance. If you have a food freezer, make it work for you.

● As a guide to amounts for a *children's party*, allow 4 – 6 savoury items (including crisps, cheese snacks or sausages), 2 sweet items, ice-cream and jelly, birthday cake and 2 cold drinks. An 850 ml bottle of Schweppes fruit squash will give 20 – 24 servings when diluted.

● For an adult tea party, allow 3 – 4 savoury items, 2 small cakes, 1 slice of a special cake and 2 cups of tea. When large numbers are to be catered for, allow a minimum of 35 g/ 1½ oz of Typhoo tea to a gallon of boiling water.

● Try not to be over-ambitious. Remember the limitations of house size or garden and your culinary ability.

● Send invitations out in plenty of time. Two or three weeks' notice is generally accepted but for formal occasions like weddings, six weeks should be allowed.

● Sort out cutlery, china and glasses the day before. For large parties, it is often a good idea to hire china and glasses. Use paper plates for informal or children's parties. Set the table the night before or designate another member of the family to do it on the day.

● Finally, allow yourself time to relax and change in peace before the guests arrive. You will enjoy the party much more.

Giving a children's party can be the most rewarding form of entertainment but takes a little more effort to organise successfully. One of the high spots of the party is undoubtedly the birthday cake although they are not always actually eaten!

There are lots of ideas in this book to bring cries of delight from all ages.

Fun invitations with matching plates, paper cups and napkins are easily available but why not make the cards yourself, or get older children to help? All that is needed is a template of the design – a teddy bear for a teddy bear's picnic or a zoo animal for an outing to the zoo are examples. Writing the message on a balloon can also be fun. Balloons are a must for games or take-home presents. Children also love streamers and blowers. The cake centrepiece should preferably fit into the chosen theme – such as the Country Cake, with each child being given a toy farm animal as a small present.

Party Games

Every family has its favourite party game and young guests come to expect it in the programme. Blend noisy and quiet games and remember to allow time for free expression – or 'fighting' time as many young boys seem to want! Eight-year olds and above seem to like educational games such as Kim's game, match stick problems, making words or odd man out.

Here are just some of my particular favourites to start you thinking.

Down on the Farm (for younger children)

Evolve a story about a farm (or zoo) mentioning the various animals. The children make the animal noises and on occasions, imitate the actions, amid shrieks of laughter.

Pass the Parcel

Wrap a small present in the centre of a large parcel with many layers of paper. Include a few sweets between the layers. Lots of mess whilst it's being undone but the children do sit down!

Scissors (older children and adults)

A game of observation, handing the scissors round a circle of people and announcing 'crossed' or 'uncrossed' as they are passed. In fact, it is not the scissors you are referring to but your legs!

Team Games

Old favourites include spoon ball (passing a ping pong ball along a line, balanced in teaspoons held in the mouth), passing oranges under the chin, blowing ping pong balls with drinking straws and fanning the kipper.

Useful Facts and Figures

Oven temperatures
The table below gives recommended equivalents.

	°C	°F	Gas Mark
Very cool	110	225	$\frac{1}{4}$
	120	250	$\frac{1}{2}$
Cool or Slow	140	275	1
	150	300	2
Warm	160	325	3
Moderate	180	350	4
Moderately hot	190	375	5
Fairly hot	200	400	6
Hot	220	425	7
Very hot	230	450	8
	240	475	9

Notes for American and Australian users
In America the 8-oz measuring cup is used. In Australia metric measures are now used in conjunction with the standard 250-ml measuring cup. The imperial pint, used in Britain and Australia, is 20 fl oz, while the American pint is 16 fl oz. It is important to remember that the Australian tablespoon differs from both the British and American tablespoons; the table below gives a comparison. The British standard tablespoon, which has been used throughout this book, holds 17.7 ml, the American 14.2 ml, and the Australian 20 ml. A teaspoon holds approximately 5 ml in all three countries.

British	American	Australian
1 teaspoon	1 teaspoon	1 teaspoon
1 tablespoon	1 tablespoon	1 tablespoon
2 tablespoons	3 tablespoons	2 tablespoons
$3\frac{1}{2}$ tablespoons	4 tablespoons	3 tablespoons
4 tablespoons	5 tablespoons	$3\frac{1}{2}$ tablespoons

Spoon measures All spoon measures given in this book are level unless otherwise stated.

✳ Denotes freezing instructions.
Denotes helpful hint.

An Imperial/American guide to solid and liquid measures

Imperial	American
Solid measures	
1 lb butter or margarine	2 cups
1 lb flour	4 cups
1 lb granulated or caster sugar	2 cups
1 lb icing sugar	3 cups
Liquid measures	
$\frac{1}{4}$ pint liquid	$\frac{2}{3}$ cup liquid
$\frac{1}{2}$ pint	$1\frac{1}{4}$ cups
$\frac{3}{4}$ pint	2 cups
1 pint	$2\frac{1}{2}$ cups
$1\frac{1}{2}$ pints	$3\frac{3}{4}$ cups
2 pints	5 cups ($2\frac{1}{2}$ pints)

Useful baking tin comparisons
There are many occasions when the exact sized baking tin may not be available or when you wish to make a particular cake recipe in another shape. The following conversions might prove useful.
800-ml/$1\frac{1}{2}$-pint pudding basin =
  14-cm/$5\frac{1}{2}$-in round deep cake tin
1.2-litre/2-pint pudding basin =
  15-cm/6-in round deep cake tin or 12.5-cm/5-in square deep tin

Loaf tins
1-kg/2-lb loaf tin =
  28 × 18-cm/11 × 7-in shallow tin
0.5-kg/1-lb loaf tin =
  18-cm/7-in square shallow cake tin or a
  33 × 23-cm/13 × 9-in Swiss roll tin
The capacity of a round tin is equal to that of a square cake tin which is 2.5 cm/1 in smaller in size, for example a 20-cm/8-in round tin holds the same quantity as an 18-cm/7-in square tin. This can be adjusted to the nearest 1.25 cm/$\frac{1}{2}$ in.

Cooking times given in the recipe will have to be adjusted to suit the new tin size.

NOTE: When making any of the recipes in this book, only follow one set of measures as they are not interchangeable

First Things First

No matter how complicated a decoration, the cake underneath tastes just as appetising as it looks. In this chapter are the basic cake and icing recipes which are used for many of the cakes in this book. You will also find clear instructions for lining cake tins and making piping bags – all the information you need for completing the design.

Chocolate Victoria Sandwich Cake

Illustrated on page 10

Metric		Imperial
175 g	margarine	6 oz
175 g	caster or soft brown sugar	6 oz
3	eggs, size 2 or 3	3
150 g	self-raising flour	5 oz
25 g	Bournville Cocoa	1 oz
	Filling	
350 g	chocolate butter icing (page 21)	12 oz
2 (19-cm)	round shallow cake tins	2 (7½-in)
	greaseproof paper	

Prepare the cake tins by cutting out two circles of greaseproof paper the same size as the base of the tins. Grease the tins, put the paper circles in them and also grease the paper.

Cream the margarine and sugar together really well until pale and soft; an electric mixer is ideal for this. Add the eggs one at a time, with a spoonful of flour if the mixture shows any signs of curdling. Sift the flour and cocoa together and fold in, adding a little milk or orange juice if the mixture is too dry, as it should have a soft dropping consistency. Divide the mixture in spoonfuls evenly between the tins, then spread the surface flat and hollow out the centres slightly. Bake in the centre of a moderately hot oven (190 c, 375 f, gas 5) for about 30 minutes until risen and springy to the touch. Leave the cakes in the tin for a moment before turning out on to a wire tray. Peel off the greaseproof paper and immediately turn the cakes over again to avoid any marks on the top. Leave to cool.

Sandwich the cakes together with half the butter icing and spread the remainder on top. Mark with a fork.

Wrap and freeze the cake complete or place greaseproof paper in between the cake layers and freeze them separately.

A 2-egg quantity of the cake mixture can be made in two 15–18-cm/6–7-in sandwich tins. If preferred, plain flour can be used instead of self-raising flour, allowing 5 ml/ 1 teaspoon of baking powder to every 50 g/2 oz of the flour and cocoa weighed together.

The cake mixture can also be cooked in a deep cake tin but increase the baking time to about 55 minutes. Cover with a piece of paper if the cake becomes too crisp on top during cooking. Stand deep and loose-based tins on baking trays.

Plain Victoria sandwich cake
To make a plain Victoria sandwich cake, omit the cocoa from the above recipe and use 175 g/6 oz self-raising flour. Continue according to the instructions.

Cutting circles of grease-proof paper for sandwich tins *It is useful to have a store of greaseproof paper circles ready cut out for instant use.*

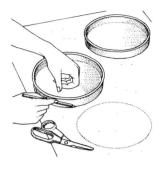

Lining a deep cake tin

1 *Cut a piece of greaseproof paper to fit the base. Cut a strip of paper, deeper than the sides of the tin and long enough to go all around the inside. Make regular snips about 1 cm/$\frac{1}{2}$ in deep along the strip of paper.*

2 *Grease the tin and ease the strip of paper in around the side, overlapping the snipped edge in the base. Lay the piece neatly in the base of the tin and grease thoroughly.*

One Stage Method

Use soft margarine. Mix all the ingredients together in a bowl; 5 ml/1 teaspoon baking powder may also be added to the cake ingredients. Beat really hard for 2–3 minutes until completely blended. Bake the cakes as usual.

Chocolate Cake

Illustrated on page 26

Metric		Imperial
1	chocolate Victoria sandwich cake	1
	double quantity chocolate butter icing	
	(see page 21)	
7	Bournville Dark plain chocolate	7
	triangles (see page 23)	
	piping bag and star pipe	

Sandwich the cakes together with the butter icing and spread it over the top and sides of the cake. Put the remainder into the piping bag. Mark a semi-circle on top of the cake and fill this in with stars of icing. Pipe stars round the top and bottom edges. Stick triangles into half the cake, dust with icing sugar.

Mocha Cake

Illustrated on page 26

Metric		Imperial
1	chocolate Victoria sandwich cake	1
about 10 ml	instant coffee powder	about 2 teaspoons
550 g	vanilla butter icing	1 lb 4 oz
	(see page 21)	
3 squares	Bournville Dark plain chocolate	3 squares
15 ml	coffee beans	1 tablespoon
	greaseproof paper piping bag	

Dissolve the coffee in a little boiling water and mix it into the butter icing. Sandwich cakes with some of the icing.

Cover the top and sides with a thick layer of icing. Make a ribbed pattern round the side by drawing a scraper with a serrated edge along the butter icing, or use a fork for a similar effect. Put the cake on to a plate. Mark into eight sections. Decorate with stars round the top and bottom and one in the centre. Melt the chocolate in a small bowl over hot water, put in a paper piping bag and cut off the tip. Make an 'S' shape pattern on each of the sections. Complete the cake by putting a roasted coffee bean on to each star; these can be eaten.

Chocolate Swiss Roll

Illustrated on page 10 and opposite

Metric		Imperial
3	**fresh eggs, size 2**	3
75 g	**caster sugar**	3 oz
	vanilla essence	
75 g	**plain flour**	3 oz
25 g	**Bournville Cocoa**	1 oz
20 ml	**warm water**	1 tablespoon
	Filling	
175 g	**plain butter icing (page 21) or**	6 oz
142 ml	**whipping cream**	¼ pint
23 × 33-cm	**Swiss roll tin, greased and lined**	9 × 13-in
	greaseproof paper	

Whisk the eggs, sugar and a few drops of essence in a bowl over a pan of hot water, or use an electric mixer. Whisk hard until the mixture is thick enough to leave a definite trail from the whisk. Sift the flour and cocoa together then fold in with a metal spoon, adding the water at the same time. Ensure there are no pockets of flour left. Turn the mixture into the prepared tin and tilt the tin to level the mixture – on no account spread it. Bake in a pre-set, fairly hot oven (200 c, 400 f, gas 6) for about 12 minutes until cooked when the sponge will be risen and springy to the touch.

Dust a large piece of greaseproof paper with caster sugar. Carefully turn the Swiss roll out on to this and gently peel off the paper. With a large sharp knife, trim off the crisp edges. Mark a dent along one short side about 1 cm/½ in from the edge. Lay another piece of greaseproof paper on top and roll the cake up, with the paper inside. Leave on a wire tray to cool.

Carefully unroll the Swiss roll and take off the paper. Spread with butter icing or whipped cream, taking it right up to the edges. Starting with the marked end, roll up as tightly as possible without squashing the cake. Dust with sugar: icing, caster or even soft brown sugar for example. Or decorate with extra cream and pieces of Cadbury's Flake as illustrated opposite.

Plain Swiss roll To make a plain Swiss roll, omit the cocoa and continue as above. Spread jam over the freshly cooked sponge and roll up as described.

Freezes well.

This type of sponge depends on the air being whisked in for its success. When the mixture is stiff enough, you should be able to write three initials in it without them disappearing immediately. If in doubt, continue whisking for a few more minutes. If you are repeatedly unsuccessful with this technique, try adding 5 ml/1 teaspoon baking powder with the flour.

To line a Swiss roll tin

1 *Cut out a rectangle of greased paper bigger than the tin itself. Grease the tin.*

2 *Lay the paper in the tin, pressing it right into the corners. Make a cut down into the corners of the paper and fold the edges behind each other to make a neat corner. Also grease the paper.*

1 Whisk until mixture is thick enough to leave a visible trail.

2 Fold in the flour and Bournville cocoa sieved together, using a light wrist action. Make sure no pockets of flour are left.

3 Turn the Swiss roll out on to a piece of sugared paper, trim the edges and roll up with the paper inside.

4 Fill and decorate the Swiss roll with whipped cream and Cadbury's Flakes.

Pudding Basin Cake

Illustrated on page 10

Metric		Imperial
175 g	**butter or margarine**	6 oz
175 g	**caster sugar**	6 oz
3	**eggs, size 3**	3
150 g	**self-raising flour**	5 oz
5 ml	**baking powder**	1 teaspoon
25 g	**Bournville Cocoa**	1 oz
1	**small orange**	1
	orange food colouring	
1.2-litre	**ovenproof basin, greased**	2-pint
	baking tray	

Cream the fat and sugar until light in colour and texture. Gradually add the eggs, then fold in the flour and baking powder sifted together. In a separate mixing bowl, blend the cocoa to a paste with a little boiling water, then add half the cake mixture to it and mix well. Finely grate the orange rind and add it to the remaining mixture with enough strained orange juice to make a soft dropping consistency. Add colouring if liked. Spoon the two mixtures alternately into the basin then swirl through *only once* so that they remain separate. Smooth the top and hollow out the centre slightly. Stand the cake on a baking tray and cook in a moderate oven (180 C, 350 F, gas 4) for 1–1¼ hours until cooked through. When cooked, a warm skewer inserted into the middle of the cake should come out cleanly. Turn out and cool on a wire tray.

Use the cake as required in a variety of recipes.

Chocolate Buns

This recipe can be made using a 3 egg quantity in which case it will make 25–30 buns. Do not be tempted to fill the paper cases too full if the buns are to be iced.

Additional flavourings are easy to add for variety. For example, try the *Frosty Bear* cheese cake mixture (page 126).

Metric		Imperial
	2 egg quantity	
	chocolate Victoria sandwich cake (page 16)	
15–20	**paper cake cases**	15–20
	bun tins or baking tray	

Make up the cake mixture, by the one-stage method if preferred. Place the paper cases in the bun tins or close together on a baking tray and put a good teaspoonful of cake mixture into each. Bake in a moderately hot oven (190 c, 375 f, gas 5) for about 15 minutes until the buns are risen and spring back when touched. *Makes 15–20*

Dariole cakes The above mixture can be cooked in 12–15 dariole (castle pudding) tins, depending on their capacity. Cook the cakes in a moderately hot oven (190 c, 375 f, gas 5) for about 20 minutes.

Chocolate Butter Icing

Metric		Imperial
25 g	**Bournville Cocoa**	1 oz
60 ml	**boiling water**	3 tablespoons
175 g	**butter or soft margarine**	6 oz
250–350 g	**icing sugar, sifted**	9–12 oz
	flavouring (optional)	

Dissolve the cocoa in the boiling water, making a paste. Cream the fat to soften it, then add the icing sugar and beat really well until the mixture becomes pale in colour and light in texture. (An electric mixer is helpful.) Mix in the cooled cocoa.

Additional flavouring of vanilla or peppermint essence, dissolved instant coffee or the finely grated rind of half an orange may be added.

Store in a covered container in the refrigerator or freezer. The quantity of butter icing given in the recipes refers to the weight of butter and sugar added together.

This recipe makes enough butter icing to fill and decorate a 20-cm/8-in sandwich cake.

Plain butter icing Omit the Bournville Cocoa but make as above, adding a few drops of vanilla essence.

Add grated lemon rind and a little juice instead of the vanilla essence to make lemon butter icing.

Melting chocolate: Place the bar of Bournville Dark plain chocolate whole, or broken into squares, in a bowl suspended over a pan of hot, not boiling, water. Leave to melt.

Making chocolate leaves: Choose unblemished rose leaves. Dip leaves into melted Bournville Dark plain chocolate, coating the veined side. Place on waxed paper. When dry, carefully peel away the leaf.

Making chocolate shapes: Trace outlines on plain paper. Cover with waxed paper. Fill a greaseproof paper piping bag with melted chocolate and follow the shape. Fill in centres as necessary.

Peel off the waxed paper carefully. If the chocolate hardens in the bag, heat in the oven or over hot water until softened. Store shapes in an airtight container.

Making chocolate curls: Scrape a vegetable peeler along the flat side of a bar of Bournville Dark plain chocolate, shaving it off into curls. Handle carefully. Alternatively, grate coarsely.

Making chocolate caraque: Spread melted Bournville Dark plain chocolate on to Formica or marble. Leave to set. Using a sharp knife, scrape the chocolate, allowing it to peel off into long curls.

Making chocolate cut-outs: Spread melted Bournville Dark plain chocolate thickly on waxed paper. Leave to set. Cut out shapes with cocktail cutters. Any chocolate remaining may be melted for use again.

Making chocolate squares or triangles: Spread melted Bournville Dark plain chocolate into a rectangle and set. Use a ruler to mark into even-sized squares. Cut squares diagonally for triangles. Cut with a sharp knife.

Glacé Icing

Metric		Imperial
225 g	**icing sugar, sifted**	8 oz
about 40 ml	**warm water or fruit juice**	about 2 tablespoons
	food colouring	

Stir the icing sugar with the water or preferably fruit juice, in a bowl, adding colouring if needed. Mix until absolutely smooth and use immediately as a skin quickly forms on the surface.

This amount is enough to coat the top of a popular sized (15–20-cm/6–8-in) sponge.

Royal Icing

Metric		Imperial
225 g	**icing sugar, sifted**	8 oz
1	**egg white, size 2**	1
5 ml	**glycerine**	1 teaspoon
5 ml	**lemon juice, strained**	1 teaspoon

Beat all the ingredients together, preferably with an electric mixer, until the icing is absolutely white and standing in peaks. The longer it is beaten, the better the icing will be. Always keep prepared icing covered until it is used.

Cup Cake Icing

Metric		Imperial
50 g	**butter**	2 oz
60 ml	**water**	3 tablespoons
225 g	**icing sugar**	8 oz
50 g	**Bournville Cocoa**	2 oz

Melt the butter and water in a saucepan. Take off the heat before sifting in the icing sugar and cocoa. Beat until smooth and glossy. Use the icing warm to coat a batch of small cakes.

This quantity will coat 25–30 small cakes.

To make a greaseproof paper piping bag

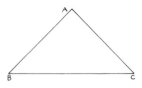

1 *Cut a square of greaseproof paper at least 25 cm/10 in. in diameter, fold in half diagonally, forming a triangle. Make a small slit in the centre of the folded line to help give a sharper point.*

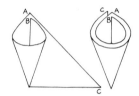

2 *Take corner (B) and roll it so that it lies inside the corner (A).*
3 *Bring corner (C) round the outside of the bag so that it lies exactly behind (A).*

4 *Adjust paper so that all corners are together and there is a sharp tip to the bag.*
5 *Fold over point (A) two or three times to keep bag together.*
6 *If an icing pipe is used, snip a small piece off the point and drop in selected pipe. To use the bag on its own, fill with icing then cut off tip.*

Family Cakes

Home-made cakes are always popular and well worth making on any occasion. We have included a selection which range from the plain and simple, requiring little time or effort to make, through to an intriguing selection of shapes and luscious flavours for family get-togethers. Careful preparation and cooking is important; weigh and measure ingredients accurately to ensure perfect results every time.

Cherry Sparkle

Illustrated on page 31

The cake would be better frozen without the topping. Wrap, seal and label. Prepare the topping while the cake is defrosting and if it is really hot, it will stick satisfactorily.

This one-stage method is excellent but a good result depends on beating the ingredients really well together.

Metric		Imperial
175 g	**self-raising flour**	6 oz
25 g	**Bournville cocoa**	1 oz
5 ml	**baking powder**	1 teaspoon
175 g	**soft margarine**	6 oz
175 g	**caster sugar**	6 oz
3	**eggs**	3
	Topping	
125 g	**glacé cherries**	4 oz
50 g	**walnut halves**	2 oz
125 g	**pineapple or apricot jam**	4 oz
	greaseproof paper	
1-kg	**loaf tin, greased**	2-lb

Cut a double piece of greaseproof paper to fit the width of the tin, allowing a bit extra at either end. Lay this in the tin and grease the paper.

Sieve the flour with the cocoa and baking powder into a bowl. Add the margarine, sugar and eggs, and cream thoroughly until well blended. Spoon the mixture into the prepared tin, hollow out the centre slightly and level off the surface. Bake in a moderate oven (180°C, 350°F, Gas Mark 4) for 50–60 minutes. Poke a skewer into the centre and if it comes out clean, the cake is ready.

While the cake is cooking, prepare the topping. Halve the cherries and put them into a pan with the walnuts and jam. Stir continuously and bring to the boil. Spread this mixture on top of the cake immediately it comes out of the oven. Leave in the tin to cool then carefully lift the cake out.

Feather Iced Cake

Illustrated opposite

Metric		Imperial
1	chocolate Victoria sandwich cake	1
	vanilla or chocolate flavoured	
	butter icing (see page 21)	
about 40 ml	warm water	about 2 tablespoons
225 g	icing sugar, sieved	8 oz
60 ml	Cadbury's chocolate spread	4 tablespoons
1	glacé cherry	1
50 g	chopped nuts	2 oz

greaseproof paper piping bag

Sandwich the cake layers together with butter icing and spread some round the edge. Beat sufficient warm water into the sieved icing sugar to make a fairly thick spreading consistency. Spread this over the top of the cake with a palette knife. Do not lift the knife or cake crumbs will be mixed into the icing. The icing can drip down the sides. Quickly mix a little hot water into the chocolate spread to make it pliable. Fill the piping bag, snip off the end and pipe evenly spaced lines across the top of the cake, in the wet glacé icing. Draw a skewer backwards and forwards, across the chocolate lines, making the feathering effect. This can be done in a fan shape, with the cherry at the base. Press the chopped nuts in to the sides of the cake and leave the icing to set.

To get a good finish with feather icing, work quickly so that the glacé icing does not form a skin before the lines are piped. Thin chocolate glacé icing may be used for the lines, which should be spaced evenly apart for a neat appearance.

Button Cake

Illustrated opposite

Metric		Imperial
1	chocolate Victoria sandwich cake	1
	vanilla butter icing (see page 14)	
1	packet Cadbury's Buttons	1

Victoria Sandwich Variations: Chocolate Cake (see page 17); Mocha Cake (see page 17); Sunshine Fruit Ring (see page 32); Christmas Tree Sparkle (see page 32); Button Cake; Feather Iced Cake

Sandwich the cakes with butter icing and spread it over the top. Mark lines with a fork in both directions so that there is a trellis effect. Stick the Buttons in at an angle round the edge.

Bournvita Loaf

Illustrated on page 31

Metric		Imperial
225 g	**self-raising flour**	8 oz
	pinch of salt	
50 g	**Bournvita**	2 oz
50 g	**soft brown sugar**	2 oz
50 g	**mixed dried fruit**	2 oz
50 g	**stoned dates**	2 oz
40 ml	**golden syrup**	2 tablespoons
125 ml	**milk**	$\frac{1}{4}$ pint
0.5-kg	**loaf tin,**	1-lb
	greased and base lined	

Wrap the loaf in foil or a polythene bag, seal and label. Freeze for up to 3 months. Defrost at room temperature, for about 4 hours.

Do not open the oven door until the minimum cooking time is completed. A draught can cause the loaf to sink in the middle. This loaf keeps well in an airtight tin.

Sieve the flour with the salt. Mix in the Bournvita, sugar and dried fruit. Chop the dates then add them too. Using a hot spoon, measure the syrup into the mixture and add enough milk to make a soft dropping consistency. Turn into the prepared tin, level the surface and bake in a moderate oven (180°C, 350°F, Gas Mark 4) for 50–60 minutes. Test with a warm skewer to see that the loaf is cooked. Cool in the tin and turn out later. Peel off the greaseproof paper.

Serve in slices with butter.

Crusted Marble Cake

Illustrated on page 35

Metric		Imperial
175 g	**margarine**	6 oz
175 g	**caster sugar**	6 oz
3	**eggs**	3
150 g	**plain flour**	5 oz
15 ml	**baking powder**	3 teaspoons
2.5 ml	**vanilla essence**	$\frac{1}{2}$ teaspoon
25 g	**Bournville cocoa, sieved**	1 oz
20 ml	**milk**	1 tablespoon
75 g	**Bournville Dark plain chocolate**	3 oz
18-cm	**square deep cake tin,**	7-inch
	greased and base lined	

Wrap, seal, label then freeze the cake complete.

Self-raising flour can be used instead of the flour and baking powder. If a square cake tin is not available, use a 19-cm/ 7½-inch round deep tin. The cake can be left whole or cut into pieces when cool.

Beat the margarine and sugar well together, and add the eggs one at a time. Sieve the flour and baking powder together and fold into the mixture. Put half the mixture into another bowl. Mix the vanilla essence into one amount and the sieved cocoa and the milk into the other, making sure they are thoroughly mixed. Place alternate spoonsful of the different coloured cake mixture in the prepared tin. Carefully smooth over the top and hollow out the centre.

Melt the chocolate in a bowl over hot water. Spread the chocolate over the chocolate cake mixture in the tin but do not worry if it spreads a little. Bake in a moderately hot oven (190°C, 375°F, Gas Mark 5) for about 40 minutes. Leave the cake in the tin just long enough for the chocolate to harden enough to handle then turn out on to a wire tray to cool.

Butterscotch Cake

Freeze the complete cake. Pack carefully, seal and label.

Substitute the milk in the frosting for some of the evaporated milk in the cake recipe, which makes an even creamier frosting. Make up the difference with water in the cake.

Metric		Imperial
200 g	**self-raising flour**	7 oz
2.5 ml	**salt**	$\frac{1}{2}$ teaspoon
40 ml	**Bournville cocoa**	2 tablespoons
225 g	**caster sugar**	8 oz
125 g	**soft margarine**	4 oz
2	**eggs**	2
I	**small can evaporated milk**	I
5 ml	**vanilla essence**	I teaspoon
	Frosting	
125 g	**butter**	4 oz
125 g	**soft brown sugar**	4 oz
60 ml	**milk**	3 tablespoons
5 ml	**vanilla essence**	I teaspoon
350 g	**icing sugar**	I2 oz
2 18-cm	**round shallow cake tins,**	2 7-inch
	greased and base lined	

Sieve the flour, salt and cocoa together. Add the sugar. Rub in the margarine. Beat the eggs with the evaporated milk and vanilla essence then beat the liquid into the dry ingredients, rather like making a batter. When it is thoroughly mixed, divide the soft cake mixture evenly between the tins and smooth over the surfaces. Bake in a moderate oven (180°C, 350°F, Gas Mark 4) for 35–40 minutes. Turn out to cool on a wire tray.

To make the frosting, place the butter and sugar in a pan. Stir gently and cook over a low heat until it comes to the boil. Take the pan off the heat, add the milk and the vanilla essence. Sieve the icing sugar into a bowl. Beat in the melted ingredients and continue beating until the frosting is really smooth and quite thick. Sandwich the cakes together with about one-third of the amount and cover the cake with the remainder. Make swirls in the frosting with a knife or teaspoon. Lift on to a plate.

Flake Slice

Illustrated opposite

Metric		Imperial
3 size 2	**eggs**	3 large
75 g	**caster sugar**	3 oz
50 g	**butter**	2 oz
75 g	**plain flour, sieved**	3 oz
	sherry or fruit juice	
	Icing	
125 g	**butter**	4 oz
25 g	**Bournville cocoa**	1 oz
200 g	**icing sugar, sieved**	7 oz
	Decoration	
50 g	**Bournville Dark plain chocolate**	50 g
4	**large Cadbury's Flakes**	4
4	**glacé cherries, halved**	4
28-cm × 18-cm	**cake tin,**	11-inch × 7-inch
	greased and base lined	
	greaseproof paper piping bag	

Freeze the cake and butter icing but omit the Flake and chocolate decoration. Pack, seal and label.

Crumbled Flake can be used to coat the sides of the cake, instead of the grated chocolate. This will give a rougher texture.

Whisk the eggs and sugar together in a fairly large bowl, over a pan of hot water. An electric mixer may be used instead. Whisk until the mixture is stiff enough to leave a good trail. Gently melt the butter. Fold in the sieved flour with the butter, making sure that no pockets of flour remain. Pour into the prepared tin. Bake in a fairly hot oven (200°C, 400°F, Gas Mark 6) for about 20 minutes until the cake is cooked and springy when touched. Turn out and cool on a wire tray.

Slice the cake lengthways through the middle then again lengthways, making four long strips of cake. Moisten these with a little sherry or fruit juice.

To make the icing, cream the butter well. Blend the cocoa with enough boiling water to make a stiff paste then add to the butter. Beat in the sieved icing sugar. Pile the cake layers on top of each other with a layer of butter icing in between each. Spread it over the top and on the sides too.

Grate the chocolate and cover the sides and the ends of the cake with it. Melt the remaining grated chocolate in a small bowl over hot water. Put the chocolate into a small paper piping bag. Cut each of the Flakes in half with a sharp knife. Arrange the halved Flakes evenly down the centre of the cake, with half a glacé cherry in between. Zigzag lines of chocolate over the top. Lift the cake on to a plate or board.

Cherry Sparkle (see page 25);
Bournvita Loaf (see page 28);
Flake Slice (see above)

Sunshine Fruit Ring

Illustrated on page 26

Metric		Imperial
I	chocolate Victoria sandwich cake	I
175 g	pineapple jam	6 oz
50 g	flaked almonds, browned	2 oz
227-g	can pineapple rings	8-oz
298-g	mandarin oranges	10½-oz
15 ml	arrowroot	3 teaspoons

Sandwich the cakes together with jam and also spread it over the sides. Roll the cake in the almonds to coat the sides. Lift on to a plate. Drain the juice from the fruit and reserve. Arrange the pineapple rings, cut into pieces, with the mandarin oranges to make an attractive pattern on the top. Blend the arrowroot with a little of the fruit juice then bring it to the boil with about 250 ml/¼ pint of juice, stirring continuously. Cover the fruit with the cold glaze.

Christmas Tree Sparkle

Illustrated on page 26

Metric		Imperial
I	chocolate Victoria sandwich cake	I
175 g	butter	6 oz
350 g	icing sugar, sieved	12 oz
5 ml	vanilla essence	1 teaspoon
40 ml	Bournville cocoa	2 tablespoons
2	Cadbury's Flakes	2
I	packet Cadbury's Buttons	I
	silver or coloured sugar balls	

	piping bag and star pipe	

To make the icing, cream the butter with the sieved icing sugar and vanilla essence. Using half the amount, sandwich the cakes together and spread a smooth layer on top. Mix the cocoa with a little boiling water and beat this paste into the remaining butter icing. Coat the sides of the cake, reserving some icing for a decorative edging. Crush the Flakes in the wrapping and press the pieces into the butter icing round the sides. Using a piping bag with a star pipe attached, pipe an edge of chocolate butter icing round the top. Practice making a Christmas tree shape with the Buttons and silver balls on the table before transferring it to the centre of the cake. Lift on to a plate or cake board.

No Bake Fudge Slice

Illustrated on page 21

Wrap, seal, label and freeze the slice complete. Use within 3 months.

Metric		Imperial
125 g	**butter**	4 oz
40 ml	**golden syrup**	2 tablespoons
225 g	**sweet biscuits**	8 oz
25 g	**seedless raisins**	1 oz
50 g	**glacé cherries, quartered**	2 oz
150 g	**Bournville Dark plain chocolate, chopped**	5 oz
	Fudge Icing	
50 g	**Bournville Dark plain chocolate**	50 g
40 ml	**water**	2 tablespoons
25 g	**butter**	1 oz
175 g	**icing sugar, sieved**	6 oz
0.5-kg	**loaf tin, greased with butter and lined**	1-lb

Lining a loaf tin

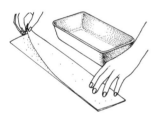

1 *Cut a double strip of paper wide enough and long enough to fit along the length of the tin and over both ends.*

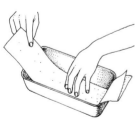

2 *Grease the tin and press the paper neatly into it. Grease the paper.*

Melt the butter and syrup in a saucepan. Crush the biscuits but do not make them too fine. Add the biscuits, raisins, quartered cherries and chopped chocolate. Stir the ingredients together then press them firmly into the tin. Leave overnight to harden. Later turn out on to a board.

To make the icing, break the chocolate into squares and melt in a pan with the water and butter. Heat gently until completely liquid. Off the heat, beat in the sieved icing sugar, beating until the icing is smooth and thick. Spread the icing over the cake then dust with icing sugar.

Holiday Layer Cake

Illustrated opposite

Metric		Imperial
100 g	**Bournville Dark plain chocolate**	$3\frac{1}{2}$ oz
60 ml	boiling water	3 tablespoons
200 g	**self-raising flour**	7 oz
25 g	**Bournville cocoa**	1 oz
175 g	**butter**	6 oz
175 g	**caster sugar**	6 oz
5 ml	**vanilla essence**	1 teaspoon
4	**eggs, separated**	4
	little milk	
	Fudge Icing	
200 g	**Bournville Dark plain chocolate**	7 oz
1	**small can evaporated milk**	1
225 g	**icing sugar, sieved**	8 oz
2 21.5-cm	**shallow cake tins,**	2 $8\frac{1}{2}$-inch
	greased and base lined	

Break up the chocolate and put it into a small bowl with the hot water. Stir until melted and smooth. Sieve the flour and cocoa together. Cream the butter then beat in the sugar and the vanilla essence. Add the soft chocolate then the egg yolks. Fold in the dry ingredients with just enough milk to make a smooth consistency. Whisk the egg whites until stiff then fold them lightly into the cake mixture, making sure no large patches of white remain. Divide the mixture between the prepared tins. Bake in a moderate oven (180°C, 350°F, Gas Mark 4) for 25–30 minutes. Turn out and cool on a wire tray.

To make the icing, break up the chocolate and place it in a fairly large bowl over a pan of hot water. When the chocolate is completely melted, add the evaporated milk and beat the mixture together whilst still over the heat. Take the bowl off the heat and allow the mixture to cool a little before stirring in the sieved icing sugar. Put the bowl of icing into the refrigerator or stand in a bowl of cold water to speed up the setting. When it is hard enough, sandwich the cakes together with about one-third of the icing and spread the rest over the cake. Dab with a knife to form peaks. Lift the cake on to a plate.

Open freeze the completed cake and when hard, wrap, seal and label.

This cake keeps exceptionally well in an airtight tin. The icing can be made separately well in advance then kept until required. It will harden but is easy to soften in a basin over a pan of hot water.

Chip Cake (see page 36); Crusted Marble Cake (see page 28); Holiday Layer Cake (see above)

34

Chip Cake

Illustrated on page 35

Metric		Imperial
275 g	**plain flour**	10 oz
5 ml	**baking powder**	1 teaspoon
175 g	**butter**	6 oz
225 g	**caster sugar**	8 oz
4	**size 2 eggs**	4
	grated rind of 1 orange	
50 g	**Bournville Dark plain chocolate**	50 g
	Icing	
100 g	**Bournville Dark plain chocolate**	4 oz
45 ml	**water**	3 tablespoons
5 ml	**flavourless salad oil**	1 teaspoon
25 g	**caster sugar**	1 oz
	Decoration	
	3 orange jelly slices	
18-cm	**round deep cake tin, greased and base lined**	7-inch

Freeze the cake without the icing. Wrap, label and seal. The icing may be put on to the cake as soon as it comes out of the freezer.

This is a plain cake which keeps well. The mixture is fairly dry and if a slightly softer texture is preferred, the juice of up to half an orange may be added before the flour.

Sieve the flour and baking powder together. Cream the butter and sugar together. Add the eggs one at a time, with a little of the sieved dry ingredients if the mixture shows any sign of curdling. Fold in the remaining dry ingredients and the orange rind. Chop the chocolate into small pieces and stir into the mixture. Place in the prepared tin, hollowing out the centre slightly. Bake in a moderate oven (180°C, 350°F, Gas Mark 4) for 1–1¼ hours. Test with a warm skewer to see that the cake is cooked through in the centre. Lift out on to a wire tray to cool. Peel off the paper.

To make the icing, break the chocolate into a pan. Measure in the water, oil and sugar. Melt the chocolate over a gentle heat, stirring occasionally to blend all the ingredients. Leave the icing to cool and thicken enough to coat the back of a wooden spoon before pouring it over the cake, still on the wire tray. Allow the icing to dribble down the sides. Cut the jelly slices in half and arrange on top. Later when the icing has set, transfer the cake to a plate.

Simply Appealing

Here is a selection of cakes which are easy to decorate and quite irresistible. Whatever the occasion, there is something for everyone – Daisy Dream Cake, perhaps, or Pretty Maid for the older members of the family or for the younger ones, the White Rabbit or Calculator. Each design has a distinct character of its own which is, indeed, simply appealing.

Clarence Caterpillar

Illustrated on page 134

The cake freezes well and can be covered with icing but it is best assembled just when it is required. The biscuits do not need freezing.

Metric		Imperial
1	chocolate Swiss roll (page 18)	1
1	plain Swiss roll (page 18)	1
25 g	Bournville Cocoa	1 oz
350 g	plain butter icing (page 21)	12 oz
	green food colouring	
80 ml	desiccated coconut	4 tablespoons
2	Cadbury's Buttons	2
1	silver doily	1
2	glacé cherries	2
2	wooden cocktail sticks	2
1 packet	Cadbury's Fingers	1 packet

62-cm (approximately)	long board	15-in (approximately)

Cut a slice off each Swiss roll, then cut the two large pieces in half lengthways. Blend the cocoa into a paste with a little boiling water and mix into half the butter icing. Colour the other half green.

Use a little icing to sandwich a chocolate and a jam piece of Swiss roll back together again. Lay the two rolls end to end on the board. Spread alternate broad stripes of chocolate and green icing along the length, covering the rolls completely. Sandwich the two reserved slices of Swiss roll together, then arrange this 'head' at an angle on one end of the roll, pressing it on firmly. Sprinkle the body with coconut. Put a small dot of icing in the centre of each Button and stick both on the front of the head. Curl the doily into a cone shape; trim the edge if it is too large but allow enough for a big, turned-back brim. Stick a cherry on the end of each cocktail stick; place the doily hat in position and press the sticks through the paper into the cake. Finally, halve all the biscuits, cut off one small piece and press it into the head to make a nose. Stick all the rest of the halved biscuits into the base for legs.

Calculator

Illustrated opposite

Metric		Imperial
50 g	**butter, softened**	2 oz
125 g	**soft brown sugar**	4 oz
150 g	**self-raising flour**	5 oz
1.25 ml	**bicarbonate of soda**	$\frac{1}{4}$ teaspoon
1	**egg**	1
2	**ripe bananas**	2
2.5 ml	**vanilla essence**	$\frac{1}{2}$ teaspoon
100 g	**Cadbury's Dairy Milk Chocolate**	$3\frac{1}{2}$ oz
40–60 ml	**milk**	2–3 tablespoons
	Filling and icing	
1 large	**Cadbury's Flake**	1 large
1 packet	**dessert topping mix**	1 packet
125 ml	**cold milk**	$\frac{1}{4}$ pint
60 ml	**Cadbury's Drinking Chocolate**	3 tablespoons
1 large packet	**Cadbury's Buttons**	1 large packet
28 × 18-cm	**cake tin, greased and base lined**	11 × 7-in
1	**greaseproof paper piping bag**	1
	plain writing pipe	
	large board or tray	

Store the completed cake in the refrigerator because of the creamy icing. This cake is easier to make on a cool day as the topping can become rather runny if it is very hot.

Measure the bicarbonate of soda carefully as a little too much can give this delicious, easy cake an unpleasant taste.

For a family cake, bake the cake mixture in a 19 cm ($7\frac{1}{2}$-in) round cake tin for the same cooking time. There is no need to ice it.

Use a potato masher to mash the butter, sugar, flour and bicarbonate of soda with the egg, bananas and essence together in a bowl until the mixture has no lumps and is well mixed. Cut each square of chocolate into four then mix into the cake mixture with enough milk to make a dropping consistency. Spread the mixture in the prepared tin and bake in a moderate oven (180 C, 350 F, gas 4) for about 50 minutes until cooked through. Turn out and cool on a wire tray.

Cut a 5-cm/2-in wide slice off one short side of the cake. Assemble the cake on the board, propping up the cut slice with the Flake so that it stands at an angle to one of the short ends.

Whisk the dessert topping with the milk until it holds its shape. Place two spoonfuls in the piping bag fitted with the plain writing pipe; add the drinking chocolate to the remainder, stirring it in evenly. Spread the chocolate mixture evenly all over the cake, including the sides. Pipe the figures and signs of a calculator on the Buttons with the plain topping mixture and place them in position. Pipe a plain white line round the edge to complete the cake. *Serves 12–16*

Animal Bricks (see page 93); Number Biscuits (see page 176); Calculator

Fantail Chicken

Metric		Imperial
3	**eggs, size 2**	3
75 g	**caster sugar**	3 oz
75 g	**plain flour**	3 oz
40 ml	**Bournville Cocoa**	2 tablespoons
5 ml	**baking powder**	1 teaspoon
	Decoration	
450 g	**plain butter icing (page 16)**	1 lb
40 ml	**Bournville Cocoa**	2 tablespoons
1 packet	**Cadbury's Buttons**	1 packet
2 (20-g) bars	**Cadbury's Dairy Milk Chocolate**	2 small bars
4	**glacé cherries**	4
2 (18-cm)	**round shallow cake tins, greased and base lined**	2 (7-in)
	star pipe	
1	**greaseproof paper piping bag**	1

Freeze complete or to save freezer space, finish off the decoration on the thawed cake.

A whisked sponge depends on the air that is whisked into it for a successful rise. If in doubt, whisk the mixture for another 5 minutes; it will not harm the cake.

Birthday candles and holders, particularly red ones, look effective arranged in a curve among the Button tail feathers.

Whisk the eggs and sugar together with an electric mixer, or stand the bowl over a pan of hot water and whisk by hand. Whisk hard until a good trail is visible from the whisk. Sift all the dry ingredients together, then lightly fold into the mixture, ensuring that no pockets of flour remain. Pour into the prepared tins and tip them to level the surface – do not spread the mixture. Bake in a fairly hot oven (200 c, 400 f, gas 6) for about 12 minutes until the cakes are springy and cooked. Cool on a wire tray and peel the paper.

Make up the butter icing. Dissolve the cocoa in a little boiling water then blend into half the icing. Sandwich the cakes together with a layer of chocolate butter icing, then cut in half. Cover one half completely with the plain icing, reserving a little for decoration, and the other half with chocolate icing. Mark the top and sides of both halves with a fork. On a large board or tray perhaps, arrange the two pieces of cake touching in the middle and protruding at either end, as shown in the picture. Fit the star pipe into the piping bag. Place the reserved plain butter icing into the bag, then pipe an eye and a small patch for the wing. Stand the lightly polished Buttons upright in the plain cake tail piece. Cut one bar of chocolate into two triangles and position as the long legs at the base of the cake. Make four triangles from the other bar of chocolate and use two as the beak and two for wings. Cut a serrated edge on the cherries and pile them up near the eye as the cock's comb.

Lucy Ladybird

Illustrated on page 42

The cake can be frozen complete if wrapped carefully, ideally in a large polythene rigid container. Otherwise, wrap in foil or a large polythene bag, seal, label and freeze. Allow about 4 hours at room temperature for the cake to thaw.

Choose a wide bowl so that the ladybird will turn out nice and round. Rub the Buttons in your hands before sticking them on to the cake.

Metric		Imperial
175 g	margarine	6 oz
175 g	caster sugar	6 oz
3	eggs	3
150 g	self-raising flour	5 oz
5 ml	baking powder	1 teaspoon
25 g	Bournville cocoa	1 oz
	Decoration	
50 g	desiccated coconut	2 oz
80 ml	water	4 tablespoons
	red food colouring	
125 g	butter	4 oz
175 g	icing sugar, sieved	6 oz
30 ml	Bournville cocoa	1 tablespoon
about 23 cm	thin strip of liquorice	about 9 in
1	packet Cadbury's Buttons	1
2	currants	2

1.2-litre	**ovenproof basin, greased**	2-pint

Cream the margarine and sugar together really well. Gradually beat in the eggs with a spoonful of the flour. Sieve the flour, baking powder and cocoa together and fold in. Add a little milk if the mixture is too dry. Turn into the prepared basin and bake in a moderate oven (180°C, 350°F, Gas Mark 4) for about 1 hour. Test with a warm skewer to see that the cake is cooked in the centre. Leave in the basin to cool then turn out.

Mix the coconut with the water and stir in some bright red colouring to make it really red. Spread the coconut on a baking tray and dry in a slow oven (140°C, 275°F, Gas Mark 1) for about 1 hour. A warm airing cupboard would also be suitable but it will take a little longer.

To make the butter icing, cream the butter with the sieved icing sugar. Blend the cocoa with a little boiling water and stir into the icing. Spread icing over the flat, top side of the cake. Cut the cake in half down the middle and press the two iced surfaces together, making a mound. Lift the cake on to a flat plate or a cake board. Cover the cake with the remaining butter icing. Shape one end slightly more into a point for the 'head'. Press the dry, red coconut on to most of the cake, leaving the front area clear. Mark a line with a skewer as a guide. Split part of the liquorice and make a 'V' on the top then continue the line down the middle of the

back. Mark lines on the face with liquorice too (as illustrated). Stick Buttons at intervals on to the coconut to make the 'spots'. Arrange two Buttons in position for the 'eyes' and stick the currants in the centre. The ladybird is now complete.

Birthday candles and holders can be stuck into the cake along the top, or extra butter icing can be piped round the base for them.

Harriet Hedgehog

Illustrated opposite

Open freeze the complete cake. Wrap in foil then in polythene; label and seal. Allow at least 4 hours for the cake to thaw at room temperature.

Metric		Imperial
1 quantity	**cake mixture for Lucy Ladybird**	1 quantity
	(see page 41), made in the	
	same size bowl	
	Decoration	
125 g	**butter**	4 oz
175 g	**icing sugar, sieved**	6 oz
30 ml	**Bournville cocoa**	1 good tablespoon
2	**large packets Cadbury's Buttons**	2
1	**glacé cherry**	1
2	**roasted coffee beans or**	2
	seedless raisins	

Have the chocolate cake ready. Make the icing by beating the butter with the sieved icing sugar. Dissolve the cocoa in a very little boiling water and mix into the butter icing.

Spread the flat, top side of the cake with butter icing then cut it in half down the middle. Sandwich the two ends covered with icing together. Spread butter icing all over the cake and lift it on to a plate or cake board. Put a little extra icing at one end and form this into a point for the 'snout'. Cut each Button in half and stick them into the butter icing at an angle, covering all the cake except the front quarter. Make the points go in the same direction as they represent 'spines'. Mark the 'face' with a fork and put the cherry on the end, with the coffee beans or raisins in position for the 'eyes'.

Harriet Hedgehog (see above); Lucy Ladybird (see page 41)

Fingers Cottage

Illustrated on front cover and page 47

Illustrated on front cover and page 47

Metric		Imperial
4 egg quantity chocolate Victoria sandwich cake		
(page 16)		
	Butter icing	
300 g	**butter or soft margarine**	10 oz
450 g	**icing sugar, sifted**	1 lb
25 g	**Bournville Cocoa**	1 oz
	Decoration	
2 packets	**Cadbury's Fingers**	2 packets
	sugar flowers	
1	**silver sugar ball**	1
	angelica diamonds	
6	**deep bun tins, greased**	6
18-cm	**square deep cake tin, greased**	7-in
	star pipe	
3	**greaseproof paper piping bags**	3
	large board	

The cottage may be wrapped loosely and frozen for about a month.

Cutting the cake

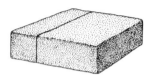

1 *Cut a 7.5-cm/3-in strip off one side of the cake.*

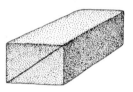

2 *Cut this strip diagonally in half, making 2 long triangular pieces.*

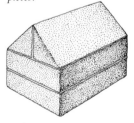

3 *Slice the large piece of cake horizontally through the middle. The triangular strips form the roof when the cake is sandwiched together.*

The cottage also looks attractive with white walls (vanilla butter icing) and chocolate doors and windows.

Winter Log Cabin
A winter log cabin may easily be made in the same way substituting 9 large, halved, Cadbury's Flakes for the Fingers on the roof and using Christmas decorations instead of the flowers.

Make up the cake mixture following the recipe, making a dropping consistency. Half fill the greased bun tins, then put the remaining mixture into the prepared square tin. Hollow out the centre slightly. Bake the cakes in a moderate oven (180 c, 350 f, gas 4), allowing about 25 minutes for the small cakes and 50–60 minutes for the large one. Turn out and cool on a wire try.

To make the butter icing, cream the butter and beating really hard, add the icing sugar. Take out and reserve two good tablespoonfuls. Blend the cocoa to a paste with boiling water and mix evenly into the larger quantity of butter icing.

Cut the cake as shown in the diagram. Slice the large piece horizontally through the middle and sandwich it back together with some of the icing. Cover the top and sides of the cake with icing, then place the two triangular pieces on top so that they form a pointed roof, as shown in the diagram. Spread butter icing over this too and make sure the whole cake is neat. Cut two Finger biscuits in half, then stand them upright in the centre of the roof, to make a chimney. Lay a Finger biscuit flat on either side of the chimney, along the top of the roof, then arrange the remaining biscuits in lines down the slope of the roof, covering the ends of the cake neatly. Lift the cake on to a suitable sized board or tray.

Fill a piping bag with the reserved butter icing. Pipe a door and windows on the cottage and press on the sugar flowers. Pipe a door knob and press in the silver ball. Press a Finger biscuit under each of the end windows and arrange flowers on them to represent window boxes.

Pipe circles of different coloured butter icing on the top of each of the little cakes. Spread the sides with any remaining butter icing and stand halved Finger biscuits round them. Decorate with angelica and a few more sugar flowers if available. Arrange these flower barrels round the cottage.

Fairy Castle

Illustrated on page 87

Shave the chocolate with a warm, sharp knife and it will be quite easy to get a good shape. Store the bits of chocolate in a screw topped jar and use to decorate a dessert or cake.

Metric		Imperial
1	**unfilled chocolate Swiss roll (page 18)**	1
40 ml	**black cherry or blackcurrant**	2 tablespoons
	jam	
142 ml	**whipping cream, whipped**	$\frac{1}{4}$ pint
$\frac{1}{2}$ quantity	**frosting for Anniversary Cake**	$\frac{1}{2}$ quantity
	(page 85)	
	pink food colouring	
2 (20-g) bars	**Cadbury's Dairy Milk Chocolate**	2 small bars
	silver sugar balls	
18-cm	**round silver cake board**	7-in
1	**greaseproof paper piping bag**	1
	plain writing pipe	
2	**silver doilies**	2

Make the Swiss roll; roll it up from the long side, without the filling, and leave to cool. Later, spread the inside with jam and whipped cream, then roll up again to make a long roll. Cut into three pieces measuring about 15-cm/6-in, 10-cm/4-in and 5-cm/2-in.

Make up the frosting according to the recipe instructions. Take out one-third and colour this a delicate pink, then swirl it on the cake board. Spread the white frosting all over the three pieces of Swiss roll and stand them upright in a triangle shape on the board. Cut each bar of chocolate into five pieces. Fill the piping bag with a little frosting and pipe a small square window and door knob on one piece of chocolate. Press a silver ball on to the door knob and press into position on the smallest piece of cake. Shave the remaining pieces of chocolate to a point at one end and pipe a trellis on them for windows. Decorate with silver balls and stick these windows in position around the castle cake. Cut the doilies in half and shape into cones, fastening them with sticky tape, then place the three turrets in position. A little fluffed-out cotton wool could be put round the cake on the table. *Serves about 8*

Rock Garden

Illustrated opposite

Metric		Imperial
1 packet	**Cadbury's Shorties**	1 packet
50 g	**butter**	2 oz
1	**egg**	1
25 g	**demerara sugar**	1 oz
125 g	**stoned dates**	4 oz
50 g	**walnut pieces**	2 oz
50 g	**crystallised ginger**	2 oz
	For the flowers	
350 g	**plain butter icing (page 21)**	12 oz
	food colourings	
225 g	**marzipan**	8 oz
about 6	**chocolate buns and dariole**	about 6
	cakes (page 21)	
1 packet	**marshmallows**	1 packet
	a few cherries, sugar balls and angelica	
19-cm	**non-stick flan tin, well greased**	7½-in
	and the centre lined with waxed paper	
	star pipe	
	several greaseproof paper piping bags	

This is an idea where you can really use your imagination. All that is necessary is the basic flan mixture on which to build the 'garden', and a few small chocolate cakes. Use ingredients at hand to make a colourful display. You are sure to have as much fun creating the garden as you will showing it off at the table.

Break up the biscuits quite roughly. Melt the butter, then cool a little before beating in the egg and the sugar. Chop the dates, walnuts and ginger then stir into the butter mixture with the biscuits, mixing really well so that everything is shiny and coated. Press firmly into the prepared flan tin and leave in the refrigerator overnight to firm up. Dip the base of the flan tin into hot water for 5 seconds then tap the mixture out on to a plate. Peel off the paper.

Divide the butter icing into two or three portions and colour each with a different food colour. Similarly, divide and colour the marzipan. Have a few small cakes ready. Roll out the marzipan and cut out 2.5-cm/1-in circles. These are arranged either round the edge of the cakes or on top, pinched in at one end to represent petals. Pipe butter icing to complete the flowers. The tall flowers are butter icing piped on the dariole cakes with a Cadbury's Finger biscuit or Flake base.

To make the marshmallow flowers, cut down into the marshmallows almost through to the base and into six wedges. Pipe a star of butter icing in the centre. Arrange the larger flower cakes on the biscuit flan and fill in the gaps with the smaller sweets, flowers, an assortment of cake decorations, Cadbury's Buttons, cherries and angelica as shown in the picture. *Serves about 8*

Butterfly Cake (see page 48);
Fingers Cottage (see page 44);
Rock Garden

46

Butterfly Cake

Illustrated on page 47

Metric		Imperial
	3 egg quantity chocolate Victoria sandwich cake	
	(page 16)	
1	**small orange**	1
	Decoration	
225 g	**icing sugar, sifted**	8 oz
	orange food colouring	
2 squares	**Bournville Dark plain chocolate,**	2 squares
	melted	
2 packets	**Cadbury's Buttons**	2 packets
350 g	**plain butter icing (page 21)**	12 oz
25 g	**Bournville Cocoa**	1 oz
1 large	**Cadbury's Flake**	1 large
1	**glacé cherry**	1
2	**thin strips angelica**	2
19-cm	**round deep cake tin, greased**	7½-in
	and based lined	
1	**greaseproof paper piping bag**	1
25-cm	**round cake board**	10-in

Wrap loosely and pack the complete cake carefully in the freezer. Keep for about a month.

To test if a deep cake is cooked, carefully insert a warm skewer into the middle of it. When it is cooked through to the base, the skewer will come out clean. Cool on a wire tray.

Make up the cake mixture, adding the finely grated orange rind and about half the juice, to make a dropping consistency. Spread the mixture in the prepared tin and hollow out the centre slightly. Stand the tin on a baking tray and bake in a moderate oven (180 C, 350 F, gas 4) for 65–70 minutes. Turn out and cool completely on a wire tray.

Cut the cake into three equal layers and decorate the top one first. Use the icing sugar and remaining orange juice left from the cake to make a stiff glacé icing, adding more water if necessary. Colour the icing orange (or yellow) and make it quite a stiff coating consistency. Fill the piping bag with the warm melted chocolate and cut just the tip off the bag. Spread the icing smoothly over the cake, letting it flow over the edge. Pipe a spiral design of chocolate as shown in the diagrams for Cobweb Cake. Draw a skewer outwards from the centre eight times. Immediately cut the cake in half and put a Button on each half as shown in the picture.

Divide the butter icing in half. Blend the cocoa to a paste with a little boiling water and add to one amount. Colour the other half with a little orange colouring. Spread the chocolate butter icing all over one of the remaining layers of cake, including the sides. Mark the top in a spiral with a fork and press polished Buttons all round the side. Place this layer on the cake board.

Cover the remaining sponge with the orange butter icing. Cut in half and arrange the semi-circles back to back, covering about two-thirds of the chocolate base as shown in the picture. Cover the cut edges with butter icing and build up a little icing on the 'wing' ends. Mark straight lines with a fork over the top and sides. Spread orange butter icing on the cut edges of the feather iced cake. Balance the two halves, again back to back, on top of the orange sponge. Rest the Flake down the centre, add a glacé cherry for the head and place the angelica in position. *Serves about 16*

Flower Power

Illustrated on page 75

The cake may be wrapped and frozen with the icing and coconut on it. Add the biscuits and sweets when the cake is thawed.

Metric		Imperial
175 g	**butter or margarine**	6 oz
175 g	**caster sugar**	6 oz
3	**eggs, size 2**	3
175 g	**self-raising flour, sifted**	6 oz
25 g	**desiccated coconut**	1 oz
1	**orange**	1
	Icing and decoration	
60 ml	**Cadbury's Chocolate Spread**	3 tablespoons
500 g	**plain butter icing (page 21)**	1 lb 2 oz
50 g	**desiccated coconut**	2 oz
1 packet	**Cadbury's Milk Assorted Biscuits**	1 packet
50 g	**small jelly sweets**	2 oz
23-cm	**round cake tin, greased and base lined**	9-in

Cream the butter and sugar well together until pale and soft. Beat in the eggs one at a time, adding a spoonful of the flour if the mixture shows any signs of curdling. Fold in the flour and coconut with the finely grated orange rind and just enough juice to make a soft dropping consistency. Spread the mixture evenly in the tin. Bake in a moderately hot oven (190 c, 375 F, gas 5) for about 30 minutes until well risen and springy to the touch. Turn out to cool on a wire tray.

Cut the cake horizontally through the middle and sandwich together again with chocolate spread. Spread the icing smoothly all over the cake, covering the sides too. Immediately press on the coconut and lift the cake on to a large plate or cake board. Decorate with an arrangement of biscuits and sweets as shown in the picture.

Pretty Maid

Illustrated opposite

Metric		Imperial
125 g	**soft margarine or butter, softened**	4 oz
125 g	**caster sugar**	4 oz
2	**eggs, size 2**	2
150 g	**plain flour**	5 oz
15 ml	**baking powder**	3 teaspoons
25 g	**Bournville Cocoa, sifted**	1 oz
	pink food colouring	
100 ml	**redcurrant jelly**	5 tablespoons
350 g	**plain butter icing (page 21)**	12 oz
2 small packets	**Cadbury's Buttons**	2 small packets
	china figure head	
1	**paper umbrella**	1
800-ml	**ovenproof basin, greased**	1½-pint
	flat, serrated icing pipe	
2	**greaseproof paper piping bags**	2

The cake and butter icing may be frozen if carefully packed. Add the Buttons when thawed.

The china heads are available from specialist cook's suppliers, quite often by mail order.

To obtain a different effect, make up half the frosting from the Pantomime Mice recipe (page 128), adding a little pink food colouring. Swirl the frosting over the cake to make a really pretty skirt then press on the Buttons. This method is particularly useful when you wish to avoid piping.

Cream the margarine or butter and sugar together until pale in colour and a light texture. Gradually add the eggs. Sift the flour and baking powder together, then fold into the mixture. Halve the mixture, add the cocoa to one portion and pink food colouring to the other. Place alternate spoonfuls of both mixtures in the basin, swirl through once with a spoon and hollow out the top slightly. Bake in a moderate oven (180 c, 350 f, gas 4) for about 1 hour, until well risen and cooked through. Turn out and cool on a wire rack.

Cut the cake horizontally into three layers, spread with the jelly and sandwich together again. Colour all but three spoonfuls of the butter icing pink. Cover the cake with pink icing and, using a round-bladed knife, mark flowing lines down the skirt. Carefully lift the cake on to a pretty plate. Fit the pipe into the piping bag and fill with pink icing. Pipe a little icing on top of the cake to secure the figure head in position. Pipe a neat row around the top rim of the cake as shown in the picture. Press the figure head firmly on top. Pipe a row of pink icing just above base of the cake, then pipe a row of plain butter icing overlapping it, right on to the plate, as shown in the picture. Polish the Buttons, then, lastly, arrange them in two rows, again following the picture. Push in the umbrella to complete the lady. *Serves about 8*

Pretty Maid; Cockle Shells (see page 125)

Country Cake

Illustrated on page 136

Metric		Imperial
250 g	**soft margarine**	9 oz
175 g	**Cadbury's Drinking Chocolate**	6 oz
140 g	**caster sugar**	4½ oz
3	**eggs**	3
75 g	**self-raising flour, sifted**	3 oz
75 g	**seedless raisins**	3 oz
	Fudge topping	
125 g	**butter**	4 oz
120 ml	**Cadbury's Drinking Chocolate**	6 tablespoons
100 ml	**milk**	5 tablespoons
350 g	**icing sugar, sifted**	12 oz
	Decoration	
25 g	**desiccated coconut**	1 oz
	green food colouring	
1 packet	**Cadbury's Fingers**	1 packet
	small toy tractor and scarecrow	
	green cake candles and holders	
28 × 18-cm	**shallow cake tin, greased and base lined**	11 × 7-in
	rectangular board	

The cake and topping may be frozen. Add the coconut and biscuits later.

The texture of the fudge topping depends on the beating so use an electric hand mixer in the pan, if you have one.

To colour coconut Dampen the coconut slightly before rubbing in food colouring with your fingers. It's messy but effective. Spread on a baking tray and either dry on a sunny shelf or in a low oven for up to 30 minutes. Store in an airtight container for a short time.

Melt 75 g/3 oz of the margarine, then stir in the drinking chocolate; cool. Cream the remaining margarine and sugar together, gradually beat in the eggs with a spoonful of the flour. Fold in the remaining flour, raisins and drinking chocolate mixture. Turn the cake into the prepared tin, spreading it evenly. Bake in a moderate oven (180 c, 350 f, gas 4) for about 50 minutes until risen and cooked. Carefully turn the cake out on to a wire tray and peel off the paper.

Melt the butter for the topping with the drinking chocolate and milk in a pan. Cool and chill in the refrigerator before beating in the icing sugar. Lift the cake on to a board then cover it all over with the chocolate topping. Using a wide-pronged fork, mark furrows on top of half the cake to represent a ploughed field. Colour the coconut with the green food colouring and sprinkle it over the other half.

Leave two Finger biscuits whole and cut a quarter off all the others. Make a fence by standing the larger pieces at intervals round the cake and slanting the smaller pieces in between. Stand the whole biscuits upright at one end with pieces of biscuit sideways between them to make a gate. Add the tractor, scarecrow and candles. *Serves 10–15*

Soldier Boy

Illustrated on page 83

The filled Swiss roll may be frozen but it is probably best to complete the decoration just before it is to be used.

With care, the cake will remain upright for several hours, supported by the large Flake inside the Swiss roll and the firm biscuits.

Add red colouring slowly as it tends to darken on standing.

Metric		Imperial
1	**unfilled chocolate Swiss roll**	1
	(page 18)	
350 g	**plain butter icing (page 21)**	12 oz
2 large	**Cadbury's Flakes**	2 large
	red food colouring	
40 ml	**Bournville Cocoa**	2 tablespoons
1 small packet	**Cadbury's Buttons**	1 small packet
4	**digestive biscuits**	4
10 ml	**desiccated coconut**	2 teaspoons
25 g	**marzipan**	1 oz
2	**pieces flaked almonds**	2
1	**greaseproof paper piping bag**	1
	cake board	

Prepare the Swiss roll according to the recipe instructions. Spread with some of the butter icing then lay a Flake along one short end and roll up the Swiss roll. Colour 75 g/3 oz of the butter icing red for the jacket, then blend the cocoa with boiling water before adding to the remaining icing.

Cover the top and bottom third of the roll with chocolate butter icing and the centre section with red icing, making it neat and smooth. Press two Buttons in the centre. Put a little red icing into the piping bag, cut off the tip and pipe a face on the top portion. Either pipe on a chin strap, or use a piece of red liquorice.

Sandwich the biscuits together with butter icing and spread a little round the edge. Roll the edge in coconut. Spread both ends of the biscuit pile with icing. Stand the decorated Swiss roll upright on the cake board. Arrange the pile of biscuits sideways as a drum, helping to support the 'soldier'. Press Buttons on to the drum sides and as feet for the soldier. Cut the Flake into smaller pieces; keep two thin pieces as drum sticks and arrange the rest round the top of the Swiss roll as a busby hat, making the top and bottom lines as even as possible.

Colour the marzipan red, then roll into two thin pieces and stick it on to the cake to represent arms. Press pieces of almond into the end of the arms and balance the Flake drum-sticks in position. *Serves 6–8*

White Rabbit

Illustrated opposite

Metric		Imperial
25 g	**Bournville Cocoa**	1 oz
150 g	**self-raising flour**	5 oz
2.5 ml	**baking powder**	½ teaspoon
175 g	**soft margarine**	6 oz
175 g	**caster sugar**	6 oz
3	**eggs, size 2**	3
	Decoration	
450 g	**plain butter icing (page 21)**	1 lb
	pink and green food colouring	
225 g	**desiccated coconut**	8 oz
4	**Cadbury's Buttons**	4
2	**silver sugar balls**	2
1	**glacé cherry**	1
1	**liquorice shoe lace**	1
	marzipan carrots (below)	
	ribbon bow	
2 (22-cm)	**shallow round cake tins, greased and base lined**	2 (8½-in)
	large board	

Sift the dry ingredients together for the cakes, then beat in the margarine, sugar and eggs, creaming all the ingredients together really well. Divide the mixture equally between the tins. Bake the cake in a moderately hot oven (190 c, 375 f, gas 5) for 25–30 minutes until well risen and cooked. Turn out and cool on a wire tray. Cut the cakes, carefully following the diagrams.

Mix a few drops of pink colouring into two spoonfuls of coconut. Press plain coconut all over the cake and make the inside of the ears and hind paws out of the pink coconut. Position the two Button eyes and use a little icing to stick a silver ball on each, add the cherry 'nose'. Cut various lengths of liquorice for feet, eyebrows, mouth and finally, long whiskers. Place the marzipan carrots on one paw and the ribbon bow on the neck with the remaining Buttons down the centre of the cake.

Any remaining coconut may be coloured green and sprinkled round the edge of the cake. *Serves about 16*

Carrots Work orange food colouring into 50 g/2 oz marzipan, then divide it into three or four pieces. Roll and shape the marzipan into carrots, mark the surface with short lines and stick pieces of angelica into the end.

The complete cake can be carefully wrapped and frozen for a short time.

To cut the cake

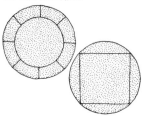

1 *Start by cutting a 4-cm/1½-in wide ring, measured from the outer edge of one cake then cut this ring into eight pieces.*

2 *Make a 16-cm/6½-in square from the other cake, cutting all the cake neatly so that no bits are wasted.*

3 *Halve both large pieces horizontally and sandwich together with butter icing. Place the round piece above the square one on a large board and proceed to assemble the rabbit shape as shown. Stick all the pieces together with butter icing before covering the cake completely with most of the remaining icing.*

White Rabbit; Big Ears (see page 132)

Circus Ring

Illustrated on page 139

Metric		Imperial
125 g	**butter**	4 oz
125 g	**caster sugar**	4 oz
2	**eggs**	2
50 g	**plain flour**	2 oz
50 g	**self-raising flour**	2 oz
25 g	**Bournville Cocoa**	1 oz
50 g	**hazelnuts, finely chopped**	2 oz
25 g	**desiccated coconut**	1 oz
2.5 ml	**vanilla essence**	$\frac{1}{2}$ teaspoon
about 60 ml	**milk**	about 3 tablespoons
	Icing	
40 ml	**blackcurrant cordial**	2 tablespoons
125 g	**plain butter icing (page 21)**	4 oz
	pink food colouring	
1 large packet	**Cadbury's Buttons**	1 large packet

20-cm	**fluted flan tin, greased and base-lined**	8-in
1	**greaseproof paper piping bag**	1
	star pipe	
	candle holders and candles	
	toy animals	

The cake will freeze.

Hollow out the cake mixture so that you can almost see the tin itself in the centre. With slow cooking, the cake should be quite flat, which is important for the appearance.

Cream the butter and sugar together until pale in colour and light in texture. Gradually beat in the eggs, then sift together the flours and cocoa and fold into the mixture. Stir in the remaining ingredients with sufficient milk to give a soft dropping consistency. Spread the mixture in the tin, hollowing out the centre really well and bake on a baking tray in a warm oven (160 c, 325 f, gas 3) for about 1 hour. Turn out the cake to cool on a wire tray.

Carefully spoon the cordial over the flan base to soften it and lift on to a plate. Add a little colouring to the butter icing. Fit the pipe into the piping bag and fill with the butter icing. Pipe a row of overlapping shells on the rim of the flan. Lay the Buttons flat on the top and sandwich two together for the centre as shown in the picture. Arrange suitable circus animals in the ring with any other appropriate figures, such as toy clowns. Keep in a cool place until required.

Serves about 8

Daisy Cream Cake

Illustrated on page 130

This is a particularly light, fresh cream cake so it should be kept in a cool place once made. The combination of flavours is delicious.

Metric		Imperial
4	**eggs, separated**	4
150 g	**icing sugar**	5 oz
65 g	**plain flour**	$2\frac{1}{2}$ oz
14 g	**cornflour**	$\frac{1}{2}$ oz
25 g	**Bournville Cocoa**	1 oz
2.5 ml	**baking powder**	$\frac{1}{2}$ teaspoon
a few drops	**vanilla essence**	a few drops
	Filling and icing	
142 ml	**whipping cream**	$\frac{1}{4}$ pint
60 ml	**redcurrant jelly**	2 good tablespoons
350 g	**plain butter icing (page 21)**	12 oz
	pink food colouring	
8	**white marshmallows**	8
4	**mimosa sugar balls**	4
4	**thin pieces angelica**	4
10 ml	**icing sugar**	2 teaspoons
20-cm	**round loose-based deep cake tin, greased**	8-in
	and base lined	
	baking tray	

Put the egg yolks into a large bowl, sift in the icing sugar, then beat really well until pale and fluffy. Whisk the egg whites stiffly and fold in carefully. Sift the dry ingredients together and fold in carefully with the essence and a little milk if the mixture is too stiff. Turn the mixture into the prepared tin and level the surface by tilting it gently. Bake on the tray in a moderate oven (180 c, 350 f, gas 4) for 40–45 minutes until cooked and springy to the touch. Cool in the tin.

Whip the cream and sieve the redcurrant jelly into it. Slice the cake into three even layers and sandwich them together again with the cream. Colour the icing pale pink and spread it all over the cake, marking smooth lines on the top and the sides with a fork or serrated cake scraper. Slice the marshmallows horizontally, then cut each piece in half. Arrange them in flower shapes on top with a mimosa ball in the centre. Cut the angelica to fit down the side of the cake and place two pieces of marshmallow at the bottom of each strip to make leaves. Sprinkle icing sugar in the centre just before serving. *Serves 8*

Cakes for Compliments

The most striking feature of any party tea table is the cake which forms the centrepiece and is the focal point of all the festivities. Children will delight in such features as the Bournville Belle, for instance, or Treasure Chest and the attractiveness of the designs will win compliments from all your guests.

The Bournville Belle

Illustrated opposite

It is easier to wrap and freeze the iced cakes *before* they are decorated.

This is definitely a party cake as the chocolate biscuits and sweets that are part of the train cake, all add to the fun of a special occasion. The cake can be completely assembled the day before it is required and stored in a cool place overnight.

Metric		Imperial
	For the engine	
1	**unfilled chocolate Swiss roll (page 18)**	1
	For the trucks	
4	**eggs, size 2**	4
125 g	**caster sugar**	4 oz
125 g	**plain flour**	4 oz
25 g	**Bournville Cocoa**	1 oz
40 ml	**warm water**	2 tablespoons
	Decoration	
1 kg	**plain butter icing (page 21)**	2 lb
225 g	**lemon curd**	8 oz
	yellow food colouring	
40 ml	**Bournville Cocoa**	2 tablespoons
2 packets	**Cadbury's Buttons**	2 packets
4	**chocolate mini-rolls**	4
6	**Cadbury's Star Bars**	6
3 large	**Cadbury's Flakes**	3 large
125 g	**fruit pastilles**	4 oz
1 packet	**Cadbury's Fingers**	1 packet
450-g	**loaf tin, greased and base lined**	1-lb
	cotton wool	
1	**greaseproof paper piping bag**	1

Make the Swiss roll according to the recipe instructions and leave rolled up but unfilled.

Make the trucks singly, using half the ingredients for each. Whisk the eggs and sugar with an electric mixer until thick and creamy, when the mixer will leave a good trail. Sift the

The Bournville Belle and Sleepers (see page 145)

59

flour with the cocoa and fold them into the mixture, with the water. Turn into the prepared loaf tin and bake the cake in a fairly hot oven (200 c, 400 f, gas 6) for 10–12 minutes until cooked. Turn the cake out on to a wire tray, clean and prepare the tin as before, then make another cake in the same way.

Prepare the large amount of butter icing with an electric mixer. Stir half the lemon curd and a little yellow colouring into two-thirds of the amount. Dissolve the cocoa to a paste with a little boiling water and blend into the remaining butter icing.

Unroll the Swiss roll, spread with lemon butter icing and roll up tightly. Following the diagrams for cutting the Swiss roll, cut off a 5-cm/2-in slice (1). Make another cut half way down through the roll 5-cm/2-in further along (2), cut horizontally through the middle of the roll, from the sliced-off end in as far as the last cut, and take out the resulting wedge (3). Stand the whole slice on the ledge to make a higher cab for the engine, and stand the smaller piece on end next to it (4). Hold all the pieces together with a little of the lemon icing, then cover the roll completely with icing. Lightly polish the Buttons and press them on to the front, sides and cab of the engine, as shown in the picture, writing the name on the front. Cut one mini-roll in half and stand these funnels on top of the engine, with a piece of cotton wool to represent smoke. Balance the engine on a halved Star Bar. Cut a mini-roll into four and place the slices in position for wheels.

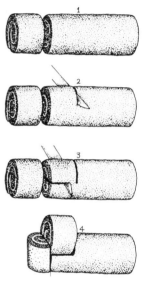

Slice the loaf cakes horizontally through the middle and sandwich them together again with the remaining lemon curd. Cover one of them completely in lemon butter icing and the other in chocolate butter icing. Press Buttons round the sides. Lay the Flakes on top of the yellow truck and pipe two thin lines of icing over the top. Pile the pastilles on the other truck. Stand the two trucks on the Star Bars in the same way as the engine and put mini-roll wheels in position. Join the engine and trucks together with Finger biscuits.

Make a track from the Sleepers (page 145), with the remaining Fingers arranged across them as railway lines.

Serves about 20

Space Invaders

Illustrated on page 63

It's very easy to vary the decorations for these buns using almost any Cadbury brand. This means that the latest space craze can be re-created by the youngsters in the family.

Metric		Imperial
125 g	**soft margarine**	4 oz
75 g	**caster sugar**	3 oz
125 g	**self-raising flour, sifted**	4 oz
20 ml	**Bournville Cocoa, sifted**	1 tablespoon
60 ml	**orange marmalade**	3 tablespoons
2	**eggs**	2
	Decoration	
450 g	**plain butter icing (page 21)**	1 lb
40 ml	**Bournville Cocoa**	2 tablespoons
7	**digestive biscuits**	7
1 packet	**Cadbury's Fingers**	1 packet
14	**glacé cherries**	14
2 small packets	**Cadbury's Buttons**	2 small packets
8	**Cadbury's Coasters**	8
15	**bun tins, greased**	15

Measure the margarine, sugar, flour and cocoa with the marmalade and eggs into a bowl and beat hard until all the ingredients are really well blended. Place a good teaspoonful of the mixture into each bun tin. Bake in a moderately hot oven (190 c, 375 f, gas 5) for 20–30 minutes until risen and springy to the touch. Turn out and cool on a wire tray.

Halve the butter icing. Blend the cocoa to a smooth paste with a little hot water, then mix it into one portion of the icing. Cover seven of the upside-down buns with the chocolate icing and stand each of them on a digestive biscuit. Halve two Finger biscuits and stick them round one bun, with another piece of Finger biscuit standing in the centre. Top the Fingers with halved cherries and a Button in the centre, as shown in the picture. Make the others in the same way.

Cover the base of the remaining buns with chocolate butter icing and the sides with vanilla-flavoured icing. Turn them over and stand them on the chocolate side of the Coaster biscuits. Stick four Buttons round the side of each and three halves of Finger biscuit at an angle on top. *Makes 15*

Flake 7 Rocket

Illustrated opposite

Metric		Imperial
125 g	**soft margarine**	4 oz
125 g	**soft brown sugar**	4 oz
2	**eggs**	2
125 g	**self-raising flour**	4 oz
25 g	**Bournville Cocoa**	1 oz
1	**filled chocolate Swiss roll (page 18)**	1
	Decoration	
450 g	**plain butter icing (page 21)**	1 lb
	yellow food colouring	
25 g	**Bournville Cocoa**	1 oz
7	**Cadbury's Flake from the Family Pack**	7
	gold and silver sugar balls	
1	**dariole tin, greased**	1
18-cm	**round shallow cake tin, greased**	7-in
	and base lined	
1	**star pipe**	1
3	**greaseproof paper piping bags**	3
23-cm	**round cake board**	9-in

The individual cakes may be packed and frozen, ready to assemble later.

It is important to match the size of the hole cut in the round cake with the circumference of the Swiss roll. As a guide, cut round a suitable jam jar or use a sharp plain pastry cutter.

Cream the margarine and sugar together, beat in the eggs, then fold in the flour and cocoa sifted together. Three-quarters fill the prepared dariole tin and tap it lightly on the work surface to remove any air pockets. Spread the remaining mixture in the round tin. Bake the cakes together on a baking tray in a moderately hot oven (190 C, 375 F, gas 5) for about 25 minutes; the smaller cake will take 5 minutes less. Turn out and cool. Have the Swiss roll completed.

Reserve 2 heaped tablespoons of the butter icing and colour this a deep yellow. Blend the cocoa with a little boiling water, then mix the paste into the remaining amount.

Cut a 6-cm/2¼-in circle out of the centre of the round cake and lift the ring on to the cake board. Stand the Swiss roll upright in the hole. Cover with chocolate icing. Stand the small circle of cake on the Swiss roll and sandwich the dariole cake securely on top with icing. Cover all the rocket shape with chocolate icing. Shave one end of six Flakes to stand angled against the Swiss roll.

Fit a bag with a star pipe and fill it with yellow icing, then pipe a zig-zag of neat stars round the rocket base, as shown in the picture. Pipe more butter icing round the nose cone end. Press the last Flake into the top, piping yellow and chocolate icing round its base. Finally, pipe the name in yellow icing and decorate with sugar balls. *Serves 8–12*

Flake 7 Rocket; Flying Saucer (see page 64); Space Invaders (see page 61)

Flying Saucer

Illustrated on page 63

Metric		Imperial
5 egg quantity chocolate Victoria sandwich cake		
(page 16)		
40 ml	**Bournville Cocoa**	2 tablespoons
500 g	**plain butter icing (page 21)**	1 lb 2 oz
1 (50-g) bar	**Bournville Dark plain chocolate**	1 (50-g) bar
8	**Cadbury's Fingers**	8
1 large	**Cadbury's Flake**	1 large
1	**Cadbury's round chocolate biscuit**	1
9	**marshmallows**	9
20-cm	**round deep cake tin, greased and base lined**	8-in
1.2-litre	**ovenproof basin, greased**	2-pint
	small star pipe	
1	**greaseproof paper piping bag**	1
23-cm	**cake board**	9-in

The cake can be frozen complete, but it may be easier to pack it without the decoration, particularly the Finger biscuits and Flake.

The cake in the basin should be cooked above the one in the tin if there is not enough room on the same shelf in the oven. Always cook the deeper mixture towards the top of the oven where the temperature is often just a little higher.

Make up the cake mixture, leaving it marbled if preferred. Spread enough mixture in the prepared tin to come about 2.5 cm/1 in high and hollow out the centre slightly. Fill the greased basin with the remaining mixture and again, hollow out the centre. Bake the cakes in a moderately hot oven (190 C, 375 F, gas 5) for 50–60 minutes. Test with a skewer to make sure the middle of the cake is cooked before turning out and cooling on a wire tray.

Blend the cocoa with a little boiling water, then mix into half the butter icing. Fit the pipe into the piping bag and fill it with the plain butter icing. Cover the flat cake with most of the remaining plain butter icing, then lift on to the board. Pipe a row of stars round the top and bottom edges. Break the chocolate into squares and space all but two of them round the sides of the iced cake as shown in the picture. Melt the two remaining squares of chocolate.

Cut the basin cake horizontally through the middle, spread with a layer of chocolate butter icing and press together again. Cover the cake with chocolate icing, then place on top of the plain iced cake. Complete the cake by pressing Finger biscuits in round the top and the Flake in the centre. Spread a little melted chocolate on the chocolate biscuit and balance it on top of the Flake. Stick the marshmallows on to the sides of the cake with more of the melted chocolate. *Serves about 16*

Hovercraft

Illustrated on page 67

The completed cake may be frozen for a short time but if it is to be kept for a longer period, freeze the undecorated cakes alone.

Both cakes take about the same time to cook because of the depth of the loaf tin.

A plain writing pipe may be used in the piping bag if preferred.

Metric		Imperial
	6 egg quantity plain Victoria sponge cake	
	(page 16)	
50 g	**Bournville Cocoa**	2 oz
1	**orange**	1
1 kg	**chocolate butter icing (page 21)**	2 lb
40 ml	**orange juice**	2 tablespoons
1 small packet	**Cadbury's Buttons**	1 small packet
225 g	**royal icing (page 24)**	8 oz
	blue food colouring	
2	**fan shaped wafer biscuits**	2
$\frac{1}{2}$ packet	**Cadbury's Fingers**	$\frac{1}{2}$ packet
1 packet	**Cadbury's Milk Digestive Biscuits**	1 packet
2	**Cadbury's Flake from the Family Pack**	2
450-g	**loaf tin, greased and base lined**	1-lb
30 × 23-cm	**roasting tin, greased and base**	12 × 9-in
	lined	
	large board	
1	**greaseproof paper piping bag**	1

Make the cake mixture with a large electric mixer or make up half at a time. Divide in half. Blend half the cocoa to a smooth paste with a little boiling water and stir this into one portion of cake mixture. Add the finely grated rind of the orange to the second portion with just enough juice to make a dropping consistency. Fill the prepared loaf tin just over half full with the chocolate mixture. Dot the remaining chocolate and orange mixtures together in the larger tin. Smooth over the top, leaving the cake marbled, and make a slight hollow in the centre. Bake both cakes in a moderately hot oven (190 c, 375 F, gas 5) for about 40 minutes. Test the cakes with a skewer to make sure they are cooked before turning out to cool.

Have the butter icing ready. Blend the 2 tablespoons orange juice into one-third of the icing. Blend the remaining cocoa with a little boiling water and add it to the larger amount of butter icing. Cut both cakes horizontally through the middle and sandwich them together with the orange-flavoured butter icing. Cut a slice about 1.25 cm/$\frac{1}{2}$ in thick off the end of the loaf cake and use a little butter icing to secure it on top. Cover both cakes completely with chocolate butter icing. Press Buttons round the top piece of the loaf cake.

Reserve a little royal icing then colour the remainder blue. Spread a blue border round the edge of the board, with a little in the centre. Lift the large cake on to the board and rest the smaller one on top in the centre. Mark the surface with a fork, as shown in the picture. Cover the wafer biscuits with chocolate butter icing and stand them at an angle, at one end of the cake. Fill the piping bag with white royal icing and cut off the tip. Cut six Finger biscuits in half. Pipe a large blob of icing in the centre of two digestive biscuits and a little along the flat side of the Fingers, near the cut end. Arrange the Fingers, iced side down, on the biscuit like the spokes of a wheel. Stick a Button in the centre of each and leave to dry for 30 minutes.

Pipe a name in icing on another round biscuit and place it on the top of the cake. Arrange five Fingers in a line round the middle layer of cake, then pipe three evenly spaced lines of white icing over them to represent windows. Halve the remaining round biscuits and stick them into the cake base at an angle round the sides. Finally, press the Flakes upright into the back of the cake and rest both biscuit 'propellors' against them for support. *Serves about 30*

Tanks

Illustrated opposite

Metric		Imperial
2 egg quantity chocolate Victoria sandwich cake		
(page 16)		
350 g	chocolate butter icing (page 21)	12 oz
1 large packet	**Cadbury's Buttons**	1 large packet
6	**Cadbury's Flake from the Family Pack**	6
18-cm	**square cake tin, greased and base lined**	7-in

The cakes may be frozen when completed.

Cutting the cake

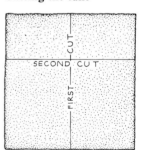

Make up the cake by the one-stage method, then spread the mixture evenly in the prepared tin. Bake in a moderately hot oven (190 c, 375 f, gas 5) for about 25 minutes until well risen and springy to the touch. Turn out and cool on a wire tray.

Cut the cake in half, then cut one-third off each piece as shown in the diagram. Spread the four pieces of cake with butter icing. Lift the smaller pieces on top of the larger ones, positioning them level with the back edge. Press five Buttons along both of the longer sides on each base cake, then tilt one more on the top for the hatch. Keep two Flakes whole and cut the others into short lengths. Arrange these like tracks along the outer edges of the base cakes, continuing over the ends as shown in the picture. Push a whole Flake into the front of the smaller pieces of cake to make a gun barrel and complete the tanks. *Makes 2 tanks each serving 4*

Hovercraft (see page 65); Tanks

Tracking Cake

Illustrated on page 175

Metric		Imperial
300 g	**soft margarine**	10 oz
300 g	**caster sugar**	10 oz
5	**eggs**	5
250 g	**self-raising flour**	9 oz
50 g	**Bournville Cocoa**	2 oz
10 ml	**baking powder**	2 teaspoons
175 g	**stoned dates, chopped**	6 oz
	Decoration	
800 g	**plain butter icing (page 21)**	1 lb 12 oz
	finely grated rind of 1 orange	
about 40 ml	**orange juice**	about 2 tablespoons
100 ml	**orange marmalade**	5 tablespoons
4	**Cadbury's Fingers**	4
2 large	**Cadbury's Flakes**	2 large
125 g	**marzipan**	4 oz
	red, green and blue food colouring	
1 small packet	**Cadbury's Buttons**	1 small packet
28 × 18-cm	**cake tin, greased and base lined**	11 × 7-in
18-cm	**square cake tin, greased and base lined**	7-in
	trefoil cocktail cutter	
	large board	

The cake will freeze complete when iced but put the tracking signs on when required. Wrap well in foil.

It is important to make the cakes the same depth in the tins so check the uncooked cake mixture with a skewer to see that it is evenly distributed before baking.
This is a cake that guides could probably make themselves and it would certainly be welcome at a guide meeting or a campfire, particularly at the end of a trail.
This cake can also be prepared by the traditional Victoria sandwich cake method.

Cutting the cakes

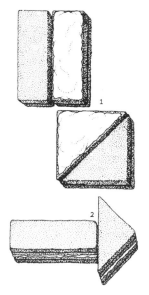

Make up the cake with a large electric mixer if possible. Place all the ingredients, except the dates, into the bowl, sifting the dry ingredients. Beat well for a good 2 minutes, then add the dates. Divide the mixture between the prepared tins and bake in a moderately hot oven (190 c, 375 f, gas 5) with the square tin above, for about 45 minutes. Cover the cakes with a piece of foil or greaseproof paper after 30 minutes to prevent them burning on top. Turn out and cool on a wire tray.

Make up the butter icing and blend in the orange rind and juice. Cut both cakes in half horizontally and sandwich together again with marmalade. Cut the oblong cake in half lengthways and the square cake in half diagonally (1). Sandwich the oblong and triangular cakes together with a little butter icing making deep cakes which fit together to form an arrow shape (2). Stick the cakes together on the board and cover them completely with the remaining icing, making it as smooth as possible.

Build a campfire of Finger biscuits on the arrow head, with some crumbs of Flake and the odd piece of marzipan, coloured red, inside. Split the Flakes into thinner pieces, reserving a big piece for the flagpole and making tracking signs with the remainder, as shown in the picture. Divide the marzipan into four and work the various colours into three portions. Roll out the marzipan and cut out two trefoil shapes of each colour, including the plain marzipan. Stick these badges in ascending order on each side of the arrow head, as illustrated. Arrange a circle of Buttons on the end of the cake, with one in the middle to represent the 'gone home' sign. Draw a World flag or substitute a Union Jack and stick it on to the Flake flagpole with a little icing. Serve slices of this cake with the traditional mug of cocoa. *Serves about 30*

Shaggy Dog Cake

Illustrated on page 102

Open freeze the cake without the biscuit tail. Later pack carefully, seal and label. Allow about 3 hours at room temperature for the cake to thaw.

A small cake can be stuck on the front of the Swiss roll to make a separate head. This is useful when you require a slightly bigger cake.

Metric		Imperial
125 g	**butter**	5 oz
225 g	**icing sugar, sieved**	8 oz
25 g	**Bournville cocoa**	1 oz
1	**chocolate Swiss roll, filled (see page 18)**	1
	Decoration	
2	**Cadbury's Buttons**	2
1	**glacé cherry**	1
1	**Cadbury's finger biscuit**	1

Cream the butter with the sieved icing sugar. Dissolve the cocoa in a little boiling water and beat into the butter icing.

Cover the Swiss roll with the butter icing, including the ends, then stick it on to a rectangular cake board or dish. Fill in the gap at the bottom of the Swiss roll too. Mark lines with a fork from the top down to the bottom of the Swiss roll, in the butter icing, flicking up the ends to make the shaggy coat. Stick the Buttons on at one end for the 'eyes', with a blob of icing in the centre of each. Place a cherry in position for the 'nose' and the biscuit standing up at the other end, for the 'tail'. This cake makes a simple and popular birthday cake.

Dartboard

Illustrated opposite

Wrap and freeze the complete cake.

If two cake tins are not available, make up all the cake mixture at once but cook the cakes separately, one after the other, in the same tin, washing it out in between.

Lemon or orange flavour butter icing tastes equally as good with the chocolate cake.

If miniature darts are not available, paper ones look most effective but they have to be stuck on with a star of butter icing.

Metric		Imperial
225 g	**butter**	8 oz
175 g	**light soft brown sugar**	6 oz
4	**eggs**	4
175 g	**golden syrup**	6 oz
225 g	**self-raising flour, sifted**	8 oz
25 g	**Bournville Cocoa**	1 oz
5 ml	**ground ginger**	1 teaspoon
5 ml	**ground mixed spice**	1 teaspoon
	Decoration	
60 ml	**apricot jam**	3 tablespoons
350 g	**plain butter icing (page 21)**	12 oz
5 ml	**ground ginger**	1 teaspoon
50 g	**Bournville Dark plain chocolate, grated**	50 g
	liquorice spiral with half a glacé cherry in the centre	
	small darts (optional)	
	cake candles and holders	
2 (25-cm)	**round shallow cake tins, well greased and base lined**	2 (10-in)
30-cm	**round cake board**	12-in
	plain writing and star pipes	
2	**greaseproof paper piping bags**	2

Cream the butter and sugar together. Gradually beat in the eggs, then the syrup. Fold in the flour and divide the mixture in half. Blend the cocoa to a thick paste with boiling water and add to one portion of cake mixture. Sift the spices into the other portion, with a little orange juice or milk if necessary to make a soft dropping consistency. Spread the two mixtures separately in the prepared tins and hollow out the centres to give a cooked cake which is flat on top. Bake in a warm oven (160 C, 325 F, gas 3) for about 35 minutes until springy to the touch and cooked. The cakes are quite shallow. Turn out and leave the cakes upside down to cool. Peel off the paper.

Place an 18-cm/7-in round cake tin base or plate on each cake in turn. Using the base or plate as a guide, cut out a circle from the middle of each of the cakes with a knife (1). Lift out the centre circles then cut each with 20 even wedges, as shown in the diagram (2). Place the ginger outer ring on the cake board and arrange the coloured sections alternately, to fill the centre (3). Spread the top with jam. Lay the chocolate ring on top and repeat the process with the remaining cake, reversing the colours to get a chequered effect (4).

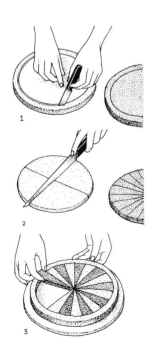

Trophy Cake (see page 72); Dartboard; Dominoes (see page 148)

Beat the butter icing with the ginger then spread some around the sides of the cake. Coat in grated chocolate. Attach the plain pipe to one of the piping bags, fill it with butter icing and pipe the numbers in the correct sequence and over the correct colour, round the 'board'. It's easiest to start at 20. Fit the star pipe in the remaining bag, fill it with butter icing and pipe lines of shells for the two scoring circles. Pipe a line round the top and bottom outer edges as shown in the picture. Stick the liquorice bull's eye in the centre, with the darts. Make an arrow shape from the candles to celebrate a birthday or to commemorate a sporting occasion.

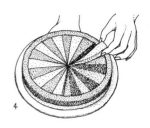

4

Trophy Cake

Illustrated on page 70

Metric		Imperial
125 g	**butter**	4 oz
175 g	**caster sugar**	6 oz
4	**eggs, separated**	4
80 ml	**milk**	4 tablespoons
1	**lemon**	1
125 g	**ground almonds**	4 oz
75 g	**Bournville Dark plain chocolate**	3 oz
175 g	**self-raising flour**	6 oz
	Filling	
60 ml	**black cherry jam**	3 tablespoons
	Crème au beurre and decoration	
225 g	**unsalted butter**	8 oz
4	**egg whites**	4
225 g	**icing sugar, sifted**	8 oz
100 g	**Bournville Dark plain chocolate**	3½ oz
20-cm	**round deep cake tin, greased and base lined**	8-in
30-cm	**square cake board (or large oblong pastry board) covered with gold foil**	12-in
	plain writing pipe	
2	**greaseproof paper piping bags**	2
	waxed paper	

Beat the butter and sugar together, then add the egg yolks and milk. Grate the lemon rind finely and keep covered to use in the cake covering. Add the strained lemon juice to the cake mixture with the ground almonds. Grate the chocolate and add it to the mixture, then stir in the flour and make sure the ingredients are well mixed. Whisk the egg whites quite

This cake keeps well and will freeze complete. Chocolate attracts moisture so it will glisten when thawed. The chocolate shapes can also be added later as they store well in an airtight container.

Chocolate Shapes
Draw or trace bold outlines of the chosen sport motifs on to a sheet of plain paper. Lay this sheet of paper flat on a board and cover with a piece of waxed paper, waxed side upwards. Pipe over the outline with melted chocolate. Try to get the chocolate at the right temperature so that it is not too thick to work. If it is too hot it will run quickly out of the bag and you will not be able to pipe the line. Leave the chocolate shapes to set completely before carefully peeling them off.

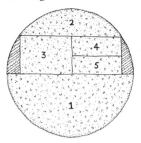

1 *Cut the cake exactly in half and cut a parallel line 5 cm/2 in from the straight edge of one half.*

2 *Trim the remaining piece to make straight ends then cut it in half. Cut one half into two more pieces.*

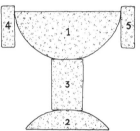

3 *Arrange the pieces of cake as shown.*

The roll freezes well – to do so, wrap the roll first in its greaseproof paper, then in foil.

stiffly and fold in carefully. Turn the mixture into the tin and bake in a warm oven (160 c, 325 f, gas 3) for about 1¼ hours. Turn out and cool on a wire tray.

Slice the cake horizontally through the middle and sandwich it back together with jam. Follow the diagram to cut the cake correctly; start by cutting the cake in half and then cut the pieces as shown. Assemble the pieces on a large board, again carefully following the diagrams.

In a bowl, soften the butter for the crème au beurre. Whisk the egg whites and icing sugar together in a basin over a pan of hot water. Whisk until the mixture is white, thick and holds its shape. Continue whisking off the heat for a few minutes, then beat in the soft butter, a spoonful at a time. Add the reserved lemon rind. Remove 2 good tablespoonfuls and spread the rest evenly over the cake, all except the base.

Melt the chocolate in a bowl over a pan of hot water. Fit the plain writing pipe into the piping bag and put two small spoonfuls of the white icing into the bag. Mix about one-third of the chocolate into the remaining icing; cover the base cake with chocolate icing. Use the white icing to pipe the words, as shown in the picture. Decorate with chocolate shapes made from the remaining Bournville Dark. *Serves about 16*

Jigsaw Roll

Illustrated on page 170

Metric		Imperial
75 g	**butter**	3 oz
75 g	**caster sugar**	3 oz
20 ml	**Bournville Cocoa**	1 tablespoon
1 packet	**Cadbury's Shorties**	1 packet
1	**egg, size 2**	1
1 packet	**marshmallows**	1 packet
about 50 g	**icing sugar**	about 2 oz

large, double piece of greaseproof paper

Melt the butter in quite a large saucepan and stir in the sugar and cocoa. Crush the biscuits roughly, leaving quite large pieces, then stir them into the butter mixture with the egg. Leave the mixture in the pan until cool and beginning to set.

Using a pair of scissors, cut the marshmallows into four pieces and stir into the chocolate mixture. Sift the icing sugar on to the greaseproof paper, then turn the biscuit mixture out on to it. Form into a 20-cm/8-in long roll using the paper to help you. Wrap up well then chill overnight. Unwrap the roll and cut it into slices. *Makes 12–14 slices*

Feather Bonnet

Illustrated opposite

The complete cake, without the marshmallow decoration, may be wrapped loosely and frozen for a short time.

Basket decoration

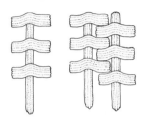

Start the basket pattern at the back of the cake where any mis-shapen lines are not likely to be noticed among the feathers. Basket work is quite easy to do and covers the cake surface remarkably quickly but if you have not tried the pattern before, practise on a clean work surface. Use only one colour of icing to practise with as the two colours, once piped together, cannot be separated to use again.

Feather Bonnet; Flower Tubs (see page 148); Flower Power (see page 49)

Metric		Imperial
	4 egg quantity plain Victoria sandwich cake	
	(page 16)	
40 ml	**Bournville Cocoa**	2 tablespoons
2.5 ml	**vanilla essence**	$\frac{1}{2}$ teaspoon
	pink food colouring	
40 ml	**red jam**	2 tablespoons
	Decoration	
800 g	**plain butter icing (page 21)**	1 lb 12 oz
	pink and yellow food colourings	
1 packet	**marshmallows**	1 packet
2	**mimosa sugar balls**	2
	angelica	
	feathers	
1.2-litre	**ovenproof basin, greased**	2-pint
24-cm	**round deep cake tin, greased and**	$9\frac{1}{2}$-in
	base lined	
	star and ribbon icing pipes	
2–4	**greaseproof paper piping bags**	2–4
30-cm	**round plate or cake board**	12-in

Make up the cake mixture then divide it into three equal portions. Add the cocoa to one amount, vanilla to a second and colour the third portion pink. Fill one-third of the basin with a little of each of the three mixtures and put the rest in the prepared tin. Do not stir the mixtures together but leave the separate colours to show attractively when the cake is cut. Smooth lightly over the top. Bake the cake in the basin above the tin in a moderately hot oven (190 c, 375 f, gas 5) for about 50 minutes until cooked through and risen. Turn out and cool on a wire tray.

Spread the top of the basin cake with jam then turn it over and press it on top of the round cake, slightly off centre. Stand the cake on the plate.

Colour 450 g/1 lb of the butter icing with pink colouring and the remainder pale yellow. Fit the star pipe into a piping bag and fill with the yellow icing. Fit a larger bag with the ribbon pipe and fill with pink icing. Using the two pipes alternately, pipe a line of yellow icing down the crown of the hat and cross it with small lines of basket weave, leaving even gaps, as shown in the diagram. Continue to make the pattern until the whole crown of the hat is covered. Do the same for the hat brim, re-filling the bags as often as necessary. Pipe a ribbon line of yellow icing.

Place a marshmallow on the top of the hat where the icing lines meet. Halve the remaining marshmallows horizontally to make them thinner, then cut these in half again and arrange alternate colours round the bottom edge of the cake as shown in the picture. Make two simple flowers from the marshmallows, with stars of butter icing and mimosa balls in the centre and a few angelica leaves. Stand the feathers in the back of the cake at a jaunty angle. *Serves about 20*

Mushroom Manor

Illustrated on page 151

Metric		Imperial
40 ml	**Bournville Cocoa**	2 tablespoons
225 g	**soft margarine**	8 oz
225 g	**caster sugar**	8 oz
60 ml	**orange marmalade**	3 tablespoons
4	**eggs, separated**	4
300 g	**self-raising flour, sifted**	10 oz
	Moulding paste	
80 ml	**liquid glucose**	4 tablespoons
2	**egg whites**	2
1 kg	**icing sugar, sifted**	2 lb
	yellow and green food colouring	
about 120 ml	**apricot jam, warmed**	about 6 tablespoons
	Decoration	
40 ml	**royal icing (page 24)**	2 tablespoons
	sugar flowers	
1 large packet	**Cadbury's Buttons**	1 large packet
	Cadbury's Drinking Chocolate	
1.2-litre	**ovenproof basin, greased**	2-pint
19-cm	**round cake tin, greased and base lined**	7½-in
4-cm	**round pastry cutter**	1½-in
	plain writing pipe	
1	**greaseproof paper piping bag**	1

Freeze the plain cakes and decorate them when required.

It is quite easy to make the paste in an electric mixer. Carefully hold a clean tea towel taut over the machine to stop the icing sugar flying all over the kitchen.

Keep the moulding paste wrapped in a polythene bag once it is coloured so that it does not dry out. It the paste becomes too firm to work comfortably, sprinkle on a few drops of water and knead it again.

Dissolve the cocoa in a little boiling water. Cream the margarine and sugar together well, then beat in the dissolved cocoa and the marmalade. Add the egg yolks, then fold in the flour. Whisk the egg whites quite stiffly and fold in evenly.

Fill the greased basin about three-quarters full with cake mixture, then spread the rest in the prepared tin. Bake in a warm oven (160 C, 325 F, gas 3) for about $1\frac{1}{4}$ hours. Test with a skewer to see that both cakes are cooked through. Turn out and cool on a wire tray.

Prepare the moulding paste by gradually blending the glucose and egg whites into the icing sugar. When there is no icing sugar left, knead the paste into a ball. Dust a work surface lightly with icing sugar and continue kneading until the paste is smooth and pliable. Divide the paste in half and knead a little yellow colouring into one portion and green into the other, making sure the colours are delicate.

Cut the round cake horizontally in half and sandwich it together with half the apricot jam. Brush both cakes all over with the remaining jam. Roll out both the coloured pastes in turn. Mould the yellow paste over the basin cake and the green paste over the round sponge, including just enough green paste to tuck neatly under the edge. Use the pastry cutter and a sharp knife to cut out a door shape and five windows from the yellow paste.

Place the round cake on top of the basin cake and lift carefully on to a suitable plate or board. Fit the pipe into the piping bag and fill it with the royal icing. Pipe the windows and round the door, pressing some flowers on to make it look really pretty. Pipe a little icing on the back of the lightly polished Buttons and arrange them over the green cake, with a few more for the path. Sift a little drinking chocolate on top of the cake. *Serves 16–20*

Treasure Chest

Illustrated opposite

Assemble the cake no longer than the day before it is required as the outside pieces may bend and soften a little.

To measure syrup accurately, use a hot metal spoon.

Cutting the biscuit mixture

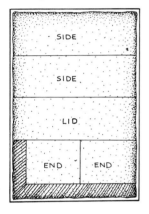

Metric		Imperial
2 egg quantity chocolate Victoria sandwich cake		
(page 16)		
50 g	butter	2 oz
150 g	soft brown sugar	5 oz
80 ml	golden syrup	4 tablespoons
175 g	self-raising flour	6 oz
50 g	Bournville Cocoa	2 oz
20 ml	milk	1 tablespoon
	Decoration	
250 g	lemon flavoured butter icing (page 21)	9 oz
450 g	royal icing (page 24)	1 lb
1 packet	Cadbury's Buttons	1 packet
	silver sugar balls	
selection of pretty sweets or Loot Biscuits (page 129)		
and Flake Envelopes (page 236)		
23-cm	square deep cake tin, greased	9-in
	and base lined	
23.5 × 33-cm	Swiss roll tin, greased	9½ × 13½-in
1	greaseproof paper piping bag	1
	small star pipe	
28-cm	square cake board	11-in

Make the sponge cake first and spread the mixture in the prepared square tin. Bake in a moderately hot oven (190 c, 375 F, gas 5) for about 30 minutes until well risen and cooked. Turn out and cool on a wire tray.

Melt the butter, sugar and syrup in a saucepan. Meanwhile, sift the flour with the cocoa. Cool the butter mixture before beating in the sifted flour and cocoa with enough milk to make a stiff dough. Wrap the dough in cling film or a butter paper and leave in the refrigerator for 30 minutes. Later, roll out the biscuit dough to fit the Swiss roll tin. Bake in a moderate oven (180 c, 350 F, gas 4) for 10–15 minutes until cooked.

Cut up the warm chocolate biscuit mixture, while it is still in the tin, to the following sizes. For the long sides and the lid, cut three pieces each measuring 23 × 7.5 cm/ 9 × 3 in. For the ends of the treasure chest, cut two smaller pieces each measuring 10 × 7.5 cm/4 × 3 in.

Assemble the chest by first cutting the cake vertically in half, then slice each oblong piece horizontally through the middle. Spread with butter icing and sandwich the layers together again, putting all four layers on top of each other.

Treasure Chest; Pirates' Puddings (see page 228); Loot Biscuits (see page 129); Flake Envelopes (see page 236)

79

Cut the end off a piping bag and drop in the pipe. Fill with royal icing. Place the oblong cake in the centre of the cake board and build the biscuit round it, sticking the edges together with stars of royal icing. Support the biscuit pieces if necessary until the icing hardens or put a dab of icing on the cake itself. Decorate one edge of the biscuit lid with stars of icing, the Buttons and silver balls, propping it up until the icing dries.

Fill the centre of the chest with a selection of sweets or Loot Biscuits and Flake Envelopes.

Attach the lid with a row of icing stars and make a lock shape on the front.

Tipsy Cake

Metric		Imperial
100 g	**Bournville Dark plain chocolate**	3½ oz
175 g	**margarine**	6 oz
175 g	**caster sugar**	6 oz
3	**eggs**	3
175 g	**self-raising flour, sieved**	6 oz
	pinch of salt	
	vanilla essence	
125 g	**granulated sugar**	4 oz
120 ml	**water**	6 tablespoons
40–60 ml	**brandy, rum or sherry**	2–3 tablespoons
275 ml	**whipping cream**	½ pint
1 tablespoon	**caster sugar**	1 tablespoon
2 20-cm	**round shallow cake tins,**	2 8-inch
	greased and base lined	
	piping bag and star pipe	

It may be easier to freeze the cake layers without the cream. Place a sheet of greaseproof or waxed paper between the cake layers, wrap, seal and label. The cake can also be frozen complete except for the chocolate triangles, in which case, open freeze first then pack.

If you are making the cake and the chocolate triangles at separate times, it may be easier to use 20 ml/1 tablespoon of Bournville cocoa dissolved in a very little boiling water, instead of melted chocolate. The marbled pattern will vary on the cakes so choose the most attractive to use on top.

Melt the chocolate in a bowl over a pan of hot water. When melted, spread half quite thickly on to waxed paper and leave to set again. Keep the remaining chocolate melted.

Cream the margarine and sugar together. Gradually beat in the eggs one at a time and fold in the sieved flour with a pinch of salt. Halve the mixture between two bowls and add a few drops of vanilla essence to one amount. Mix the melted chocolate into the other. Place alternate spoonsful of the vanilla and chocolate cake mixture in the prepared tins, dividing it between both tins. Swirl the colours together slightly and smooth over the top, hollowing out the centre slightly. Bake the cakes in a moderately hot oven (190°C, 375°F, Gas Mark 5) for about 25 minutes. Turn the cakes out on to a wire tray to cool.

Dissolve the granulated sugar in the water over gentle heat. When the sugar crystals have disappeared, increase the heat and boil rapidly for about 3 minutes. Take the syrup off the heat and cool slightly before adding the brandy. Pour over the cakes just before they are to be assembled.

With a sharp knife, cut the set chocolate into 3.5-cm/ 1½-inch squares; you will need at least 4 good ones but any extra will keep in a screwtop jar. Cut the squares across into 2 triangles. Whip the cream until it will hold its shape then fold in the tablespoon of caster sugar. Pipe a circle of rosettes round the edge of one cake, upside-down so that the marbled pattern shows. Sandwich the cakes together with the remaining cream. Place the chocolate triangles in position.

Loch Ness Monster

Illustrated on page 143

The iced cake may be frozen but thaw carefully as the icing tends to become very moist.

It is important to beat the icing really hard and an electric mixer is ideal for this. The thickness and gloss of the finished icing will depend on the beating.

Metric		Imperial
175 g	**butter or margarine**	6 oz
125 g	**caster sugar**	4 oz
	grated rind of 1 orange	
75 g	**black treacle**	3 oz
3	**eggs**	3
150 g	**self-raising flour**	5 oz
25 g	**Bournville Cocoa**	1 oz
	Icing	
65 g	**butter**	2½ oz
60 ml	**milk**	3 tablespoons
80 ml	**Cadbury's Drinking Chocolate**	4 tablespoons
225 g	**icing sugar, sifted**	8 oz
	Decoration	
2	**chocolate mini rolls**	2
1	**round Cadbury's biscuit**	1
3 or 4	**small pieces of angelica**	3 or 4
1	**glacé cherry**	1
2	**pieces flaked almonds**	2
15-cm	**round deep cake tin, greased and base lined**	6-in
	large board or tray covered with coloured foil paper	

Make the cake by creaming the butter, sugar and orange rind together until soft and light. Beat in the treacle, then the eggs, one at a time. Sift the flour and cocoa together and fold into the mixture, ensuring no pockets of flour are left. Turn into the prepared tin and bake in a moderate oven (180 C, 350 F, gas 4) for about 1 hour 10 minutes, until reasonably firm but not overcooked. Turn out carefully and cool on a wire tray. Peel off the greaseproof paper when cold.

To make the icing, melt the butter, milk and drinking chocolate together in a pan. Allow to cool before beating in the icing sugar until fairly thick and quite smooth.

Slice the cake horizontally into three equal layers, then sandwich two together again with a little of the icing. Halve the remaining layer of cake, then sandwich together with a little icing, making a semi-circle. Cut the large cake into two, making one piece quite a lot larger than the other, ending up with a total of three different sized pieces of cake. Cover each piece with icing, making the surface rough. Arrange the pieces of cake on the tray, in a line or semi-circle, cut sides down as shown in the picture. Cut one mini roll diagonally in half with a sharp knife and cover one piece with icing. Place in position for the tail. Cover the remaining halved and whole mini rolls with icing, then assemble both on top of the biscuit to form a head, as shown. Stick in a crest of angelica, 2 slices of glacé cherry for eyes and the almonds sticking out behind. The Monster is now ready to eat. *Serves about 12*

Soldier Boy (see page 53); *Birthday Parade*

Birthday Parade

Illustrated opposite

Metric		Imperial
2 egg quantity chocolate Victoria sandwich cake (page 16)		
350 g	**chocolate butter icing (page 21)**	12 oz
2 packets	**Cadbury's Fingers**	2 packets
18-cm	**round deep cake tin, greased and base lined**	7-in
	candles and soldier candle holders	
	sentry box and a toy soldier	

Make up the chocolate sponge cake according to the recipe instructions and spread the mixture evenly in the prepared tin. Bake in a warm oven (160 c, 325 f, gas 3) for 35–40 minutes. Turn out and cool on a wire tray.

Slice the cake in half and spread about one-third of the butter icing in the centre before sandwiching together again. Cover the top and sides of the cake with the remaining icing. Mark the top into lines with a small palette knife. Lift the cake on to a plate or board before pressing the Finger biscuits upright on to the side. Arrange the appropriate number of candles in their soldier holders in lines on the cake and stand the toy soldier in the sentry box. *Serves about 16*

The iced cake may be frozen but the Finger biscuits are more difficult to stick on to hard icing. It may be necessary to make up a little more chocolate butter icing to coat the sides before pressing on the biscuits, or spread with apricot jam.

Soldier candle holders can be bought from some newsagents or department stores. If they are the wrong colour, paint over them with a permanent ink pen.
If soldier candle holders are difficult to obtain, it looks equally effective to stand a toy soldier beside the ordinary birthday candles.

Sweetheart Surprise

Illustrated on page 139

Metric		Imperial
175 g	**caster sugar**	6 oz
125 ml	**bland vegetable oil**	$\frac{1}{4}$ pint
150 g	**natural yogurt**	5 oz
80 ml	**golden syrup**	4 tablespoons
3	**eggs, size 2**	3
a few drops	**almond essence**	a few drops
225 g	**self-raising flour**	8 oz
90 ml	**Bournville Cocoa**	3 rounded tablespoons
2.5 ml	**bicarbonate of soda**	$\frac{1}{2}$ teaspoon
2.5 ml	**salt**	$\frac{1}{2}$ teaspoon
	Frosting and decoration	
350 g	**apricot jam**	12 oz
175 g	**caster sugar**	6 oz
2	**egg whites**	2
1.25 ml	**cream of tartar**	$\frac{1}{4}$ teaspoon
40 ml	**water**	2 tablespoons
	pink food colouring	
4	**glacé cherries**	4
	angelica	
18-cm	**round deep cake tin, greased and base lined**	7-in
18-cm	**square deep cake tin, greased and base lined**	7-in
30-cm	**heart-shaped or round cake board**	12-in

Beat the sugar, oil, yogurt, syrup, eggs and almond essence together in a large bowl, preferably with an electric mixer, until pale in colour. Sift the dry ingredients together, then fold them into the mixture, making sure no lumps of flour remain. Divide the mixture *equally* between the two prepared tins and bake the cakes in a warm oven (160 C, 325 F, gas 3) for 70–80 minutes until risen, springy to the touch and cooked. Turn out both cakes and cool on a wire tray.

Slice both cakes in half and sandwich them back together with jam. Cut the round cake in half. Assemble the cakes on the board: place the two semi-circles on two sides of the square cake as shown in the diagram. Stick them together with a little jam.

To make the frosting, mix the sugar, egg whites, cream of tartar and water in a large bowl. Stand the bowl over a pan of simmering water, then whisk hard for at least 8 minutes until the frosting thickens, forms soft peaks and becomes really shiny. About half way through, slowly add a few drops of

Freeze the complete cake without covering and when hard, wrap loosely in foil and label. Be careful the icing is not knocked off in the freezer. Alternatively, freeze the cakes alone and decorate them later.

Fold the flour in with a large metal spoon or spatula to ensure the air is not knocked out and that all the flour gets mixed in from the bottom of the bowl. A flat cake generally means too vigorous mixing at this stage. Make sure that the cakes are the same depth in the tin before baking.

An electric hand mixer is best for making this icing as it really needs to be whisked hard. As the frosting thickens, it becomes harder to work but it is essential to make it thick enough or it will not harden on the cake. About 8–10 minutes with an electric mixer is generally enough, but keep the bowl standing over hot water.

Paper doilies make an attractive edge for this cake. Before the cake is assembled secure the doilies in the centre of the board with sticky tape.

Cutting and assembling the cakes

colouring. When the right texture is reached, quickly spread the frosting all over the cake, including the sides, swirling it into soft peaks. Cut three of the cherries into long pieces and cut the last one in half. Arrange a simple flower design on the cake, as shown in the picture, with stalks and leaves of angelica. Leave the icing to harden on the surface, although the underneath remains moist. *Serves 12–16*

Anniversary Cake

Illustrated on page 87

The complete cake may be frozen but be careful to put it on a board or plate suitable for cold temperatures.

The frosting keeps the cake moist and it can therefore be made a couple of days in advance.

This cake can be decorated with any colour icing and ribbon; for example pink or blue for a christening or yellow for a golden wedding anniversary.

Metric		Imperial
50 g	**Bournville Cocoa**	2 oz
175 g	**self-raising flour**	6 oz
2.5 ml	**bicarbonate of soda**	$\frac{1}{2}$ teaspoon
good pinch	**salt**	good pinch
125 g	**soft margarine**	4 oz
225 g	**dark soft brown sugar**	8 oz
2	**eggs**	2
150 g	**natural yogurt**	5 oz
2.5 ml	**vanilla essence**	$\frac{1}{2}$ teaspoon
	Filling and frosting	
100 ml	**redcurrant jelly**	5 tablespoons
2	**egg whites**	2
350 g	**icing sugar, sifted**	12 oz
1.25 ml	**cream of tartar**	$\frac{1}{4}$ teaspoon
80 ml	**water**	4 tablespoons
	Decoration	
about 15	**sugar bells (page 86)**	about 15
40 ml	**thick glacé or royal icing**	2 tablespoons
	(page 24), coloured yellow	
2 (19-cm)	**round shallow cake tins,**	2 (7-in)
	greased and base lined	
1	**greaseproof paper piping bag**	1
	appropriate coloured ribbon	
23-cm	**round plate or cake board**	9-in

Sift all the dry ingredients for the cake into a bowl. Add all the remaining ingredients and beat for a good three minutes until thoroughly mixed. Divide the mixture between the prepared tins. Bake in a moderately hot oven (190 c, 375 f, gas 5) for about 35 minutes until well risen and cooked. Turn out and cool on a wire tray.

Split both cakes in half, then spread the bottom layer of each with redcurrant jelly and sandwich together again. Do not put the two cakes on top of each other.

Prepare the frosting by measuring all the ingredients into quite a large bowl and standing it over a pan of hot water. Beat, preferably with an electric hand mixer, until stiff peaks form and the icing is satin smooth and white, which will usually take 8–10 minutes. Spread some frosting over one cake, then sandwich the two together to make one deep cake. Without picking up any crumbs on the knife, spread the cake liberally with frosting; cover it completely leaving definite swirls and peaks. Carefully lift the cake on to the plate.

Before the frosting sets, arrange a pattern of sugar bells on top. Pipe bows of yellow icing on the edge and arrange an attractive bow of ribbon in the centre (paper ribbon stands up particularly well).

Fairy Castle (see page 45); Anniversary Cake (see page 85)

Sugar Bells

Metric		Imperial
125 g	**granulated sugar**	4 oz
40 ml	**royal icing (page 24),**	2 tablespoons
	coloured yellow	
	mimosa sugar balls	
	metal bell shapes	
1	**greaseproof paper piping bag**	1

Small metal bells are usually available in different sizes at large department stores, particularly around Christmas time. Take out the piece in the middle so that a bell mould shape remains. Clean thoroughly before using.

The dry sugar bells keep well in a clean dry place.

Put the sugar in a bowl and carefully add only about three or four drops of water, making the sugar just moist. Be very careful not to add too much water. Pack the sugar into the bell moulds as tightly as possible then tap it out on to a clean surface (1). Use up all the sugar in the same way. Leave the bells long enough for the sugar on the outside to harden enough to handle.

When the outside is hard, lift the bell very carefully and with a skewer, scrape out the soft sugar inside, leaving a hard bell-shaped shell (2). It is important to catch the sugar before it is too hard in the centre of the bells. Leave all the shells to dry completely.

Put the icing into the piping bag then pipe a line in the middle of each bell. Stick a mimosa (or silver) sugar ball on each one (3). *Makes 15–30 bells, depending on size*

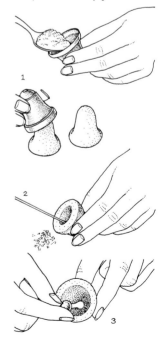

Cadbury's Chocolate Box

Illustrated on page 234

Metric		Imperial
100 g	**Bournville Dark plain chocolate**	3½ oz
60 ml	**boiling water**	3 tablespoons
175 g	**butter**	6 oz
175 g	**caster sugar**	6 oz
5 ml	**vanilla essence**	1 teaspoon
4	**eggs, separated**	4
25 g	**Bournville Cocoa**	1 oz
200 g	**self-raising flour**	7 oz
	Sugar syrup	
50 g	**granulated sugar**	2 oz
125 ml	**water**	scant ¼ pint
20 ml	**maraschino liqueur**	1 tablespoon
175 g	**black cherry jam**	6 oz
	Moulding paste	
25 g	**Bournville Cocoa**	1 oz
450 g	**icing sugar**	1 lb
20 ml	**glucose syrup**	1 tablespoon
5 ml	**glycerine**	1 teaspoon
60–80 ml	**maraschino liqueur**	3–4 tablespoons
	Cadbury's Drinking Chocolate	
	Decoration	
350 g	**royal icing (page 24)**	12 oz
	green food colouring	
1 large packet	**Cadbury's Buttons**	1 large packet
	sugared flowers	
225 g	**Rose's Milk Chocolates**	8 oz
22-cm	**square deep cake tin, greased and fully lined**	8½-in
20 × 8-cm	**stiff card, covered in foil**	8 × 3-in
	star and plain writing pipes	
2	**greaseproof paper piping bags**	2

To test if the sugar syrup has reached the short thread stage, dip a wooden spoon into the pan. Lightly oil your fingers and pinch a little of the syrup off the spoon, pulling it away so that it comes away in short threads. If the syrup does not form threads then boil and test again.

Melt the chocolate in a small pan with the water. Cream the butter, sugar and essence until light in colour and texture. Fold in the egg yolks and melted chocolate, then the cocoa and flour sifted together. Add a little milk if necessary to give the correct soft consistency. Whisk the egg whites until stiff then fold them into the mixture and turn it into the prepared tin, hollowing out the centre slightly. Bake in a moderate oven (180 c, 350 f, gas 4) for about 1 hour until risen and firm to the touch. Turn out and cool on a wire tray.

1 *Lightly whip one egg white in a bowl and paint this over each individual petal.*

2 *Dust the flower with caster sugar, separating each petal, using a paint brush to help coat them completely. Leave the flowers to dry in a sunny warm place for a day. Store in a clean dry place, ready to use as required.*

Dissolve the sugar in the water for the sugar syrup and when quite clear, boil rapidly for about three minutes until the short thread stage is reached. Stir in the liqueur and allow to cool. Pour the cool syrup over the cake.

Cut the cake in half horizontally to give two layers, then cut each layer in half again, vertically across the middle to make four rectangles. Spread two of them with half the jam, then sandwich three layers together, leaving the fourth for the lid. Brush all the cake, including the lid, with jam.

To make the moulding paste, sift the cocoa and icing sugar into a bowl. Stir in the glucose syrup and glycerine with enough liqueur to make a mouldable paste. The easiest way to complete the mixing, though messy, is with your hands. Cut off one-third of the paste and keep it moist in a polythene bag. Dust a clean work surface with drinking chocolate and roll the larger portion of paste into a thin strip 12 × 65 cm/5 × 25 in or make two shorter pieces if it is easier. Wrap the rolled-out paste round the sides of the large piece of cake, taking it just over the top edge and smoothing it carefully with your fingers to make it as even as possible. Roll out the remaining paste to fit the lid, covering the top, sides and overlapping underneath. Place this piece of cake on the foil covered card.

Mark even diagonal lines about 2.5 cm/1 in apart on the paste, as a guide for piping. Colour the royal icing pale green. Fit the pipes in the two piping bags and fill them both with the royal icing. Pipe plain lines over the marks on the paste, making diamond shapes. Where the piped lines cross, pipe a small star of icing and press on alternate Buttons and flowers before the icing dries. Lift the base cake on to an oblong plate. Pipe a shell edging round the lid and cake base. Cover the top of the cake with a selection of Rose's chocolates and the home-made sweets, then prop the lid on top as shown in the picture. Leave the icing to dry before serving the cake.

Serves about 16

Desert Fort Cake

Illustrated opposite

Metric		Imperial
350 g	**margarine**	12 oz
350 g	**caster sugar**	12 oz
6	**eggs**	6
350 g	**self-raising flour, sieved**	12 oz
25 g	**Bournville cocoa, sieved**	1 oz
50 g	**ground almonds**	2 oz
	Icing	
450 g	**chocolate butter icing**	1 lb
	(double quantity recipe, see page 21)	
	Decoration	
150 g	**chocolate finger biscuits**	$5\frac{1}{4}$ oz
	soft brown sugar	
	toy soldiers and flags	
25-cm	**square cake tin, greased and lined**	10-inch
30-cm	**square cake board**	12-inch

The cake may be frozen undecorated, or when covered with the butter icing, without the finger biscuits or decorations. Pack carefully, seal and label. Open freeze first if decorated.

If you have an oven that bakes very evenly, it is probably unnecessary to line the cake tin completely. With a cake this size, a paper lining helps to prevent the edges from burning. Warm the mixer bowl and beater before beginning.

Use an electric mixer for making this large amount of mixture, if available. Beat the margarine and sugar together until they are thoroughly mixed and smooth. Add the eggs one at a time by hand, with a little of the sieved flour and cocoa. Fold in the remaining dry ingredients, including the ground almonds. Add a little milk if necessary to make a dropping consistency. Turn the mixture into the prepared tin, hollow out the centre so that when the cake rises, it will be flat. Bake in a moderately hot oven (190°C, 375°F, Gas Mark 5) for about 45 minutes. Test with a warm skewer to see if it is cooked through. Cover with a piece of paper if the cake seems to be getting too brown. Cool in the tin slightly before turning out on to a wire tray.

Prepare the chocolate butter icing. Carefully measure a 13-cm/5-inch square in the centre of the cake and cut it out. Cut the centre square into four, making smaller squares. Lift the larger square carefully on to the centre of the cake board. Stick the smaller squares on to each of the corners, with butter icing, to make the 'turrets'. Very carefully, spread the whole cake, inside and out, with the butter icing, making it as smooth as possible.

Divide the finger biscuits into four. Stand them up between the 'turrets', pressing them into the icing. Sprinkle soft brown sugar in the centre and round the edge to represent the 'sand'. Arrange the soldiers and flags on the 'fort'. Birthday candles may be stuck into the 'turrets'.

Desert Fort Cake

Merry-Go-Round

Illustrated on page 170

Metric		Imperial
175 g	**soft margarine**	6 oz
175 g	**light soft brown sugar**	6 oz
3	**eggs**	3
200 g	**self-raising flour**	7 oz
75 g	**Cadbury's Drinking Chocolate**	3 oz
50 g	**walnuts, chopped**	2 oz
20 ml	**coffee essence**	1 tablespoon
100 g	**Cadbury's Dairy Milk Chocolate**	3½ oz
	Icing and decoration	
400 g	**plain butter icing (page 21)**	14 oz
25 g	**ground almonds**	1 oz
2 packets	**Cadbury's Fingers**	2 packets
1 large	**Cadbury's Flake**	1 large
1 packet	**Cadbury's Animals**	1 packet
.40 ml	**royal icing (page 24)**	2 tablespoons
1 packet	**Cadbury's Buttons**	1 packet
15	**silver sugar balls**	15
20-cm	**round deep cake tin, greased and lined**	8-in
7	**wooden cocktail sticks**	7
	paper canopy	
75 cm	**red ribbon**	30 in
	star pipe	
1	**greaseproof paper piping bag**	1

Cream the margarine and sugar together until soft and light, then gradually stir in the eggs. Sift the flour and drinking chocolate together and fold them into the mixture with the walnuts and coffee essence, making a soft dropping consistency. Cut each square of chocolate into six, then fold the pieces into the cake. Turn the mixture into the tin, hollow out the centre slightly and bake the cake in a moderate oven (180 C, 350 F, gas 4) for about 1¼ hours. Turn out and cool on a wire tray.

Prepare the butter icing and beat in the ground almonds. Cover the top and sides of the cake with this icing, forking over the top. Lift the cake on to a large flat plate or board. Lightly polish the Finger biscuits before pressing them upright against the side of the cake. Stand the Flake in the centre, pressing it in firmly. Stick six Animal biscuits on to cocktail sticks and arrange them near the cake edge, at different heights to resemble a merry-go-round. Stand more Animals round the Flake. Prepare the paper canopy according to the instructions.

Freeze the cake without the biscuits and canopy.

If coffee essence is not available, dissolve 15 ml/3 teaspoons instant coffee in a very little hot water and add to the cake mixture.

To make a paper canopy

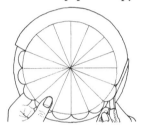

1 *Draw a 20-cm/8-in circle on to some coloured card. On the reverse side, mark the circle into 16 equal segments.*

Cut out a scalloped edge slightly away from the drawn circle.

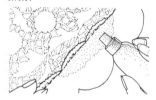

2 *Stick the doily on to the right side, with a little glue.*

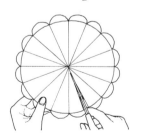

3 *Turn the card over and cut up one line in towards the centre of the circle. Glue down one complete segment.*

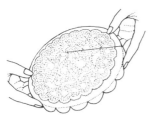

4 *Make a sharp fold round the scalloped edge. Cut out a triangular paper flag.*

Fit the star pipe into the piping bag and spoon the royal icing into it. Pipe a large star of icing on top of the Flake then one on each of the Buttons. Press on a silver ball. Pipe a star on the scalloped edges of the prepared canopy, press on the Buttons and balance the canopy on the Flake in the centre – as the royal icing sets, it will become firm. Stick a paper flag on a cocktail stick in the top and secure the ribbon round the cake to complete the merry-go-round. *Serves 12–16*

Animal Bricks

Illustrated on page 39

The iced cakes will freeze but do not add the biscuits until the cakes are thawed again.

Alphabet letters can easily be substituted for the numbers, perhaps choosing childrens' names or the animals themselves.

A good game to encourage younger children to mix at a party is to give each child an animal noise to make and encourage them to find another child making the same noise. As a reward, give the pair their Cadbury's Animal biscuits.

Metric		Imperial
3 egg quantity plain Victoria sandwich cake (page 21)		
5 ml	**ground ginger**	1 teaspoon
1	**small lemon**	1
350 g	**chocolate butter icing (page 16)**	12 oz
25 g	**butter**	1 oz
40 g	**icing sugar, sifted**	1½ oz
1 packet	**Cadbury's Animals**	1 packet
18-cm	**square deep cake tin, greased and base lined**	7-in
	small star pipe	
1	**greaseproof paper piping bag**	1

Make up the sponge mixture, adding the ground ginger and finely grated lemon rind to the mixture. Mix in enough lemon juice to make a soft dropping consistency. Spread the mixture in the prepared tin and bake in a moderate oven (180 c, 350 f, gas 4) for about 50 minutes until well risen and cooked. Turn out and cool on a wire tray. Cut into 9 squares.

Cover the pieces of cake with chocolate butter icing, making them as smooth and square as possible. Beat the butter and icing sugar together until soft and pale. Fit the pipe into the piping bag, fill with the icing then pipe a selection of numbers on the bricks. Stand one Animal biscuit on top of each brick cake and press others on the sides. *Makes 9*

Seasonal Style

Every seasonal feast calls for a celebration cake and the exciting ideas in this chapter will appeal to all the family. There are special themes for Easter and Christmas and even Chocolate Cat motifs suitable for a Hallowe'en party – a host of good ideas to celebrate the seasonal mood.

Santas

Illustrated opposite

Metric		Imperial
40 ml	**Bournville Cocoa**	2 tablespoons
75 g	**self-raising flour**	3 oz
2.5 ml	**baking powder**	$\frac{1}{2}$ teaspoon
125 g	**soft margarine**	4 oz
125 g	**caster or soft brown sugar**	4 oz
25 g	**ground almonds**	1 oz
2	**eggs**	2
	Decoration	
450 g	**icing sugar, sifted**	1 lb
	bright red food colouring	
2	**glacé cherries**	2
20 cm	**round cake tin, greased and base lined**	8-in
1	**greaseproof paper piping bag**	1

Sift the cocoa, flour and baking powder into a bowl, then beat in the soft margarine, sugar, ground almonds and eggs. Beat the mixture for a good 2 minutes until really well mixed, then spread it evenly in the prepared tin. Bake in a moderately hot oven (190 c, 375 f, gas 5) for 25–30 minutes until cooked. Turn out and turn the cake over to avoid marks on top. Cool.

Reserve about 75 g/3 oz of the icing sugar, then blend the remainder with enough red food colouring and water or fruit juice, to make a strong-coloured, coating glacé icing. Cut the cake into 6 wedges and cut off the bases to make triangles, (see diagram). Coat each cake with icing; dry, then trim the edges.

Use the remaining icing sugar with a little water or lemon juice to make a stiff glacé icing, fill the piping bag with this icing. Cut off just the tip of the bag and pipe a face and the line of buttons on each Santa. Cut the hole a little larger to mark the wavy lines and a blob for a hat at the top. Stick a thin piece of cherry in each and leave to dry. *Makes 6*

The uniced, whole or cut cake may be frozen.

Coloured icing darkens on standing so do not worry if it looks rather pink at first. To get a good result, spread the icing with a small palette knife and do not lift the knife off the surface at all until completely coated. This helps prevent the cake crumbs mixing into the soft icing.

Cutting the cake

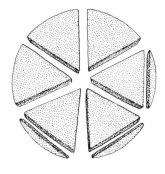

Chimney Christmas Cake (see page 96); Santas; Mini Mountains (see page 103); Star Sparkles (see page 97)

Chimney Christmas Cake

Illustrated on page 95

Metric		Imperial
225 g	**plain flour**	8 oz
40 ml	**Bournville Cocoa**	2 tablespoons
7.5 ml	**baking powder**	1½ teaspoons
5 ml	**ground mixed spice**	1 teaspoon
175 g	**butter**	6 oz
175 g	**soft brown sugar**	6 oz
4	**eggs**	4
450 g	**mixed dried fruit**	1 lb
50 g	**blanched almonds, chopped**	2 oz
50 g	**glacé cherries, quartered**	2 oz
50 g	**chopped mixed peel**	2 oz
40 ml	**rum, sherry or fruit juice**	2 tablespoons
	Decoration	
675 g	**icing sugar, sifted**	1½ lb
10 ml	**glycerine**	2 teaspoons
3	**egg whites**	3
225 g	**Cadbury's Fingers (about 1½ packets)**	8 oz
	Father Christmas figure	
	Christmas cake decorations	
16-cm	**deep square cake tin, greased and lined**	6½-in
25-cm	**square cake board**	10-in

The cake itself may be wrapped and frozen but the icing and decorations should only be added when the cake is to be used.

Do not remove the paper lining from fruit cakes if they are to be stored; it helps to keep them moist. Peel off the paper just before use.

Sift the dry ingredients together. Cream the butter and sugar, then gradually beat in the eggs with a spoonful of flour. Stir in all the remaining cake ingredients, mixing well to make a dropping consistency that is not too stiff. Turn the mixture into the prepared tin and hollow out the centre. Stand the tin on a baking tray and bake in the centre of a warm oven (160 c, 325 f, gas 3) for about 2 hours until cooked through. Cool in the tin.

Use the icing sugar, glycerine and egg whites to make up the royal icing as described on page 24. Secure the cake on to the centre of the board with a little icing, then cover both the cake and board, leaving the icing standing in peaks. Place eight Finger biscuits horizontally on each side, as shown in the picture. Encourage the icing to flow over the top biscuits.

Arrange a circle of halved Fingers on the top of the cake. Leave the icing to dry before putting the Father Christmas in position in the middle of the Finger chimney. Add the cake decorations.

This cake is not a rich fruit cake so it should be eaten within a fortnight.

Star Sparkles

Illustrated on page 95

These biscuits are quite effective hung on a Christmas tree but should be placed high enough to be out of the way of dogs or small children. For extra brightness, stick a silver sugar ball on each point.

Metric		Imperial
125 g	**butter**	4 oz
75 g	**caster sugar**	3 oz
1	**egg yolk**	1
225 g	**plain flour, sifted**	8 oz
50 g	**Cadbury's Bournvita**	2 oz
	Icing	
25 g	**Cadbury's Bournvita**	1 oz
175 g	**icing sugar, sifted**	6 oz
75 g	**coloured sugar crystals**	3 oz
	star-shaped biscuit cutter	
2	**baking trays, greased**	2
7 metres	**gold coloured string**	8 yards

Cream the butter and sugar together until pale and soft, then beat in the egg yolk. Add the flour, then the Bournvita and mix until the mixture forms a dough. Roll out on a lightly floured surface to about 3 mm/$\frac{1}{8}$ in thick. Cut out the biscuits; the exact number will depend on the size of your cutter. Place the biscuits slightly apart on the baking trays and bake in a moderate oven (180 c, 350 f, gas 4) for about 10 minutes. Cool on a wire tray. With a skewer, carefully make a hole in each warm biscuit, big enough for the string to go through later.

Dissolve the Bournvita for the icing in two spoonfuls of boiling water. Gradually blend in the icing sugar, making a smooth, fairly thick icing. Spread the icing neatly on each biscuit, taking it right up to the points. Sprinkle on the coloured sugar and leave to dry. Thread a piece of cord through each biscuit so that they can be hung on the Christmas tree. Store in an airtight container. *Makes about 30*

Forest Fruit Cake

Illustrated opposite

Metric		Imperial
175 g	**butter**	6 oz
175 g	**caster sugar**	6 oz
3	**eggs, size 2**	3
175 g	**plain flour, sifted**	6 oz
5 ml	**baking powder**	1 teaspoon
50 g	**ground almonds**	2 oz
1	**small orange**	1
75 g	**Cadbury's Dairy Milk Chocolate**	3 oz
75 g	**glacé cherries**	3 oz
50 g	**glacé pineapple**	2 oz
50 g	**chopped mixed peel**	2 oz
50 g	**sultanas**	2 oz
	Decoration	
400 g	**chocolate butter icing (page 21)**	14 oz
5 large	**Cadbury's Flakes**	5 large
	ribbon decoration	
18-cm	**deep round cake tin, greased and lined**	7-in

Wrap the complete cake in foil and freeze for up to a month.

Clean and dry fruit should always be used when making any type of fruit cake. If cherries are sticky, wash them and leave to dry before use.

Cream the butter and sugar together. Gradually beat in the eggs, then fold in the flour and baking powder with the ground almonds. Finely grate the orange rind, and add to the cake mixture. Squeeze out the juice. Cut each square of chocolate into four. Chop the cherries and pineapple quite roughly. Mix all the fruit and chocolate into the mixture with enough orange juice to make a fairly stiff dropping consistency. Spoon the mixture into the prepared tin and level the surface, slightly hollowing out the centre. Place the tin on a baking tray and bake the cake in a moderate oven (180 c, 350 f, gas 4) for 1–1½ hours until cooked through. Allow to cool a little in the tin before turning out on to a wire tray. Later, peel off the greaseproof paper.

Cover the cake liberally with the chocolate butter icing and mark the top into rings with a fork. Lift the cake on to an attractive flat plate or board. Cut the Flakes into thinner pieces, keeping them as long as possible. Carefully press upright pieces of Flake on to the side of the cake, mixing the large and smaller pieces to resemble the bark of a tree – this is remarkably realistic. Dust with sifted icing sugar and place a neat bow on top.

Forest Fruit Cake; Festive Yule Log (see page 101); Christmas Tree Biscuits (see page 100)

Christmas Tree Biscuits

Illustrated on page 99

Metric		Imperial
125 g	**plain flour, sifted**	4 oz
25 g	**ground almonds**	1 oz
50 g	**caster sugar**	2 oz
125 g	**butter**	4 oz
20 ml	**Bournville Cocoa**	1 tablespoon
20 ml	**Cadbury's Drinking Chocolate**	1 tablespoon
	Decoration	
120 ml	**icing sugar, sifted** 3 heaped tablespoons	
	green and red food colouring	
25 g	**coloured sugar balls**	1 oz
7	**Cadbury's Flake from the Family Pack**	7
225 g	**marzipan**	8 oz
	Christmas tree biscuit cutter	
1	**baking tray, greased and floured**	1
1	**greaseproof paper piping bag**	1

The undecorated biscuits may be frozen, or stored in an airtight container for a short time.

Draw a pointed triangle on cardboard, making it fit the centre of the tree shape. Allow at least 0.5 cm/¼ in from the edge or else the uncooked mixture could break. Use the cut-out cardboard shape for all the biscuit centres.

The biscuit dough can be made in one colour for speed. The plain mixture could be flavoured with a little finely grated lemon or orange rind.

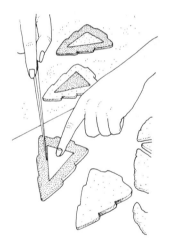

Measure 100 g/3 oz of the flour into a bowl. Add the ground almonds and sugar, then rub in the butter until the mixture resembles breadcrumbs. Divide the dry mixture in half. Knead the extra flour into one amount and the sifted cocoa and drinking chocolate into the other. On a lightly floured surface, roll out the mixtures in turn to a thickness of about 0.5 cm/¼ in. Cut out as many trees as possible, using the tree cutter, making an even number in both colours. Cut out a triangle of mixture from the middle of each biscuit, then interchange the triangular centres to alternate the colours. Press the pieces lightly together and transfer the biscuits to the baking tray. Bake in a moderate oven (180 c, 350 f, gas 4) for about 12 minutes until cooked. Leave the cooked biscuits to harden and cool a little before lifting them off the tray.

Mix the icing sugar with just enough water or lemon juice and a few drops of green colouring to make a fairly stiff glacé icing. Fill the piping bag with the icing, cut off the tip, then pipe zig-zag lines on each tree to represent the coloured lights. Press on the sugar balls. Cut each Flake into three equal pieces and use a dot of icing to secure a piece of Flake to the base of each biscuit tree. Leave to set for about an hour.

Knead a little red colouring evenly into the marzipan, then roll out to about the same thickness as the biscuits. Cut into strips measuring 6 cm/2¼ in. in length and about 2 cm/¾ in wide, making the same number as there are biscuits. Wrap the marzipan round the base of the Flake and biscuit, with the join at the back. The trees should now stand up. *Makes about 20*

Cutting the Flake
1 *To halve Flake, cut across the middle with a sharp knife in one definite movement.*

2 *Split the Flake lengthways to make thinner strips. Put the point of a plain sharp knife between the grooves and press gently but evenly.*

Festive Yule Log

Illustrated on page 99

Metric		Imperial
1	**unfilled chocolate Swiss roll (page 18)**	1
300 g	**plain butter icing (page 21)**	10 oz
10	**Cadbury's Flake from the Family Pack**	10
25 g	**Bournville Cocoa**	1 oz
	icing sugar	

Make up the Swiss roll and spread the inside with just under half the butter icing. Lay two Flakes along one short end, then roll up the cake as tightly as possible. Blend the cocoa to a paste with a little boiling water, then mix into the remaining butter icing, but do not make it too stiff. Cover the length of the roll with the soft icing, leaving the ends uncovered. With a sharp knife, cut off a good slice of cake at an angle and secure it on one side of the roll with a little icing. Assemble the cake on a plate or square cake board. Cut the Flakes into smaller pieces (see diagram) and neatly press them into the icing, ensuring that all the pieces lie in the same direction. Sprinkle the Flake crumbs over the top to fill any gaps and dust with icing sugar. *Serves 6*

Yuletide Cake

Illustrated on page 102

Open freeze the Yule Log. Wrap carefully in foil when the cake is hard. Allow a minimum of 3 hours for the cake to defrost.

Metric		Imperial
	icing sugar	
350 g	**chocolate butter icing**	12 oz
	(1½ quantities, page 21)	
2	**chocolate Swiss rolls, filled (page 18)**	2
28-cm	**square cake board**	11-inch
	Christmas cake decorations	

Cover the cake board with sieved icing sugar. Spread butter icing over both the Swiss rolls. Put one on the board. Cut a slice off one end of the second Swiss roll then another third, cut at an angle. Stick the pieces on as 'branches', with the icing, covering all the ends. Place the slice on the top of the roll. Form lines in the icing to give the log texture. Arrange Christmas trees, robins and any other decorations in position. Dust with icing sugar.

Party Candles

Illustrated opposite

Peach slices are equally effective on the candles. White glacé icing (see page 21) may be used instead of the butter icing but it should be quite thick so that it does not run off.

Metric		Imperial
I	**chocolate Swiss roll**	I
8	**Cadbury's Flake from the Family Pack**	8
312-g	**can mandarin oranges**	11-oz
about 50 g	**vanilla butter icing (see page 21)**	about 2 oz
2	**glacé cherries**	2

greaseproof paper piping bag

Cut the Swiss roll into 8 even slices. Stand a Flake in the centre of each, sticking it through the cake. Drain the juice from the mandarin oranges. Arrange the mandarin segments on the slices of Swiss roll, round the Flake. Fill a paper piping bag with the butter icing, cut off the tip and pipe dribbles of the icing coming down from the top of each Flake. Cut the cherries into four and stand one piece upright on the top of each Flake, to represent the candle 'flame'. *Makes 8*

Mini Mountains

Illustrated on page 95

Open freeze the complete cakes. Wrap carefully, label and freeze for up to a month.

An individual cake would make a welcome small gift for someone living alone. They also look very nice as part of an edible Christmas table decoration.

Metric		Imperial
50 g	**butter, softened**	2 oz
50 g	**light soft brown sugar**	2 oz
1	**egg**	1
50 g	**self-raising flour**	2 oz
30 ml	**mincemeat**	1 good tablespoon
	Decoration	
225 g	**chocolate butter icing (page 21)**	8 oz
3 large	**Cadbury's Flakes**	3 large
50 g	**marzipan**	2 oz
	red and green food colouring	
4 (125-ml)	**individual round moulds,**	4 (4–5-fl oz)
	greased	

Party Candles; Yuletide Cake (see page 101); Shaggy Dog Cake (see page 69)

Beat the butter, sugar, egg and flour together thoroughly, then stir in the mincemeat. Divide the mixture equally between the moulds, place them on a baking tray and bake in a moderate oven (180 c, 350 f, gas 4) for 20–25 minutes. Turn out and cool on a wire rack.

Spread the cakes with the butter icing. Using a sharp knife, cut the Flakes into small neat pieces and press on to the cakes as shown in the picture. Dust with icing sugar.

Work red colouring into one-third of the marzipan and green colouring into the remaining portion. Roll small pieces of red marzipan into balls. Roll out the green marzipan and make holly leaves as described on page 236. Arrange leaves and berries on top of each litte cake. Lift the cakes on to individual paper plates or arrange them together attractively on a board. *Makes 4*

Fir Cone Cakes

Illustrated on page 154

Metric		Imperial
20 ml	**Bournville cocoa**	1 tablespoon
50 g	**self-raising flour**	2 oz
	pinch of salt	
50 g	**soft margarine**	2 oz
50 g	**caster sugar**	2 oz
1	**egg**	1
	Butter icing	
50 g	**butter**	2 oz
125 g	**icing sugar, sieved**	4 oz
20 ml	**Bournville cocoa**	1 tablespoon
20 ml	**boiling water**	1 tablespoon
	vanilla essence	
	Decoration	
2	**large packets Cadbury's Buttons**	2
10	**bun tins, greased**	10

Open freeze the cakes covered with the butter icing but omit the Buttons as they come off easily in the freezer. Wrap, seal and label the cakes. Use within 3 months. Cover with Buttons when the cakes are thawed.

The number of buns will vary according to the size of your tins.

Sieve the cocoa and flour with a pinch of salt into a bowl. Add the margarine, sugar and egg then beat thoroughly until well mixed. Divide mixture between the tins, shaking each one so that the mixture settles. Bake in a moderately hot oven (190°C, 375°F, Gas Mark 5) for 15–20 minutes. Turn out and cool on a wire tray.

Make the butter icing by creaming the butter with the sieved icing sugar. Mix the cocoa with the boiling water then add to the butter icing with a few drops of vanilla essence. Mix well. Turn the buns upside down and cover the tops and sides with butter icing.

Divide the Buttons evenly between the cakes; polish them in the palm of your hand and arrange in overlapping rows. A small piece of fir may be stuck into one end of each cake.

Makes 10

Easter Celebration Cake

Illustrated on page 107

Pack, label and freeze complete for up to a month.

To ensure that the decoration is even, giving a more professional finish, pipe the loops at each quarter of the cake before filling in the loops between.

If a quicker decoration is preferred, crumbled Flake can be used to coat the sides of the cake.

Metric		Imperial
4	**eggs, separated**	4
1	**lemon**	1
150 g	**icing sugar, sifted**	5 oz
75 g	**plain flour**	3 oz
25 g	**cornflour**	1 oz
120 ml	**apricot jam**	6 tablespoons
125 g	**marzipan**	4 oz
	yellow food colouring	
350 g	**plain butter icing (page 21)**	12 oz
10	**Cadbury's Flake from the Family Pack**	10
20-cm	**deep round cake tin, greased and base lined**	8-in
	star vegetable pipe	
	small star pipe	
	nylon piping bag	
2	**greaseproof paper piping bags**	2

Beat the egg yolks with the finely grated lemon rind, half the strained juice and the icing sugar until pale and fluffy. Carefully fold in the stiffly beaten egg whites, then the flours, sifted together. Pour the mixture into the prepared tin and bake in a moderate oven (180 C, 350 F, gas 4) for about 45 minutes until the sponge springs back when touched. Turn out and cool on a wire tray.

Cut the cake in half and sandwich it together again with half the jam. Mark a 7.5-cm/3-in circle in the centre of the cake with a skewer, then spread the remaining jam over the outside ring, leaving the centre clear. Soften the marzipan with enough lemon juice to give a piping consistency. Fill the nylon bag, with the large pipe attached, with the marzipan then pipe 16 loops round the inner circle, as shown in the picture. Place the cake under a hot grill for a few minutes to brown lightly and cook the marzipan.

Beat a little yellow colouring into the prepared butter icing, then spread it quite liberally over the sides of the cake, using about two-thirds of the icing. Lift the cake on to a plate or board. Halve the Flakes, then shave them into smaller pieces to stand round the edge of the cake, pressing them in well. Fit the smaller star pipe in a piping bag and pipe an edge of the remaining icing on the cake. Decorate with Easter decorations.

Valentine Spectacular

Illustrated opposite

Metric		Imperial
6	**eggs, separated**	6
225 g	**icing sugar, sifted**	8 oz
1	**orange**	1
50 g	**cornflour**	2 oz
150 g	**plain flour**	5 oz
	Decoration	
80 ml	**Cadbury's Chocolate Spread**	4 tablespoons
80 ml	**seedless raspberry jam**	4 tablespoons
350 g	**plain butter icing (page 21)**	12 oz
	pink food colouring	
12	**Cadbury's Flake from the Family Pack**	12
350 g	**royal icing (page 24)**	12 oz
80 ml	**glacé icing (page 24),**	4 tablespoons
	coloured pink	
18-cm	**round deep cake tin, greased**	7-in
	and base lined	
18-cm	**square deep cake tin, greased**	7-in
	and base lined	
	small star pipe	
	star vegetable pipe	
1	**nylon piping bag**	1
1	**greaseproof paper piping bag**	1
35-cm	**heart-shaped or round cake board**	14-in
1	**rose**	1

The complete cake may be frozen. Wrap carefully. Allow at least 4 hours for the cake to thaw.

This is not really a difficult cake to prepare but it needs time, particularly for the decoration. It's worth practising the loops on the kitchen surface first. The finish is all important. Pipe the loops at all four quarters first and space the others evenly in between.

For ease, plain butter icing may be piped round the edge instead of the royal icing, but the white royal icing gives a particularly attractive, crisp finish and enhances the overall look of the cake.

Warming the chocolate spread makes it easier to spread on the soft sponge.

Whisk the egg yolks, icing sugar, finely grated orange rind and the strained juice until fluffy and pale in colour. Whisk the egg whites to the soft peak stage and carefully fold them into the yolks together with the flours, sifted together. Divide the mixture equally between the prepared tins and bake in a moderate oven (180 c, 350 f, gas 4) for about 25 minutes, until well risen and cooked. Turn out and cool the cakes on wire trays.

Cut the cakes horizontally through the centre and fill them with chocolate spread. Sandwich together again. Cut the round cake in half. Arrange the square cake diagonally on the board, with the semi-circles at the top. (See Sweetheart Surprise page 84) Stick the cakes together with a little jam. Mark out a heart shape in the centre of the cake, making it 8 cm/3 in. in from the outside edge. Spread this wide outer border with the remaining jam.

Colour the butter icing pink. Fit a large nylon piping bag with the vegetable pipe and fill it with butter icing. Pipe

Valentine Spectacular; Easter Celebration Cake (see page 105)

loops of butter icing over the jam as shown in the picture. Spread the cake sides with the remaining butter icing. Halve all but one of the Flakes, then cut them into thin strips with a sharp knife. Press the cut Flakes upright round the edge of the cake, using all the very small pieces too. Using the small pipe fitted in the greaseproof paper piping bag, pipe a shell edge of royal icing round the inside heart. Cover the loop ends and top and bottom cake edges. Flood the centre with glacé icing. Allow to set. Complete the cake by arranging the whole Flake and a rose on top. *Serves about 16*

Bunny Biscuits

Illustrated on page 114

Metric		Imperial
75 g	**butter**	3 oz
75 g	**caster sugar**	3 oz
1	**egg**	1
	finely grated rind of 1 orange	
225 g	**self-raising flour**	8 oz
2.5 ml	**ground mixed spice**	$\frac{1}{2}$ teaspoon
50 g	**currants**	2 oz
40 ml	**milk**	2 tablespoons
50 g	**Bournville Dark plain chocolate**	50 g
1 large packet	**Cadbury's Buttons**	1 large packet
	rabbit-shaped biscuit cutter	
2	**baking trays, greased**	2
	paint brush	

To get a particularly shiny, golden finish, add an egg yolk to the milk when brushing over the biscuits.

Cream the butter and sugar together until pale and soft, then beat in the egg and orange rind. Sift in the flour and mixed spice, then mix in the currants. Mix well to make a pliable dough, knead quickly then roll out on a lightly floured surface to just under 1 cm/$\frac{1}{4}$ in thick. Cut out shapes with the cutter, rolling the dough trimmings again in between. Arrange the biscuits on the prepared trays and bake carefully in a moderate oven (180 c, 350 f, gas 4) for 10 minutes only.

Brush the biscuits with milk, then return them to the oven for a further 10 minutes until crisp and nicely coloured. Be careful that the edges are not too brown. Lift off and cool.

Melt the chocolate in a small bowl. With the paint brush, brush all the ears, then the paws of the bunny biscuits with chocolate. Dab a little on the tails and stick on a Button. *Makes about 24*

Cute Chicks

Illustrated on page 114

The cakes will freeze complete but do not store them too long as small cake items tend to dry out more than larger ones.

The dariole tins are available in different sizes. Make these cakes in the larger ones if possible; although there will be less chicks, they will look more effective.

Press the top of each cake on to a fork so that they are easily held to spread with butter icing. If the icing is not too hard, the crumbly cake mixture will be easier to coat.

Metric		Imperial
125 g	**soft margarine**	4 oz
125 g	**caster sugar**	4 oz
2	**eggs**	2
1	**small orange**	1
125 g	**self-raising flour, sifted**	4 oz
	Decoration	
400 g	**plain butter icing (page 21)**	14 oz
40 ml	**Bournville Cocoa**	2 tablespoons
	yellow food colouring	
125 g	**desiccated coconut**	4 oz
10–14	**sugar orange slices**	10–14
30–40	**silver sugar balls**	30–40
1	**Cadbury's Flake**	1
1 small packet	**Cadbury's Buttons**	1 small packet
15–20	**dariole cake tins, well greased**	15–20
	baking tray	

Cream the margarine and sugar together. Beat in the eggs and the finely grated orange rind. Fold in the flour, then add enough orange juice to make a fairly soft dropping consistency. Three-quarter fill the prepared tins, tapping them on the surface so that the mixture reaches the bottom. Stand on a baking tray and bake in batches according to the number of tins available, in a moderately hot oven (190 c, 375 f, gas 5) for about 25 minutes. Turn out and cool on a wire tray. This mixture will make between 15–20 cakes depending on the actual size of the tins.

Prepare the butter icing according to the recipe instructions. Mix the cocoa with a little boiling water, or hot orange juice and beat it into the icing. Turn the cakes upside down and cover with chocolate icing. Work a few drops of colouring into the coconut, blending it in evenly. Spread on a plate then roll the iced cakes in it.

Cut the orange slices into three triangles. Stick two pieces into each cake, with the points outwards to represent beaks. Press silver balls in for eyes. Cut the Flake into short pieces and use it to make a crest and tail for each of the chick cakes, as shown in the picture. Halve the Buttons and stick them in the sides as flapping wings. *Makes 15–20*

Easter Egg Cake

Illustrated opposite

Metric		Imperial
1	**pudding basin cake (page 20)**	1
	almond essence	
	pink food colouring	
	Decoration	
550 g	**plain butter icing (page 21)**	1 lb 4 oz
20 ml	**Bournville Cocoa**	1 tablespoon
$\frac{1}{2}$	lemon	$\frac{1}{2}$
	yellow food colouring	
about 18	**yellow sugar primroses and daffodils**	about 18
1.2-litre	**ovenproof basin, greased**	2-pint
1	**greaseproof paper piping bag**	1
	small star pipe	

Freeze the cake without the sugar flowers, which will store very well in a dry, clean place.

Making sugar flowers is a good way of using small quantities of left-over royal icing. This is an easy method of decorating cakes at a moment's notice.

Make up the cake mixture as described in the recipe, but do not mix in the cocoa. Divide the mixture into three. Now add the cocoa to one amount, a little essence to a second portion and pink colouring to the third. Spoon the mixtures alternately into the basin, fold through only once to give the cake a marbled effect. Smooth over the top, hollowing out the centre slightly. Bake in a moderate oven (180 C, 350 F, gas 4) for about 1–1¼ hours until well risen and cooked. Test with a skewer to make sure the middle of the cake is cooked. Leave briefly in the basin before turning out to cool on a wire tray.

Have the butter icing made. Blend the cocoa with a spoonful of boiling water then mix into a quarter of the icing. Add the strained lemon juice to the remainder with a little yellow food colouring.

Spread yellow butter icing over the flat side of the cake then cut it in half down the middle. Press the iced surfaces together. Cover the cake with yellow butter icing, spreading it evenly. Lift the cake on to an oval plate. Fit the star pipe into the piping bag and fill the bag with chocolate butter icing. Pipe diagonal lines over the cake in opposite directions so that they cross, making a diamond pattern. Complete the piping with a shell border round the base. Arrange the flowers over the surface, like a traditional chocolate Easter egg.

Serves at least 8

Humpty Dumpty (see page 112); Easter Egg Cake; Crispie Nests (see page 113)

Humpty Dumpty

Illustrated on page 111

Metric		Imperial
3 egg quantity plain Victoria sandwich cake		
(page 16)		
40 ml	**Bournville Cocoa**	2 tablespoons
350 g	**chocolate butter icing (page 21)**	12 oz
1	**Cadbury's Chocolate Easter Egg**	1
2 squares	**Bournville Dark plain chocolate,**	2 squares
	melted	
	red food colouring	
175 g	**marzipan**	6 oz
18-cm	**square cake tin, greased and base lined,**	7-in
	divided in half with greased, foil-covered card	
7.5-cm	**fluted biscuit cutter**	3-in
	wooden board	

The wall of cake may be frozen.

A divided cake tin, giving two different coloured cakes, makes a more effective wall than using a marbled cake mixture.

To divide the tin, cut a thin piece of card the depth of the cake tin and wrap it in foil. It should be as tight a fit as possible so that no cake mixture seeps through. Grease this foil-covered card as well as the cake tin.

Make up the cake mixture, then divide it in half. Dissolve the cocoa in a little boiling water and mix into one amount. Spread this in half the prepared tin, with the plain mixture in the other half. Bake in a moderately hot oven (190 c, 375 f, gas 5) for about 30 minutes until well risen and cooked. Turn out carefully and cool on a wire tray.

Have the butter icing ready. Slice both cakes horizontally through the middle, then cut all four pieces into four again, widthways across the cake into small rectangles. On a suitable wooden board, build up a wall of cake in alternate colours, making it four layers high. Stick each piece of cake to the other with butter icing and spread a layer on top, reserving just a little butter icing to use later.

Unwrap the egg and paint the rim with melted chocolate, then stick the two halves together. Stand in a jug to set.

Knead red colouring into just over half the marzipan. Roll out the red marzipan about 0.5 cm/¼ in thick and cut out a circle with the biscuit cutter. Place this circle of marzipan in a patty tin or cup and leave it in the refrigerator for about 15 minutes until hard enough to handle. Stand the marzipan cup in the centre of the wall of cake, put a little butter icing in the base then stand the egg in it. Using the red marzipan, cut out two strips for the trousers, a small circle and a round piece for Humpty's hat. Cut two small stars from the scraps of red marzipan to make eyes. Take the plain marzipan and mould thin rolls for arms and legs; a small ball for the nose; a ring for the mouth and two pieces for eyes as shown in the picture. Assemble Humpty Dumpty on the wall. *Serves about 8*

Crispie Nests

Illustrated on page 111

Stand the paper cases in a tray of patty tins as they are easier to fill when the paper cannot bend too much.

Metric		Imperial
50 g	**butter**	2 oz
1 packet	**marshmallows**	1 packet
125 g	**'Rice Krispies'**	4 oz
225 g	**Cadbury's Mini-Eggs**	8 oz
18	**paper cake cases**	18

Melt the butter and marshmallows slowly in quite a large pan. When melted and mixed, stir in the krispies and coat them completely in the marshmallow mixture. Divide the mixture evenly between the paper cases pressing it together slightly. Make a hollow in the centre with the back of a spoon, then leave to get quite cold before filling with mini-eggs.

Makes 18

Chocolate Caramels

Use a heavy saucepan with a thick base for making sweets. Sugar reaches a high temperature but must not be allowed to burn as this will spoil the taste.

Metric		Imperial
50 g	**Cadbury's drinking chocolate**	2 oz
165 g	**golden syrup**	6 oz
225 g	**sugar**	8 oz
284 ml	**single cream**	$\frac{1}{2}$ pint
16-cm	**square shallow cake tin, lightly oiled**	$6\frac{1}{2}$-inch

Measure the drinking chocolate, syrup, sugar and cream into a fairly large, heavy saucepan. Stir until the sugar has dissolved then bring slowly to the boil. Continue cooking gently for about 1 hour, leaving the pan uncovered. Do not allow the base to catch. Stir occasionally if necessary. The mixture will thicken considerably and reduce by half. Pour into the tin and leave to cool. Before it is quite hard, mark into squares. The caramels may be wrapped in squares of waxed or cellophane paper and stored in a dry place. Use in place of Cadbury's Mini-Eggs to fill Crispie Nests, if liked.

Nest Cake

Illustrated opposite

The cake may be frozen without the decoration which does not freeze well. Have the chocolate cereal mixture quite hot to press on to a cold cake.

Although rather messy, the easiest way to press on the chocolate cereal mixture is with your fingers; but be careful not to handle it when it is too hot.

The nest is also most effective decorated with thin strips of Flake. Cover the ring cake with 175 g/6 oz chocolate butter icing (page 21), then press on 4 or 5 large Cadbury's Flakes, using the small cut pieces and the crumbs sprinkled over the top. Both cakes may be decorated with the traditional Easter chicks or made at other times of the year. Cadbury's Creme Eggs are generally available all year if the smaller eggs are difficult to find.

Metric		Imperial
20 ml	**Bournville Cocoa**	1 tablespoon
100 g	**self-raising flour**	3½ oz
1.25 ml	**salt**	light ¼ teaspoon
125 g	**dark soft brown sugar**	4 oz
50 g	**soft margarine**	2 oz
1	**egg**	1
	finely grated rind and juice of ½ orange	
2.5 ml	**vanilla essence**	½ teaspoon
	Decoration	
100 g	**Bournville Dark plain chocolate**	3½ oz
50 g	**butter**	2 oz
3	**'Shredded Wheat'**	3
80 ml	**Cadbury's Chocolate Spread**	4 tablespoons
1 large	**Cadbury's Flake**	1 large
125 g	**Cadbury's Mini-Eggs**	4 oz
18-cm/700-ml capacity	**ring mould tin, well greased**	7-in/1¼-pint capacity

Sift the cocoa, flour and salt together into a bowl. Add the sugar, then rub in the margarine. Beat in the egg, finely grated orange rind, strained juice and the essence. Pour this soft batter-type mixture into the prepared tin and bake in a moderate oven (180 C, 350 F, gas 4) for 35–40 minutes until well risen and cooked through. Gently turn out to cool on a wire tray.

Melt the chocolate and butter together in a good sized saucepan. Crumble in the breakfast cereal and stir until it is completely coated in chocolate. Warm the chocolate spread separately, then quickly spread it over the cake and press on the 'Shredded Wheat' mixture. Leave the centre clear but if some mixture remains, put it into the hole once the cake is on a board or plate. Cut the Flake into thin pieces and sprinkle over the top. Leave the chocolate to cool and set before filling the centre with mini-eggs.

Nest Cake; Cute Chicks (see page 109); Bunny Biscuits (see page 108)

Cobweb Cake

Illustrated on page 118

Metric		Imperial
150 g	**self-raising flour**	5 oz
50 g	**Bournville Cocoa**	2 oz
2.5 ml	**bicarbonate of soda**	½ teaspoon
125 g	**soft margarine**	4 oz
225 g	**dark soft brown sugar**	8 oz
2	**eggs**	2
10 ml	**peppermint essence**	2 teaspoons
25 g	**ground almonds**	1 oz
142 ml	**soured cream**	¼ pint
	Decoration	
50 g	**Bournville Dark plain chocolate**	50 g
175 g	**icing sugar, sifted**	6 oz
	green food colouring	
1 packet	**Cadbury's Buttons**	1 packet
225 g	**plain butter icing (page 21)**	8 oz
	peppermint essence	
1	**liquorice shoe lace**	1
6	**marshmallows**	6
2 (19-cm)	**round cake tins, greased**	2 (7½-in)
	and base lined	
1	**greaseproof paper piping bag**	1

Freeze the plain cake and decorate when required.

Be careful when adding peppermint flavouring. Peppermint oils are generally much stronger than essences, but it is wise to add any kind of peppermint flavouring slowly.

Warm the chocolate in the piping bag, if it gets too thick. A plain writing pipe may be used but this tends to clog up first and good results can be obtained with just a small hole in the end of the greaseproof paper piping bag.

Icing the cake

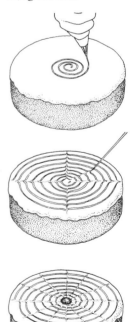

Sift the dry ingredients into a bowl, then add all the other cake ingredients and beat well for about three minutes until thoroughly blended.

Divide the mixture between the tins, hollowing out the centres slightly. Bake in a moderately hot oven (190 c, 375 f, gas 5) for about 35 minutes until well risen and cooked. Turn out and cool on a wire tray.

Melt *half* the chocolate in a small bowl over a pan of hot water. Mix the icing sugar with enough water (or fruit juice) and colouring to make an icing with a fairly thick coating consistency. Put the soft chocolate into the piping bag and cut off the very tip to make a small hole. Spread the icing evenly over one sponge. Immediately pipe a spiral of chocolate from the centre of the cake outwards, as shown in the diagram. Draw twelve straight lines out from the centre with a skewer then place a Button in the centre. Leave to set.

Colour the butter icing green and add essence to taste. Sandwich the cakes together with a little of this butter icing and spread some round the side. Wrap a narrow strip of greaseproof paper round the top half of the side of the cake. Grate the remaining chocolate and press this on to the butter icing below the paper, all round the cake. Take off the paper, carefully easing it away from the butter icing with a knife. Press on a Button below each chocolate line, as shown in the picture. Carefully lift the cake on to a suitable plate or board.

Cut the liquorice into pieces about 2 cm/¾ in long. Press eight pieces into each marshmallow, using a skewer to make holes. Pipe two chocolate eyes and top each with a Button to complete the spiders. Arrange them around the cake.

Serves 10–12

Halloween Magic

Illustrated on page 118

Freeze the cake filled and covered in butter icing but without the chocolate decorations.

Children's books are a useful source of inspiration for cake decorations. Trace an outline then prick it on to the cake or pipe it straight on to waxed paper. Chocolate or royal icing decorations will keep for some time in a cool dry place and are handy to have around for an unexpected treat.

Metric		Imperial
50 g	**Bournville Dark plain chocolate**	50 g
125 g	**butter**	4 oz
175 g	**soft brown sugar**	6 oz
2	**eggs, separated**	2
175 g	**self-raising flour**	6 oz
2.5 ml	**salt**	½ teaspoon
2.5 ml	**ground mixed spice**	½ teaspoon
2.5 ml	**ground cinnamon**	½ teaspoon
25 g	**chopped candied peel**	1 oz
80 ml	**milk**	4 tablespoons
	Decoration	
80 ml	**lemon curd**	4 tablespoons
225 g	**plain butter icing (page 16)**	8 oz
5 ml	**ground mixed spice**	1 teaspoon
	yellow food colouring	
50 g	**Bournville Dark plain chocolate**	50 g
4	**Cadbury's Flake from the Family Pack**	4
10	**chocolate cats (page 119)**	10
20-cm	**round deep cake tin, greased and base lined**	8-in
1	**greaseproof paper piping bag**	1
	waxed paper	

Melt the chocolate for the cake. Cream the butter and sugar, stir in the egg yolks and melted chocolate. Sift all the dry ingredients together and fold them into the mixture, followed by the peel and milk, mixing well. Whisk the egg whites until stiff and fold them in before turning the mixture into the prepared tin, levelling it carefully. Bake in a warm oven (160 c, 325 f, gas 3) for 1–1¼ hours until well risen and cooked. Turn out and cool on a wire tray.

Slice the cake horizontally through the middle and sandwich

it back together with half the lemon curd. Beat the remaining curd into the butter icing with the mixed spice and enough yellow colouring to make a rich colour. Spread this icing all over the cake, making it as smooth as possible.

Trace a suitable witch's outline, first on to a piece of paper and then on the centre of the cake. Melt the chocolate, fill the piping bag with it and cut off just the tip. Follow the marked outline with chocolate, filling in the hair, feet and other suitable features. Pipe star and moon shapes on to the waxed paper, shiny side up, and fill them in with more chocolate. Leave the chocolate to dry completely before peeling the shapes off the paper and placing them on the cake. Make a broomstick of Flakes and arrange a thin piece on top as the hat brim. Fill in the witch with crumbled Flake.

Lift the cake on to a brightly coloured plate before standing the chocolate cats round the edge. The ones at the back can be made to peep over the top, depending on where the cake is placed on the table. *Serves 10*

Chocolate Cats

Illustrated opposite

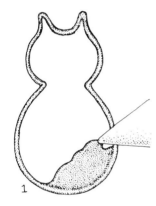

Metric		Imperial
100 g	**Bournville Dark plain chocolate**	$3\frac{1}{2}$ oz
20–30	**red sugar balls**	20–30
2	**glacé cherries**	2
5	**red liquorice shoe laces**	5
1	**greaseproof paper piping bag**	1
	waxed paper	

Melt the chocolate carefully in a small bowl over a pan of hot water. Meanwhile, draw or trace one or several cat outlines, each about 6 cm/$2\frac{1}{4}$ in high, on to a piece of white paper. Place waxed paper on top of the drawing, waxed side upwards. Fill the piping bag with melted chocolate, cut off just the tip, then pipe the cat outlines and fill in the centres (1). Make more than you require for the cake in case of breakages. If the chocolate hardens as you are working, put the bag in a warm place to melt the chocolate again.

Press two red eyes in position and cut up small pieces of cherry for noses and liquorice for whiskers and tails (2). Leave the cats to harden for between 1–2 hours, depending on how warm the kitchen is, before carefully peeling them off the paper.

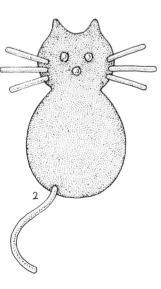

Cobweb Cake (see page 116);
Halloween Magic (see page 117);
Shiny Black Hats (see page 120)

Shiny Black Hats

Illustrated on page 118

Metric		Imperial
1 packet	**any round Cadbury biscuit**	1 packet
40 ml	**apricot jam**	2 tablespoons
10	**marshmallows**	10
100 g	**Bournville Dark plain chocolate**	3½ oz
5 ml	**bland corn oil**	1 teaspoon
25 g	**caster sugar**	1 oz
40 ml	**water**	2 tablespoons
3	**glacé cherries**	3

Select ten biscuits and spread a little jam on the centre of the plain side of each. Stick a marshmallow on each, with the wide end downwards. Place on a wire tray.

Carefully melt the broken up chocolate, oil, sugar and water together in a small pan over a low heat, stirring until melted and quite smooth. Leave the icing to cool and thicken enough to be able to coat each marshmallow and biscuit completely. Leave the coating to set. Stick a piece of cherry at a jaunty angle on the side of each hat. *Makes 10*

Firework Fountains

Illustrated on page 123

Metric		Imperial
250 ml	**condensed milk**	8 fl oz
350 g	**icing sugar, sifted**	12 oz
100 g	**Cadbury's Roast Almond, grated**	3½ oz
	grated rind of ½ lemon	
175 g	**desiccated coconut**	6 oz
50 g	**Bournville Dark plain chocolate**	50 g
	knob of butter	
2	**glacé cherries**	2

Mix the condensed milk and icing sugar together. Stir in the grated almond chocolate and lemon rind, then work in the coconut until the mixture is pliable. Divide into 15 equal amounts and shape them into pyramids, rolling in between your hands. Stand the pyramids on a tray.

Melt the plain chocolate in a small bowl with the butter. Dip the pointed end of each pyramid into the chocolate and let it run down the sides. Stand a small piece of cherry upright in the top of each cake. Leave to set. *Makes 15*

Bonfire Cake

Illustrated on page 123

The cake may be wrapped and frozen complete and kept for about a month.

An artistic person could model a head out of marzipan or fondant. It needs to be about 5 cm/2 in high, with a black paper or marzipan hat on top. A whole small Flake may be pushed in behind the guy to represent the stake.

Metric		Imperial
1	**pudding basin cake (page 20)**	1
	Decoration	
350 g	**plain butter icing (page 21)**	12 oz
	yellow and red food colouring	
12–16	**Cadbury's Flake from the Family Pack**	12–16
1.2-litre	**ovenproof basin, greased**	2-pint
	guy's head, made from card or marzipan	

Make up and bake the cake as described in the recipe.

Divide the butter icing in half and colour one portion bright yellow and the other a good red. It does not matter if the icing gets a little soft. Spread nice thick lines of alternate colours of butter icing, from the top to the bottom of the turned-out cake, covering it completely. Dip a paint brush into neat food colouring and brush short strokes at irregular intervals over the icing, to highlight the 'flames'. Alternatively, for speed and simplicity, cover the cake completely with just yellow butter icing. Cut the Flakes into thinner strips with a sharp knife. Press the pieces into the icing, letting the brilliant colours show through. Sprinkle the Flake crumbs over the top.

Make the guy's head out of card, drawing on the features, and place it in the centre of the cake. Lift the cake on to a plate or board. *Serves 10–12*

Catherine Wheel Cake

Illustrated opposite

Metric		Imperial
175 g	**soft margarine**	6 oz
175 g	**caster sugar**	6 oz
3	**eggs**	3
175 g	**self-raising flour, sifted**	6 oz
20 ml	**Bournville Cocoa**	1 tablespoon
	pink and green food colouring	
	Decoration	
350 g	**chocolate butter icing (page 21)**	12 oz
175 g	**plain butter icing (page 21), coloured pink**	6 oz
3 (19-cm)	**shallow cake tins, greased and**	3 (7½-in)
	base lined	
2	**greaseproof paper piping bags**	2
	small star pipe	
8	**green or pink cake candles and holders**	8
1	**red cake candle and holder**	1

Freeze the cake complete, wrapping it very carefully. It may be easier to let the icing harden first in the freezer before the cake is wrapped.

The cake can be made in a deep cake tin of the same diameter, with the various colours layered on top of each other. They do run into each other a little, but the cooked cake is still quite effective. Bake for about 55 minutes at the same oven temperature. Cut the cake into three layers, then sandwich together with butter icing.

Cream the margarine and sugar together until pale and light. Beat in the eggs individually, then fold in the flour. Divide the mixture equally into three bowls. Sift the cocoa into one amount, colour another portion pink and add green colouring to the remaining mixture. Spread each colour separately in the prepared cake tins and bake in a moderately hot oven (190 C, 375 F, gas 5) for 20–25 minutes until well risen and cooked. Turn out and cool on a wire tray.

Spread each cake with a little chocolate butter icing and sandwich them together. Reserve equal quantities of both colours of icing, then spread the remaining chocolate icing over the sides of the cake. Run a serrated cake scraper round the side or mark the cake with a fork. Place the pipe in the piping bag, then fill the bag with pink icing. Working from the centre outwards, pipe a spiral scroll of butter icing, leaving space in between as shown in the picture. Empty and discard the bag, clean the pipe, then fill the other bag with chocolate icing and repeat the process, piping a spiral in between the lines of pink icing. Lift the cake on to a suitable plate. Stick the candles in their holders at an angle round the side of the cake with the red one standing straight on the top for the taper. *Serves 10–12*

Bonfire Cake (see page 121); Catherine Wheel Cake; Cannon Balls (see page 135); Firework Fountains (see page 120); Jumping Jacks (see page 137)

Individual Ideas

Small children love small cakes and when you make the delicious examples from this chapter you will find that adults love them, too! Cupid Hearts, Viennese Slices and Scottish Fingers are favourites of children and adults alike, whilst Frosty Bears or Clown Cakes will bring a smile to every child's face.

Sausage Dogs

Metric		Imperial
2	**eggs, size 2**	2
50 g	**caster sugar**	2 oz
50 g	**plain flour**	2 oz
15 ml	**Bournville Cocoa**	3 teaspoons
5	**glacé cherries**	5
20	**currants**	20
1	**Cadbury's Flake, crumbled**	1
142 ml	**double cream**	¼ pint
10	**short strips angelica**	10

tray of sponge finger tins, greased and floured
nylon piping bag
medium star pipe

Whisk the eggs and sugar with an electric mixer or in a bowl over hot water, for about 10 minutes until the whisk leaves a definite trail in the mixture. Fold in the flour and cocoa, sifted together, being careful not to knock out the air but leaving no pockets of flour in the mixture. Spoon the mixture neatly into each tin. Place half a cherry at one end for a nose and two currants just behind for eyes, on only half the total number of cakes. Bake in a fairly hot oven (200 c, 400 f, gas 6) for 10–12 minutes until firm and springy to the touch. Turn out to cool on a wire tray. Bake another batch in the same way, making about 20 sponge fingers in all. Sprinkle the crumbled Flake along the top of the decorated sponges whilst they are still hot. Leave to cool completely.

Whisk the cream until it will hold its shape. Fit the pipe into the piping bag and fill with the cream. Pipe quite a thick layer of cream on the underside of the plain sponges, then sandwich a decorated and plain sponge finger together. Put a star of cream at the tail end of each and stand a small piece of angelica in it. *Makes about 10*

Freeze complete for up to a month, standing them in a firm container so that they do not break or become squashed.

As the cooking time is short, the whisked sponge mixture should stay firm enough for it to be cooked in batches if enough sponge finger tins are not available to cook it all at once. Make an even number.

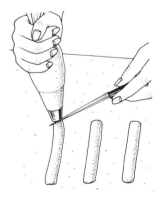

The mixture can also be piped on to well greased and floured baking trays, with a 2-cm/¾-in plain nozzle. Make them the same length by marking straight lines at least 7.5 cm/3 in long on the trays, spacing them well apart.

Cockle Shells

Illustrated on front cover and page 51

It is easy to make the shell shapes smaller for younger children, making double the number of biscuits. The mixture can also be adapted into Iced Gems by making smaller individual stars, baking for about half the time then placing a Button or sugar strands in the centre whilst the biscuits are still hot.

Metric		Imperial
125 g	**butter**	4 oz
25 g	**icing sugar, sifted**	1 oz
125 g	**plain flour**	4 oz
40 ml	**Cadbury's Drinking Chocolate**	2 tablespoons
1 small packet	**Cadbury's Buttons**	1 small packet
225 g	**plain butter icing (page 21)**	8 oz
	pink food colouring	
5 ml	**fresh lemon or orange juice**	1 teaspoon
20 ml	**coloured sugar strands**	1 tablespoon
	icing sugar	
	large nylon piping bag	
	star vegetable pipe	
	baking tray	

Cream the butter, gradually adding the icing sugar. Sift the flour and drinking chocolate together and gradually add to the creamed mixture, beating until quite pliable. Fit the star pipe into the piping bag, fill with the mixture and pipe ten shell shapes on to the baking tray. Bake in a moderately hot oven (190 c, 375 f, gas 5) for 15 minutes. Immediately the biscuits are removed from the oven, press two Buttons on to the narrow end of each biscuit. Lift carefully on to a wire rack to cool.

Match the biscuits into pairs. Colour the butter icing pink and beat in the fruit juice. Spoon into the washed and dried pipe and piping bag, then pipe a generous whirl on one biscuit of each pair and sandwich together. Sprinkle with sugar strands and dust with a little icing sugar before placing on a plate. *Makes 5*

Frosty Bears

Illustrated opposite

Metric		Imperial
50 g	**soft margarine**	2 oz
50 g	**soft brown sugar**	2 oz
2	**eggs**	2
50 g	**self-raising flour**	2 oz
40 ml	**Bournville Cocoa**	2 tablespoons
125 g	**soft cream cheese**	4 oz
25 g	**caster sugar**	1 oz
	Decoration	
1.5 litres	**vanilla ice cream**	2½ pints
1 packet	**Cadbury's Buttons**	1 packet
14 g	**seedless raisins**	½ oz
1	**liquorice shoe lace**	1
12	**paper cake cases**	12
	baking tray	

The cakes can be packed and frozen separately, ready to use later or complete the bears and freeze them in a rigid container for about a week.

To speed assembly, scoop out the ice cream on to a baking tray and leave in the freezer until required.

Beat the margarine, brown sugar, 1 egg, flour and cocoa together in a bowl for about 2 minutes until well mixed and smooth. Divide the mixture equally between the cake cases. Beat the cream cheese to soften, then add the caster sugar and remaining egg. Drop a good teaspoonful of the cheese mixture on to each little cake. Arrange them fairly close together on the baking tray and bake in a moderate oven (180 C, 350 F, gas 4) for about 30 minutes until well risen and cooked. Cool the cakes in their cases on a wire tray.

Just before they are required, place a good scoopful of ice cream on each little cake, pressing it on quite firmly. Press two Buttons into the top of each one for ears, three raisins for the eyes and nose and a small piece of liquorice for the mouth. Complete all of them in the same way and serve immediately. *Makes 12*

Frosty Bears; Sunbathing Penguins (see page 217); Frogland (see page 229)

Pantomime Mice

Illustrated on page 130

Metric		Imperial
125 g	**plain flour**	4 oz
25 g	**Bournville Cocoa**	1 oz
10 ml	**baking powder**	2 teaspoons
25 g	**ground almonds**	1 oz
150 g	**caster sugar**	5 oz
2	**eggs, separated**	2
100 ml	**milk**	5 tablespoons
120 ml	**bland salad oil**	6 tablespoons
2.5 ml	**vanilla essence**	$\frac{1}{2}$ teaspoon
60 ml	**Cadbury's Chocolate Spread**	3 tablespoons
	Icing	
2	**egg whites, size 2**	2
350 g	**icing sugar, sifted**	12 oz
1.25 ml	**cream of tartar**	$\frac{1}{4}$ teaspoon
pinch of	**salt**	pinch of
80 ml	**water**	4 tablespoons
	Decoration	
	red food colouring	
75 g	**marzipan**	3 oz
1 small packet	**Cadbury's Buttons**	1 small packet
16	**red sugar balls**	16
1	**glacé cherry**	1
2	**thin liquorice shoe laces**	2
1.2-litre	**ovenproof basin, well greased**	2-pint
2.5-cm	**round pastry cutter**	1-in

The frosting is easiest to make with an electric hand mixer and will probably take between 8–10 minutes. It is worth timing the whisking the first time you make the frosting, as it is quite difficult to know when it is whisked enough. If too soft, it will not harden on the outside and retain its shape. Work as quickly as possible once the frosting is whisked to retain the glossy appearance.

Using a small palette (flat-bladed) knife helps avoid cake crumbs mixing with the frosting. Keep the knife level on the surface of the frosting as much as possible.

Heat the chocolate spread a little if it is difficult to spread.

Sift the flour, cocoa and baking powder into a bowl. Add the almonds and sugar. Mix in the egg yolks, milk, oil and essence until quite smooth. Whisk the egg whites fairly stiffly and fold in carefully, then pour the soft mixture into the greased bowl. Bake in a moderate oven (180 c, 350 f, gas 4) for about 55 minutes until well risen and cooked through. Test with a skewer before turning out. Immediately slice the cake in half horizontally and sandwich together again with chocolate spread. Leave to cool before cutting into 8 wedges.

Measure all the icing ingredients into a fairly large bowl and stand this over a pan of hot water. Whisk hard until the frosting is glossy, white and smooth, standing in stiff peaks. Spread the frosting over the triangular pieces of cake, covering them liberally and leaving the surface in peaks. Keep the bowl of frosting over the hot water while you cover the cakes.

Work a little colouring evenly into the marzipan then roll

128

out and cut out 16 circles with the cutter. Pinch one side of the circles to form ears and stand two ears in the icing on the top of each cake as shown in the picture. Stick a sugar ball on to the centre of each Button with a little icing and place these eyes on each cake. Cut the cherry into eight triangles and place one piece as a nose on each cake with small pieces of liquorice for the whiskers. Stick a longer piece of liquorice in to form a tail. Allow the icing to harden for a couple of hours. *Makes 8*

Loot Biscuits

Illustrated on page 78

The biscuits will keep quite well if stored in an airtight container, but they will go soft if left in the open air too long.

Children might well enjoy creating their own designs on the biscuits. The decoration can easily be altered to fit into the theme of a party.

Metric		Imperial
175 g	**plain flour**	6 oz
50 g	**rice flour**	2 oz
50 g	**caster sugar**	2 oz
125 g	**butter**	4 oz
10 ml	**lemon juice**	2 teaspoons
	yellow and green food colouring	
a few drops	**almond essence**	a few drops
5 ml	**milk**	1 teaspoon
	a little icing sugar, sifted	
	Decoration	
225 g	**royal icing (page 24)**	8 oz
3 small packets	**Cadbury's Buttons**	3 small packets
75 g	**glacé cherries**	3 oz
	tree and star-shaped biscuit cutters	
2	**baking trays, well greased**	2
1	**greaseproof paper piping bag**	1
	plain writing pipe	

Mix the flours and sugar together and rub in the butter until the mixture resembles fine breadcrumbs. Divide the mixture in half, adding lemon juice and a little yellow colouring to one amount and the green colouring, essence and milk to the other portion. Knead both mixtures separately, then roll out the biscuit doughs in turn on a lightly sugared surface. Cut out yellow stars and green trees, making about 18 of each. Bake the biscuits on the prepared baking trays in a moderate oven (180 C, 350 F, gas 4) for 10–15 minutes until cooked. Lift off and cool on a wire tray.

Cut the tip off the piping bag and drop in the pipe. Fill with royal icing and pipe a variety of designs on the biscuits, using the Buttons and cherries as decoration, as shown in the picture. Leave to dry. *Makes about 36*

Clown Cakes

Illustrated opposite

These could be used as place names at a party, with gaily coloured cards, particularly if a suitable theme is chosen.

Metric		Imperial
	Hats	
50 g	**Bournville Dark plain chocolate**	50 g
	knob of butter	
40 ml	**water**	2 tablespoons
25 g	**icing sugar**	1 oz
4	**wafer ice cream cones**	4
1 large packet	**Cadbury's Buttons**	1 large packet
	Base	
4	**chocolate buns (page 21)**	4
175 g	**chocolate butter icing (page 21)**	6 oz
1 large packet	**Cadbury's Buttons**	1 large packet
	Heads	
75 g	**chocolate cake crumbs**	3 oz
75 g	**ground almonds**	3 oz
20 ml	**orange juice or sherry**	1 tablespoon
30 ml	**apricot jam, heated**	1 good tablespoon
40 ml	**icing sugar, sifted**	2 tablespoons
50 g	**plain butter icing (page 21)**	2 oz
12	**silver sugar balls**	12
2	**glacé cherries, halved**	2
4	**deep Yorkshire pudding tins**	4
4	**decorative paper cake cases**	4
	greaseproof paper piping bag	
	star pipe	

Melt the chocolate, butter and water together in a pan. Sift the icing sugar into a small, deep bowl, then beat in the chocolate mixture until smooth. Dip the cones into the chocolate, using a pastry brush to completely cover them. Place six Buttons round each base and set on waxed paper.

Make the chocolate buns according to the recipe instructions. Cover each up turned cake with the butter icing, cut the Buttons in half and arrange them round the cake bases, then lift carefully on to small up turned saucers.

Work the cake crumbs, ground almonds, orange juice or sherry and jam together, divide into four and roll into balls. Use icing sugar to prevent the mixture sticking to your hands. Stand a paper case on each base, with the pattern upwards as shown in the picture and place a ball shape on top. Press a hat on to each. Fit the star pipe into the piping bag and fill with butter icing. Pipe a ruff round the neck of each cake, two eyes on each face and a pom-pom on the hats. Press silver balls on the eyes and hats. Add a cherry nose. *Makes 4*

Pantomime Mice (see page 128);
Circus Ring (see page 56);
Clown Cakes

131

Big Ears

Illustrated on page 55

Metric		Imperial
125 g	**butter**	4 oz
75 g	**caster sugar**	3 oz
1	**egg yolk**	1
75 g	**Cadbury's Bournvita**	3 oz
175 g	**plain flour, sifted**	6 oz
	Topping	
1 packet	**marshmallows**	1 packet
25 g	**butter**	1 oz
20 ml	**golden syrup**	1 tablespoon
75 g	**Bournville Dark plain chocolate**	3 oz
65 g	**'Rice Krispies'**	$2\frac{1}{2}$ oz
	Decoration	
1 packet	**Cadbury's Fingers**	1 packet
24	**silver sugar balls**	24
14 g	**flaked almonds**	$\frac{1}{2}$ oz
	heart-shaped biscuit cutter	
	baking tray, greased	
12	**deep patty tins**	12

Cream the butter and sugar together until pale and soft. Beat in first the egg yolk, then the Bournvita and flour, mixing until the ingredients form a dough. Roll out to approximately 0.5 cm/$\frac{1}{4}$ in thick and cut out the biscuits with the cutter. Space out the biscuits on the prepared baking tray and bake in a moderate oven (180 c, 350 f, gas 4) for about 15 minutes. Allow to stand on the tray until the biscuits are firm before lifting off to cool on a wire tray.

Reserve six marshmallows, then melt the remainder gently in a large pan with the butter, syrup and broken-up chocolate. When liquid, take off the heat and stir in the krispies, coating them completely. Divide the mixture between the patty tins, pressing it in slightly. Leave to set for a couple of hours in the refrigerator.

Turn out the krispie toppings and press them firmly on to the biscuits. Push two Finger biscuits in at an angle in the krispies at the wider end of each heart biscuit. Cut the marsh-mallows horizontally through the centre, then in half across. Press a silver ball into each piece of marshmallow and position these to represent eyes as shown in the picture. Complete by adding pieces of almond for teeth. *Makes about 12*

Continental Cases

Glacé cherries are sometimes very sticky. Wash them in warm water to remove the syrup, using a sieve, then dry in an airy place, on kitchen paper.

Metric		Imperial
6–8	**individual meringue cases**	6–8
150 g	**Bournville Dark plain chocolate**	5 oz
40 g	**unsalted butter**	$1\frac{1}{2}$ oz
125 ml	**single cream**	$\frac{1}{4}$ pint
40 ml	**rum**	2 tablespoons
50 g	**glacé cherries**	2 oz
50 g	**cake crumbs**	2 oz
35 ml	**apricot jam**	1 heaped tablespoon

piping bag and star vegetable pipe

Have the meringue cases ready. Break the chocolate into a pan and melt it with the butter and cream. Take the pan off the heat and beat the mixture quite hard until it thickens. Add half the rum and leave to cool.

Keep 3 or 4 of the cherries aside for the decoration and chop the remainder. Stir them into the cake crumbs and bind the mixture together with the jam and remaining rum. Divide the filling between the meringue cases. Fill the piping bag with the chocolate mixture and pipe a large whirl on top of each meringue case. Decorate with half a glacé cherry.

Makes 6–8

Krackolates

Metric		Imperial
50 g	**butter or margarine**	2 oz
25 ml	**Cadbury's drinking chocolate**	2 tablespoons
40 ml	**golden syrup**	2 tablespoons
75 g	**cornflakes**	3 oz

baking tray, greased

Melt the butter in a fairly large pan with the drinking chocolate and syrup. Stir continuously and bring to the boil, making a thin sauce. Stir in the cornflakes, making quite sure they are completely covered. Leave the mixture in the pan for about 20 minutes to cool so that it becomes sticky. Spoon the mixture into heaps on a greased baking tray and leave until they cool completely and set quite hard. The mixture may also be placed straight into paper cake cases.

Makes 12

Artillery Cannons

Illustrated opposite

❄

The Swiss roll will freeze but it is better to assemble the cakes as required.

Metric		Imperial
1	**chocolate Swiss roll, filled (page 18)**	1
50 g	**butter**	2 oz
75 g	**icing sugar, sifted**	3 oz
	vanilla essence	
4 large	**Cadbury's Flakes**	4 large
50 g	**aniseed balls**	2 oz
	small star pipe	
1	**greaseproof paper piping bag**	1

Prepare and fill the Swiss roll as described in the recipe. Cream the butter with the icing sugar and a few drops of essence until soft and pale. Fit the star pipe into the piping bag and fill with the butter icing. Cut the Swiss roll into twelve even slices, then cut four slices in half. Place two halves together side by side, flat sides down and press two whole slices on either side. Pipe a zig–zag of icing down the middle and rest a Flake on it at an angle as shown in the picture. Make all the cannons in the same way. Pile up the aniseed balls beside the cannons and arrange toy soldiers round about if available. *Makes 4*

Cannon Balls

Illustrated on page 123

This is another recipe that older children can make. These cannon balls are very tempting so try to see that all the delicious, sticky mixture goes round the marshmallows.

Metric		Imperial
40 g	**butter or hard margarine**	1½ oz
40 ml	**Bournville Cocoa**	2 tablespoons
60 ml	**condensed milk**	3 tablespoons
50 g	**light soft brown sugar**	2 oz
150 g	**desiccated coconut**	5 oz
125 g	**marshmallows**	4 oz

Melt the butter or margarine, cocoa, condensed milk and sugar together, in a saucepan, stirring continuously. Reserve 25 g/1 oz of the coconut before stirring the remaining coconut into the melted mixture, with the pan off the heat. When the mixture is cool enough to handle, divide it into 12 equal amounts. Flatten the rather sticky mixture between the palms of your hands, then mould this round a marshmallow and roll into a ball. Make them all in the same way before tossing in the reserved coconut, pressing it on slightly. Leave to harden a little before eating. *Makes 12*

Clarence Caterpillar (see page 37); Country Cake (see page 52); Artillery Cannons

Strawberry Chocolate Boxes

Metric		Imperial
200 g	**Bournville Dark plain chocolate**	7 oz
125 g	**soft margarine**	4 oz
125 g	**caster sugar**	4 oz
2	**eggs**	2
125 g	**self-raising flour, sieved**	4 oz
125 g	**granulated sugar**	4 oz
125 ml	**water**	$\frac{1}{4}$ pint
20 ml	**curaçao or orange juice**	1 tablespoon
60–80 ml	**strawberry jam**	3–4 tablespoons
90 ml	**double cream**	6 tablespoons
12	**fresh strawberries**	12
12	**chocolate leaves (see page 22)**	12
28-cm × 18-cm	**Swiss roll tin,**	11-inch × 7-inch
	greased and base lined	

Melt the chocolate in a bowl placed over a pan of hot water. Have a large piece of waxed paper ready and spread the chocolate on to it, forming a rectangle measuring 31 cm × 23 cm/12 inches × 9 inches. Leave to set.

Measure the margarine and sugar into a bowl. Add the eggs and sieved flour. Beat the mixture together for a good 2 minutes so that it is well blended. Spread in the prepared tin and bake the cake in a moderately hot oven (190°C, 375°F, Gas Mark 5), for about 20 minutes. Turn out on to a wire tray to cool.

Dissolve the granulated sugar with the water in a saucepan, over gentle heat. When the sugar granules have completely disappeared and the liquid is clear, bring the syrup to the boil. Cook rapidly for a minute. Add the curaçao or orange juice off the heat. Cool the syrup a little.

Slice the cake through the centre. Spread one piece with jam and sandwich the cake together again. Trim the edges. Pour over the syrup and leave it to soak through. Cut the cake into 12 squares, measuring 3.5 cm/1½ inches. Melt a little more jam and brush it over the sides of the cake squares. Cut the chocolate into the same sized squares, using a sharp knife. Press one on to each side of each cake. Whip the cream and pipe a whirl on top or put it on with a spoon. Make sure the strawberries are clean then place one on each of the cakes, with a chocolate leaf sticking out at an angle. Arrange the cakes on a plate. *Makes 12*

Jumping Jacks

Illustrated on page 123

These biscuits freeze well if they are carefully packed to avoid breakages.

Use butter in this recipe as the biscuits tend to spread unevenly if other fat is used – which rather spoils the effect.

The two-colour mixture is particularly attractive. Endeavour to keep the two mixtures from blending together in the piping bag by not adding too much at one time.

Metric		Imperial
175 g	**butter**	6 oz
50 g	**caster sugar**	2 oz
175 g	**plain flour**	6 oz
20 ml	**Bournville Cocoa**	1 tablespoon
	green food colouring	
	peppermint essence	
5	**glacé cherries, quartered**	5
50 g	**Bournville Dark plain chocolate**	50 g
	large nylon piping bag	
	large star pipe	
	baking tray, greased	

Cream the butter and sugar together really well, until very soft and creamy, then fold in the flour. Halve the mixture and sift the cocoa into one amount, blending it in well. Add a few drops of green colouring and essence to taste to the other portion. Fit the pipe into the bag and fill one side of the bag with the green mixture. Using a spoon, push the chocolate mixture down into the other side of the bag. Pipe four short lines in a close zig-zag on to the prepared baking tray as shown in the picture. Allow room for the biscuits to spread and bake them in batches if necessary. Place a piece of cherry at one end for the taper. Bake in a moderately hot oven (190 c, 375 f, gas 5) for 10–12 minutes until a good colour and cooked. Cool the biscuits on the baking tray for a short while before lifting them on to a wire tray.

Melt the chocolate and either dribble it in lines with a spoon over the biscuits, or fill a greaseproof paper piping bag and pipe lines. Leave to set for a short time. *Makes 18–20*

Cupid Hearts

Illustrated opposite

Metric		Imperial
50 g	**plain flour**	2 oz
50 g	**ground almonds**	2 oz
50 g	**butter**	2 oz
40 ml	**caster sugar**	2 tablespoons
40 ml	**Cadbury's Drinking Chocolate**	2 tablespoons
1	**egg yolk**	1
	Icing	
225 g	**sugar, sifted**	8 oz
	lemon juice	
	pink food colouring	
4	**Cadbury's Flake from the Family Pack**	4
50 g	**Bournville Dark plain chocolate**	50 g
	heart-shaped biscuit cutter	
	baking tray, greased	
1	**greaseproof paper piping bag**	1

As these biscuits are quite sweet, use a sharp fruit juice, not water, to make up the icing. They look effective and children also like to see their initials on their own biscuit. Store in an airtight container when the icing is absolutely dry.

Halve Cadbury's Flake by cutting it down the middle lengthways, with a sharp knife, in one definite movement. It should not flake up. A whole Flake looks too heavy on these biscuits.

If a heart-shaped cutter is not available, trace a suitable sized heart shape on to clean cardboard and cut it out. Use this shape to cut out the biscuits.

Mix the flour and ground almonds together, then rub in the butter. Add the sugar and drinking chocolate and bind the mixture together with the egg yolk. Roll out on a lightly floured surface to about 0.5 cm/$\frac{1}{4}$ in thick and cut out heart-shaped biscuits. Knead and roll the biscuit dough in between. Arrange on the prepared baking tray and bake in a moderate oven (180 c, 350 f, gas 4) for about 12 minutes. Leave to harden slightly before lifting off the baking tray.

Make up a fairly thick coating icing with the icing sugar and lemon juice, adding colouring to make a pretty pink. Carefully ice each biscuit, letting the icing flow smoothly over the edges. Lift them on to a wire tray. Cut the Flake straight down the middle and lay one piece diagonally across each biscuit, before the icing has set. Leave to harden.

Melt the chocolate, then pour into the piping bag. Cut off the tip and pipe chocolate initials on each biscuit. *Makes 8*

Sweetheart Surprise (see page 84); Cupid Hearts; Daisy Cream Cake (see page 57)

Viennese Slices

Metric		Imperial
175 g	**butter**	6 oz
50 g	**caster sugar**	2 oz
125 g	**plain flour, sieved**	4 oz
25 g	**cornflour, sieved**	1 oz
25 g	**Bournville cocoa, sieved**	1 oz
	few drops of vanilla essence	
	Butter icing	
175 g	**icing sugar**	6 oz
25 g	**Bournville cocoa**	1 oz
75 g	**butter or soft margarine**	3 oz
20 ml	**warm water**	1 tablespoon
	Decoration	
	icing sugar, sieved	

piping bag and star vegetable pipe
baking tray, greased

Pack the fingers very carefully and freeze with or without the butter icing. Seal and label.

The finely grated rind of a small orange, or a lemon, may be added to the mixture. Use only the zest, never the white part which is bitter.

Make up the biscuit mixture by softening the butter then creaming it with the sugar. Fold in the sieved flour, cornflour and cocoa then add a little vanilla essence. Mix all the ingredients together until the mixture is really well blended and fairly soft. Fill the piping bag then pipe lengths about 9 cm/3½ inches long on to a greased baking tray. There should be between 20 and 24. Make an even number if possible. Bake in a moderate oven (180°C, 350°F, Gas Mark 4) for 15 minutes. As the biscuits are quite short, leave them on the tray to harden before cooling completely.

Sieve the icing sugar and cocoa into a bowl. Beat in the butter and warm water, making a nice light consistency. Sandwich two of the finger biscuits together with a thick layer of the butter icing, which can be either spread or piped in between. Dredge with sieved icing sugar.

Makes about 12 complete slices

Chocolate Gems: Pipe the biscuits into small stars. Place a piece of glacé cherry in the centre and bake for 10 minutes. They can also be decorated with coloured glacé icing (see page 24).

Coconut Heaps

Rice paper can be eaten. This is a lighter mixture than the more traditional coconut pyramids.

Metric		Imperial
2	**egg whites**	2
125 g	**caster sugar**	4 oz
50 g	**Cadbury's drinking chocolate, sieved**	2 oz
125 g	**desiccated coconut**	5 oz
	about 5 glacé cherries	
2	**baking trays**	2
	rice paper or Bakewell paper	

Prepare the trays first by covering them with the rice paper or Bakewell paper cut to fit. Whisk the egg whites until really stiff. Add the sugar and whisk again until the mixture is stiff again and thick. Stir in the sieved drinking chocolate and the coconut. Drop spoonsful of mixture on to the baking trays, making at least 10. Stick half a cherry on top of each. Bake in a slow oven (150°C, 300°F, Gas Mark 2) for about 45 minutes. Lift them off the Bakewell paper or peel off any excess rice paper and cool.

Makes 10

Chocolate Sponge Fingers

Illustrated on page 227

These fingers freeze well. Pack, label and freeze.

The sponge fingers can be sandwiched together with whipped cream, butter icing (see page 21) or jam. For a special treat, melt about 100 g/3½ oz Bournville Dark plain chocolate and dip both ends of the sponge fingers into it.

Metric		Imperial
2	**size 2 eggs**	2
50 g	**caster sugar**	2 oz
50 g	**plain flour, sieved**	2 oz
15 ml	**Bournville cocoa**	1 tablespoon
	sponge finger tins	

Whisk the eggs and the sugar in a fairly large bowl over a pan of hot water, or use an electric hand beater. Continue whisking until the mixture will leave a very definite trail. Fold in the sieved flour with the cocoa and 15 ml/1 tablespoon of warm water. Spoon the mixture into the greased sponge finger tins. There will be about 20. The cooking time is fairly quick so the mixture will keep to cook a second batch. Bake in a fairly hot oven (200°C, 400°F, Gas Mark 6) for 10–12 minutes. Turn out and cool on a wire tray.

Makes 20–24

Braemar Men

Illustrated on front cover and opposite

Metric		Imperial
175 g	**plain flour**	6 oz
pinch of	**salt**	pinch of
125 g	**butter**	4 oz
50 g	**caster sugar**	2 oz
	Decoration	
50 g	**icing sugar, sifted**	2 oz
1 metre	**tartan ribbon**	39 in
6	**Cadbury's Buttons**	6
12	**currants**	12
2	**glacé cherries**	2
6	**Cadbury's Flakes**	6
	gingerbread man cutter	
	baking tray, lightly floured	
1	**greaseproof paper piping bag**	1

Do not roll the shortbread too thin or the biscuits tend to break. The quantity of mixture is exactly right to make six biscuits. Either size of Flake may be used: the larger size looks more correct but the smaller Flakes are not so heavy on the biscuits.

Should you only have a gingerbread woman cutter, make a sharp cut through the skirt with a knife and divide the legs.

Sift the flour and salt together. Rub in the butter until the mixture resembles breadcrumbs, then add the sugar. Knead the mixture into a pliable dough. Roll out on a lightly floured surface to just under 1 cm/¼ in thick. Cut out the shapes with the cutter, rolling the excess dough again in between, making six in all. Move one arm of each man closer to his side. Bake on the prepared baking tray in a warm oven (160 c, 325 F, gas 3) for about 30 minutes until pale brown. Cool before lifting off the tray.

Blend the icing sugar with just enough water or fruit juice to make a thick glacé icing and fill the piping bag. Cut the ribbon into six even lengths. Cut the tip off the bag and secure the ribbon over the shoulder of each man, sticking the ends at the back with icing. Use a little icing to stick a Button in position on the heads, two currants for eyes and a piece of cherry for a cheerful mouth. Finally add a Flake 'caber' (see picture). Allow the icing to dry. *Makes 6*

Braemar Men; Scottish Fingers (see page 149); Lock Ness Monster (see page 81)

Fancy Cakes

Illustrated on page 147

Metric		Imperial
125 g	**soft margarine or butter**	4 oz
125 g	**caster sugar**	4 oz
2	**eggs**	2
125 g	**self-raising flour, sieved**	4 oz
20 ml	**Bournville cocoa, sieved**	1 tablespoon
20	**paper cake cases**	20

Cream the margarine and the sugar until lighter in colour and texture. Gradually beat in the eggs and fold in the sieved flour with the cocoa. Add a little milk if necessary to make a soft dropping consistency. Place the paper cases close together on a baking tray, or put the cases into a tray of bun tins. Fill with mixture and bake in a moderate oven (180°C, 350°F, Gas Mark 4) for 12–15 minutes. Cool on a wire tray.

Makes 20

Top Hats

Make up a batch of Fancy Cakes. With a small plain pastry cutter measuring about 2.5 cm/1 inch, cut out centre but do not cut right through the cakes. Fill the centres with a whirl of the economical vanilla icing. Replace the centre piece of cake and dust with icing sugar.

Economical Vanilla Icing

Beat 75 g/3 oz soft margarine with 225 g/8 oz sieved icing sugar and 45 ml/3 tablespoons milk until it is light in colour and texture. Add 2.5 ml/$\frac{1}{2}$ teaspoon vanilla essence and any food colouring that may be needed.

To make chocolate icing: dissolve 25 g/1 oz Bournville cocoa in a little boiling water and stir into the icing.

Decorated Cakes

Make a variety of designs by piping vanilla or chocolate icing on the small cakes. Decorate with Cadbury's Buttons, Flake and some softened jam. Cherries, nuts and angelica are also colourful additions. Grated Bournville Dark plain chocolate over vanilla icing makes a simple decoration. The small cakes may also be feather iced, made in the same way as the Feather Iced Cake (page 27).

For Madeleines, see Owl Madeleines, page 154.

Sleepers

Illustrated on page 58

Inaccurately measured syrup can mean that the recipe will not work. Always measure syrup with a hot, metal tablespoon, holding the spoon with an oven cloth. If the syrup is very thick in the tin, pop it into a warm oven for a short time to melt so that it is easier to spoon out.

Metric		Imperial
50 g	**Bournville Dark plain chocolate**	50 g
75 g	**butter**	3 oz
60 ml	**golden syrup**	3 tablespoons
75 g	**sugar**	3 oz
225 g	**rolled oats**	8 oz
pinch of	**salt**	pinch of
50 g	**sultanas**	2 oz
	Icing	
100 g	**Bournville Dark plain chocolate**	$3\frac{1}{2}$ oz
10 ml	**bland salad oil**	2 teaspoons
60 ml	**water**	3 tablespoons
50 g	**butter**	2 oz
18 × 28-cm	**shallow tin, greased**	7 × 11-in

Break the chocolate into a pan and melt it with the butter, syrup and sugar without boiling. Off the heat, stir in the oats, salt and sultanas to make a flapjack mixture, then press the mixture evenly into the prepared tin. Bake in a moderate oven (180 c, 350 f, gas 4) for 20–25 minutes. Whilst still hot, cut the flapjack lengthways down the middle and then into 1.25-cm/ $\frac{1}{2}$-in wide pieces, making 24 pieces in all. Leave to cool completely before lifting out of the tin.

Melt all the icing ingredients together in a small bowl over a pan of hot water. Dip both ends of the flapjack pieces into the icing and leave to dry on a wire tray. *Makes 36*

Marzipan Log Cakes

Illustrated opposite

Metric		Imperial
125 g	**butter**	4 oz
125 g	**caster sugar**	4 oz
2	**eggs**	2
125 g	**self-raising flour, sieved**	4 oz
80 ml	**apricot jam**	4 tablespoons
225 g	**marzipan**	8 oz
	red and green food colouring	
5 ml	**Bournville cocoa**	1 teaspoon
	Icing	
200 g	**Bournville Dark plain chocolate**	7 oz
25 g	**slightly salted butter**	1 oz
45 ml	**water**	3 tablespoons
50 g	**icing sugar**	2 oz
18-cm	**square cake tin,** · **greased and base lined**	7-inch

Cream the butter and sugar together until quite soft. Add the eggs then fold in the sieved flour. Turn into the prepared tin and bake in a moderately hot oven (190°C, 375°F, Gas Mark 5) for about 20 minutes. Turn out and cool on a wire tray.

Trim the cake edges and split the cake in half. Spread the cake with jam and sandwich together again. Spread the jam thinly over the top. Cut the cake in half.

Divide the marzipan into three. Work a few drops of red colouring into one amount, green colouring into another and the cocoa into the third amount, kneading it well so that the colours are thoroughly blended. Divide each colour into two then form into six rolls the same length as the cake strips. Lay two rolls together along the centre of each cake strip, with one on the top, making a triangle. Lift the pieces of cake on to a wire tray.

Melt the chocolate with the butter and water in a small saucepan and stir gently until melted. Beat in the icing sugar off the heat. Carefully spoon this icing over the cake strips and marzipan. Spread the sides with the icing too. It is a little difficult to get the texture smooth but when the cakes are completely covered, shake the wire tray slightly to level the icing. Leave to set. Later cut each cake strip diagonally into about 4 slices, with a piece at either end. *Makes 8 slices*

Fancy Cakes (see page 144); Marzipan Log Cakes; Madeleines (see page 154)

Dominoes

Illustrated on page 70

Metric		Imperial
50 g	**butter**	2 oz
40 ml	**golden syrup**	2 good tablespoons
75 g	**Cadbury's Drinking Chocolate**	3 oz
100 g	**'Rice Krispies'**	3½ oz
40 ml	**royal icing or plain butter icing (pages 24 and 21)**	2 tablespoons
30 × 20-cm	**Swiss roll tin, greased**	12 × 8-in
1	**greaseproof paper piping bag**	1

It is worth using a ruler to make the pieces as even in size as possible. It will be necessary to make double quantities of the recipe if a fun game of dominoes is to be played at the tea table.

Melt the butter and syrup in a saucepan. Remove the pan from the heat and stir in the drinking chocolate and rice krispies, mixing thoroughly until completely coated. Press this mixture firmly into the tin, without breaking up the krispies, and leave to harden.

Cut the mixture in half lengthways, then cut each strip into nine even-sized finger-shaped pieces. Put the icing into the piping bag and cut off the tip. Pipe a line and the required number of dots across each domino, remembering to include a double six or the game cannot start! *Makes 18*

Flower Tubs

Illustrated on page 74

Metric		Imperial
100 g	**Bournville Dark plain chocolate**	3½ oz
125 g	**margarine**	4 oz
125 g	**caster sugar**	4 oz
2	**eggs**	2
175 g	**self-raising flour, sifted**	6 oz
80 ml	**concentrated orange squash**	4 tablespoons
	Decoration	
175 g	**chocolate butter icing (page 21)**	6 oz
1 packet	**marshmallows**	1 packet
20	**mimosa sugar balls**	20
20	**paper cake cases**	20
	baking tray	

The easiest way to cut marshmallows is to use scissors which are first dipped in warm water.

Other decorations can be used with the marshmallows: Cadbury's Buttons, sugar strands or coloured small sweets look nice.

Chop the chocolate into small pieces. Cream the margarine and sugar well together. Stir in the eggs, then the flour, chocolate and orange squash to make a dropping consistency. Divide the mixture between the cake cases and bake them on the tray in a moderately hot oven (190 c, 375 f, gas 5) for 12–15 minutes until lightly browned, well risen and cooked. Cool on a wire tray.

Prepare the butter icing and spread it neatly on top of the cakes. Slice each marshmallow horizontally into three circles. Pinch one end to elongate each piece into the shape of a petal. Arrange the petals on top of the cakes, with a mimosa ball in the centre of each. *Makes 20*

Scottish Fingers

Illustrated on page 143

Should the caramel be ready before the base is cooked, stand the pan in cold water to prevent it cooking any further. It is most important to cook the caramel correctly.

This is a recipe that would be particularly popular at fund raising events. Cut the fingers in half with a sharp knife to make them go further.

Metric		Imperial
175 g	**butter**	6 oz
75 g	**caster sugar**	3 oz
175 g	**plain flour**	6 oz
75 g	**cornflour**	3 oz
	grated rind of 1 orange	
25 g	**chopped nuts, for example walnuts,**	1 oz
	hazelnuts or peanuts	
25 g	**seedless raisins**	1 oz
	Topping	
125 g	**butter or margarine**	4 oz
125 ml	**condensed milk**	scant $\frac{1}{4}$ pint
125 g	**caster sugar**	4 oz
40 ml	**golden syrup**	2 tablespoons
1	**Cadbury's Flake Family Pack**	1
28 × 18-cm	**Swiss roll tin**	11 × 7-in

Cream the butter and sugar together thoroughly for the shortbread base. Sift together the flours and add them to the creamed mixture with the finely grated orange rind, nuts and fruit, mixing well. If the mixture becomes sticky, sprinkle in a little extra flour. Press into the tin and level the surface with a knife before pricking all over with a fork. Bake in a warm oven (160 c, 325 f, gas 3) for 25–30 minutes until golden brown. Leave in the tin.

Meanwhile prepare the topping by dissolving all the ingredients except the Flakes in a saucepan over a low heat, stirring occasionally. When the sugar grains have disappeared completely and the mixture is smooth, bring to the boil and continue cooking carefully for 5 minutes, stirring continuously so the base does not burn. When it is a nice rich colour, pour over the shortbread base in the tin. Cut into 18 even-sized fingers and place a Flake on each whilst the caramel is still quite hot. Leave to cool before lifting the fingers out of the tin. Store in an airtight container.

Makes 18

Mushroom Cakes

Illustrated opposite

Metric		Imperial
225 g	**marzipan**	8 oz
	a little icing sugar, sifted	
75 g	**butter**	3 oz
100 g	**Bournville Dark plain chocolate**	3½ oz
125 g	**desiccated coconut**	4 oz
50 g	**glacé cherries, chopped**	2 oz
50 g	**sweet biscuits, crushed**	2 oz
20 ml	**brandy or fruit juice**	1 tablespoon
6	**Cadbury's Flake from the Family Pack**	6
	a little Cadbury's Drinking Chocolate	
7-cm	**plain cutter**	2½-in
	12 patty tins	

Pack the mushroom cakes carefully and freeze complete.

Choose a tray of fairly shallow, *plain* patty tins. The fluted or decorative tins are not suitable as they do not look like mushrooms when turned out, and the marzipan is more likely to stick to the tins.

Roll out the marzipan on a surface lightly dusted with icing sugar. Using the biscuit cutter, cut out twelve circles, re-rolling the trimmings in between. Line the patty tins with the marzipan, rather like pastry tarts. Melt the butter with the broken up chocolate, coconut, chopped cherries and crushed biscuits in a saucepan, heating gently and stirring frequently. Stir in the brandy or fruit juice and mix well before dividing this mixture between the marzipan cases. Fork over the top of the mixture, towards the centre then leave to cool.

Cut the Flakes in half and stand a piece in the centre of each mushroom cake, pushing it in gently but firmly. Leave the mixture to set completely before removing from the tins with a palette knife. Be careful not to mark the marzipan. Dust the marzipan with a little sifted drinking chocolate. *Makes 12*

Mushroom Manor (see page 76) and Mushroom Cakes

Cream Puffs

Illustrated on front cover

Metric		Imperial
1 quantity	**choux pastry (see page 184)**	1 quantity
75 g	**Bournville Dark plain chocolate**	3 oz
60 ml	**water**	3 tablespoons
1	**egg yolk**	1
125 ml	**double cream**	¼ pint
	good pinch of ground cinnamon	
25 g	**icing sugar, sieved**	1 oz
	Decoration	
	little icing sugar	

Open freeze the completed puffs. Later, wrap, label and seal. Use within 3 months.

There are several methods for cooking choux pastry but we have found a rising temperature to be consistently the most successful.

piping bag and star vegetable pipe

Make up the choux pastry as described. Place the mixture into the piping bag. Grease a baking tray then dust it with flour, shaking off any excess. Pipe 4 large stars on the tray, using half the mixture. Space them well apart as they will rise and puff out. Bake in a moderate oven (180°C, 350°F, Gas Mark 4) for 10 minutes then increase the heat to moderately hot (190°C, 375°F, Gas Mark 5) for another 10 minutes. Now increase the heat again to fairly hot (200°C, 400°F, Gas Mark 6) for about 20 minutes until the puffs are golden brown and crisp on the base. Cool on a wire tray, making a slit in the side with a knife to let the steam escape. Make a second batch in the same way.

Break the chocolate into a small pan. Add the water and egg yolk. Stir over a low heat until the chocolate has completely melted and the mixture thickens. Cool completely. Whip the cream, cinnamon and sieved icing sugar together until it will hold its shape nicely. Fold the cold chocolate into the cream. Divide the cream filling between the puffs, using a piping bag if it is more convenient. Dust with icing sugar. *Makes 8*

Merry Mice

Illustrated on page 155

Metric		Imperial
20 ml	**Bournville cocoa**	1 tablespoon
50 g	**self-raising flour**	2 oz
50 g	**soft margarine**	2 oz
50 g	**caster sugar**	2 oz
1	**egg**	1
	Icing	
100 g	**Bournville Dark plain chocolate**	$3\frac{1}{2}$ oz
45 ml	**water**	3 tablespoons
5 ml	**flavourless salad oil**	1 teaspoon
25 g	**caster sugar**	1 oz
	Decoration	
10	**marshmallows**	10
1	**large packet Cadbury's Buttons**	1
50 g	**vanilla butter icing (see page 21)**	2 oz
	glacé cherries and currants	
about 5 cm long	**angelica strips**	about 2 inches long
	thin strips of liquorice	
10	**paper cake cases**	10
10	**bun tins**	10

Sieve the cocoa and flour into a bowl. Add the margarine, sugar and the egg. Beat the mixture together until thoroughly blended. Put the paper cases into the bun tins and divide the mixture between them. Place on a baking tray. Bake in a moderately hot oven (190°C, 375°F, Gas Mark 5) for 15–20 minutes until springy to the touch and cooked. Leave to cool.

Break up the chocolate and melt in a small pan, with the water, oil and sugar. Stir gently until melted. It should be a really glossy icing. Press a marshmallow on to each cake. Cool the icing slightly then spoon it over the top of the cakes. Leave the icing to set. With a hot, sharp knife, make two slits at either side of the marshmallow and press Buttons into these for the 'ears'. Pipe two small stars of butter icing in the centre for the 'eyes' and stick a currant on. Pipe another star of icing for the 'mouth', with a quarter of a cherry on top. Stick thin strips of angelica in at either side for the 'whiskers'. Finally, use a skewer to make a hole in the back in which to stick a liquorice 'tail'. Complete all the cakes in the same way.

Makes 10

Owl Madeleines

Illustrated opposite

Metric		Imperial
25 g	**Bournville cocoa**	1 oz
125 g	**self-raising flour**	4 oz
	pinch of salt	
2	**eggs**	2
125 g	**soft margarine**	4 oz
125 g	**caster sugar**	4 oz
	Decoration	
about 60 ml	**apricot jam**	about 3 tablespoons
40 ml	**water**	2 tablespoons
50 g	**desiccated coconut**	2 oz
	little plain or chocolate butter icing or	
	glacé icing (pages 21 and 24)	
1	**large packet Cadbury's Buttons**	1
4	**glacé cherries**	4

The cakes may be frozen complete but the Buttons and cherry may need sticking on again when the cakes are thawed. Open freeze then pack, label and seal.

The easiest way to coat these cakes is to stick each one on a skewer before covering with jam and coconut.

dariole moulds, greased

Sieve the cocoa, flour and salt into a bowl. Add the eggs, margarine and sugar. Beat the ingredients together, making the cake by the one-stage method. When quite smooth, spoon enough mixture into the moulds to come halfway up. There will be enough for between 12 and 15 cakes, depending on the size of the dariole moulds. Bake the cakes in batches if necessary. Place on a baking tray and bake in a moderately hot oven (190°C, 375°F, Gas Mark 5) for about 20 minutes. Test with a warm skewer to see if they are cooked through. Shake out on to a wire tray and bake the next batch, removing any cake crumbs that may be left in the moulds.

Melt the jam with the water. Coat each cake with jam then roll in the coconut. Stick two Buttons on each cake with the icing, for the 'eyes', with a spot in the centre of each. Complete the 'owls' with a piece of cherry sticking out as the 'beak'. The cakes can be placed in paper cake cases if wished.

Makes about 15

Madeleines: Follow the above recipe but omit the Buttons and add a whirl of cream on top with a cherry.

Fir Cone Cakes (see page 104);
Owl Madeleines (see above);
Merry Mice (see page 153)

Patrol Tents

Illustrated on page 175

Metric		Imperial
25 g	**Bournville Cocoa**	1 oz
125 g	**self-raising flour**	4 oz
2	**eggs**	2
125 g	**soft margarine**	4 oz
125 g	**caster sugar**	4 oz
	Decoration	
100 ml	**red jam**	5 tablespoons
150 ml	**desiccated coconut** 4 heaped tablespoons	
125 g	**chocolate butter icing (page 21)**	4 oz
2 packets	**Cadbury's Fingers**	2 packets
9	**dariole moulds, well greased**	9
	baking tray	
	small star pipe	
	greaseproof paper piping bag	
9	**paper cake cases**	9
	patrol badges and flags	

The cakes, coated with jam and coconut may be frozen. Pack in a rigid container and keep for about a month. Complete the decoration as required.

Tap the tins, filled with the uncooked cake mixture, on the work surface so that no pockets of air are left and the cakes bake evenly.

The easiest way to spread these small castle cakes with jam is to push them on to a short skewer, brush with jam then roll in the coconut.

Sift the cocoa and flour into a bowl, then add the remaining cake ingredients. Beat really well, making the cake by the one-stage method. Half fill the prepared tins with mixture, stand them on the baking tray and bake in a moderately hot oven (190 c, 375 f, gas 5) for about 25 minutes until well risen and cooked right through. Shake out on to a wire tray to cool.

Melt the jam with two spoonfuls of water. Brush the cakes with jam and roll them in the coconut spread on a plate. Fit the pipe into the piping bag and fill with chocolate butter icing. Pipe a good whirl on the top of each cake. Stand them on the flattened paper cases and lean five or six Finger biscuits against each cake, to make tents. Allocate tents to a 'patrol' with a badge as shown in the picture and stick flags in some cakes. *Makes 9*

Popper Bars

Illustrated on page 2

Experiment with other types of cereal mixed into the cocoa mixture. This is an easy recipe for children to make.

Metric		Imperial
25 g	**butter**	1 oz
20 ml	**golden syrup**	1 tablespoon
20 ml	**sugar**	1 tablespoon
20 ml	**Bournville cocoa**	1 tablespoon
25 g	**'Puffed Wheat'**	1 oz
10	**Cadbury's Flakes**	10
10	**paper cake cases**	10

Put the butter, syrup, sugar and cocoa into a fairly large pan then stir over a gentle heat to melt. Stir in the 'Puffed Wheat' off the heat. Place one Flake into each paper case, flattening the paper slightly. Divide the mixture between the Flakes and press it on the centre, sticking it all together. Leave to set which will only take a short time. *Makes 10*

Munchies

Illustrated on page 2

Children will enjoy making this recipe as it is very easy to do. The best way to accurately measure golden syrup is to heat a metal spoon, or a metal scale pan if larger amounts are required. The syrup then slides off the spoon easily.

Metric		Imperial
100 g	**butter**	4 oz
80 ml	**golden syrup**	4 tablespoons
40 ml	**Bournville cocoa**	2 tablespoons
225 g	**Swiss style breakfast cereal**	8 oz
16	**small paper cake cases**	16

Melt the butter and syrup in a good sized pan with the cocoa and when it is dissolved, bring to the boil. Take it off the heat and stir in the cereal. Press the mixture into a round spoon, or use a small ice cream scoop and make heaps. Arrange these in the paper cases and leave in the refrigerator for a couple of hours. *Makes 12–16*

Biscuits and Bakes

There are comparatively few people who are not called upon at one time or another to give produce for a local market or fund-raising activity. What better than biscuits, cookies and bakes that can be made quite easily and relatively cheaply? Home-made biscuits look and smell particularly appetising. There are recipes for all kinds, both cooked and uncooked. Plain, iced, blends of fruit and spice, novelty ideas to ring the changes.

Many of the goodies can be packed in the food freezer ready for use at a moment's notice — that is if there are any left after the scrumptious smells have wafted out from the kitchen. Make some to keep in the biscuit tin too, for nibbling on the many occasions when we all want a biscuit.

Swiss Circles

Illustrated opposite

Metric		Imperial
175 g	**butter**	6 oz
25 g	**icing sugar, sieved**	1 oz
125 g	**self-raising flour**	4 oz
25 g	**cornflour**	1 oz
25 g	**Cadbury's drinking chocolate**	1 oz
	few drops of vanilla essence	
2	**baking trays, greased**	2
	piping bag and star pipe	

Cream the butter with the sieved icing sugar until light in colour. Sieve the flour, cornflour and drinking chocolate together. Beat them in gradually, making sure there are no pockets of flour left. Beat in the essence and continue to beat until the mixture is soft enough to pipe. Fill the piping bag then pipe circles on to the trays, spacing them apart as the mixture will spread. Bake in a hot oven (220°C, 425°F, Gas Mark 7) for 6 minutes then lower the heat to moderate (180°C, 350°F, Gas Mark 4) for about a further 6 minutes, until the biscuits are cooked. Cool before carefully lifting from the tray. The mixture is very short so has to be handled carefully. *Makes 10*

The biscuits will freeze but should be packed very carefully in a rigid container as they break easily. Wrap, seal and label. Keep up to 2 months.

25 g/1 oz extra flour may be added if the mixture is too short for your liking. The biscuits can be finished off with half a glacé cherry on the join, or sprinkled with flaked almonds, added before baking.

Island Slices (see page 165); Swiss Circles; Bourbon Dominoes (see page 160); Crunchy Cookies (see page 164)

Bourbon Dominoes

Illustrated on page 159

Metric		Imperial
125 g	**butter or soft margarine**	4 oz
125 g	**caster sugar**	4 oz
I	**egg, beaten**	I
250 g	**plain flour**	9 oz
25 g	**Bournville cocoa**	I oz
	pinch of salt	
	Butter icing	
75 g	**butter**	3 oz
175 g	**icing sugar, sieved**	6 oz
2.5 ml	**vanilla essence**	$\frac{1}{2}$ teaspoon
2	**baking trays, greased**	2

The dominoes can be frozen complete. Pack in a rigid container, seal and label.

When making the holes, twist the skewer round so that they become big enough for the butter icing to come through later.
For older tastes, make the butter icing coffee flavoured.

Cream the fat and sugar, and gradually add the beaten egg. Sieve in the flour and cocoa with a pinch of salt and blend the mixture together with a wooden spoon. Knead lightly in the bowl. Place the biscuit dough between 2 sheets of grease-proof paper to avoid marking it with flour and roll out to about 3-mm/$\frac{1}{8}$-inch thickness. Accurately mark rectangles with a ruler, measuring 3 cm × 7 cm/$1\frac{1}{4}$ inches × $2\frac{3}{4}$ inches; cut out and lift on to greased baking trays. Roll out the dough again as necessary. Make an even number of biscuits, there should be about 48. Mark a line across the centre with a skewer. Make holes in half the biscuits to represent the dominoe numbers and remember to have a double six to start the game. Leave the biscuits on their trays for about 30 minutes to relax, then bake in a moderate oven (180°C, 350°F, Gas Mark 4) for 10–15 minutes. It may be necessary to cook a second batch, or rotate the trays in the oven. Cool the biscuits on a wire tray.

To make the icing, soften the butter then beat the sieved icing sugar into it so that it becomes much lighter. 20 ml/1 tablespoon of hot water may be added if the butter icing is too stiff. Beat in the essence. Spread the underside of the plain biscuits quite thickly with butter icing and sandwich the others to them, pressing them together so that the icing comes through the holes. Scrape off any excess icing. The dominoes are now ready. *Makes about 24 biscuits*

Farmhouse Biscuits

Pack in a rigid container, seal and label before freezing.

It does not really matter if these biscuits are uneven in size. If you want to be particularly accurate, form the dough into a roll and cut it into 24 even-sized pieces. Roll these into balls and proceed.

Metric		Imperial
50 g	lard	2 oz
50 g	soft margarine	2 oz
75 g	caster sugar	3 oz
20 ml	Bournville cocoa	1 tablespoon
150 g	self-raising flour	5 oz
75 g	porridge oats	3 oz
2.5 ml	vanilla essence	$\frac{1}{2}$ teaspoon
2	baking trays, greased	2

Beat the lard and margarine together, then beat in the sugar. Sieve the cocoa and flour into the mixture. Mix it all together with the oats and vanilla essence. If it is too crumbly, knead the mixture by hand. Roll small amounts of the dough into balls between the palms of your hands. Arrange them on the baking trays and flatten each one with a fork. Do not make them too thin. There will be enough for two trays so either alternate the trays in the oven halfway through cooking time or bake them in batches. The biscuits do not spread much. Bake in a slow oven (150°C, 300°F, Gas Mark 2) for about 35 minutes. Lift off and cool on a wire tray. *Makes 24*

No Bake Squares

The recipe varies each time it is made, depending on the kind of biscuit that is used. This is an ideal recipe to use up the bits in the bottom of the biscuit tin, or broken biscuits. Home-made ones can also be used.

Metric		Imperial
175 g	mixed digestive and sweet biscuits	6 oz
50 g	hazelnuts	2 oz
50 g	seedless raisins	2 oz
50 g	Bournville Dark plain chocolate	50 g
30 ml	golden syrup	2 tablespoons
75 g	butter	3 oz
19-cm	square tin, greased	$7\frac{1}{2}$-inch

Crush the biscuits but do not make them too fine. Chop the hazelnuts and add to the biscuits, with the raisins. Break up the chocolate and melt it with the syrup and butter. When it is quite smooth, stir the liquid into the biscuit crumbs and mix thoroughly. Press into the tin and leave to harden. Cut into squares. *Makes 16*

Frosted Malted Bars

Illustrated opposite

Metric		Imperial
125 g	**margarine**	4 oz
175 g	**plain flour**	6 oz
125 g	**soft brown sugar**	4 oz
	Filling	
25 g	**plain flour**	1 oz
2.5 ml	**baking powder**	½ teaspoon
25 g	**Bournvita**	1 oz
50 g	**caster sugar**	2 oz
2	**eggs**	2
5 ml	**vanilla essence**	1 teaspoon
50 g	**desiccated coconut**	2 oz
50 g	**walnuts, chopped**	2 oz
	Frosting	
50 g	**Bournvita**	2 oz
2.5 ml	**instant coffee**	½ teaspoon
40 ml	**hot water**	2 tablespoons
25 g	**margarine or butter**	1 oz
225 g	**icing sugar, sieved**	8 oz
2.5 ml	**vanilla essence**	½ teaspoon

Freeze complete.

A 19-cm/7½-inch square cake tin may also be used.

18-cm × 28-cm   **shallow cake tin, greased**   7-inch × 11-inch

Rub the margarine into the flour then stir in the brown sugar. Press the mixture into the tin, prick the surface and bake in a moderate oven (180°C, 350°F, Gas Mark 4) for 10 minutes.

Meanwhile make the filling. Sieve the flour and baking powder into a bowl. Mix in the Bournvita, sugar, eggs, vanilla essence, coconut and walnuts. Spread this mixture evenly over the pastry in the tin and return to the oven for a further 25–30 minutes. Cool in the tin.

For the frosting, mix the Bournvita and coffee with the hot water. Beat in the margarine, sieved icing sugar and essence until really smooth. Spread frosting over the mixture in the tin and mark the surface with a fork. When set, cut into half down the centre and then across several times.

Makes 12 or 14

Chocolate Concrete (see page 161); Crackle Snaps (see page 168); Topsy Turvy Bars (see page 168); Peppermint Squares (see page 169); Frosted Malted Bars

Crunchy Cookies

Illustrated on page 159

Metric		Imperial
125 g	**margarine**	4 oz
125 g	**caster sugar**	4 oz
I	**egg, beaten**	I
2.5 ml	**vanilla essence**	½ teaspoon
125 g	**plain flour, sieved**	4 oz
2.5 ml	**bicarbonate of soda**	½ teaspoon
50 g	**Bournvita**	2 oz
50 g	**rolled oats**	2 oz
2	**baking trays, greased**	2

Beat the margarine and sugar together. Add the beaten egg and essence then the sieved flour and bicarbonate of soda. Finally stir in the Bournvita and rolled oats. Place teaspoonsful of mixture on greased baking trays, allowing room for them to spread. Bake in a moderately hot oven (190°C, 375°F, Gas Mark 5) for 10–12 minutes until browned nicely. Cool for a few minutes then lift on to a wire tray.

Makes about 32

These cookies freeze well. Place in a rigid container, seal and label.

For a special occasion, glacé icing (see page 14) can be zigzagged over the cookies, or perhaps piped as initials for children.

Chocolate Concrete

Illustrated on page 163

Metric		Imperial
75 g	**margarine**	3 oz
50 g	**white fat**	2 oz
50 g	**caster sugar**	2 oz
175 g	**plain flour**	6 oz
25 g	**Bournville cocoa**	I oz
50 g	**biscuit crumbs or**	2 oz
	browned breadcrumbs	
	Icing	
350 g	**icing sugar**	12 oz
30 g	**Bournville cocoa**	I oz
20-cm × 30-cm	**Swiss roll tin, greased**	8-inch × 12-inch

Beat the fats together really well, then add the sugar. Sieve the flour with the cocoa and work into the mixture with the finely crushed biscuits or breadcrumbs. Spread evenly in the tin, using a palette knife. Bake in a moderate oven (180°C,

Freeze the biscuits cut up in the tray, without the icing. Wrap, seal and label.

Do not be put off by the name, which is local to the Midlands. The biscuits are light in texture. They keep exceptionally well when kept in an airtight tin. Home-made breadcrumbs should be used for this recipe, or the broken biscuits from the biscuit tin.

350°F, Gas Mark 4) for 25 minutes. Cut up the biscuits straight away, making 24 pieces. Cool in the tin.

Sieve the icing sugar and cocoa into a bowl. Slowly mix in just enough water to make a spreading consistency. Pour all the icing on to the centre of the biscuits in the tray then with a palette knife, spread it over the surface. Do not lift up the knife at all. Carefully lift the biscuits on to a wire tray. Trim the edges with a sharp knife. *Makes 24 biscuits*

Island Slices

Illustrated on page 159

Freeze the slices before icing with chocolate, preferably whilst still in the tin. Wrap, seal and label. Defrost at room temperature. Cover with melted chocolate and cut into slices.

Melted Bournville plain chocolate may be substituted for the milk chocolate, if a stronger taste is preferred.

Metric		Imperial
125 g	**plain flour**	4 oz
10 ml	**Bournville cocoa**	2 teaspoons
	pinch of salt	
50 g	**butter**	2 oz
50 g	**caster sugar**	2 oz
1	**egg yolk**	1
	Filling	
50 g	**butter**	2 oz
1	**small can condensed milk**	1
60 ml	**icing sugar**	3 tablespoons
20 ml	**Bournville cocoa**	1 tablespoon
225 g	**desiccated coconut**	8 oz
	Icing	
125 g	**Cadbury's dairy milk chocolate**	4 oz

18-cm × 28-cm	**cake tin, about 2.5 cm/ 1-inch deep**	7-inch × 11-inch

Sieve the flour and cocoa with a pinch of salt. Rub in the butter until the mixture resembles breadcrumbs, then add the sugar. Bind the mixture together with the egg yolk and a very little water if necessary. Roll out the pastry to fit the tin and line it carefully. Prick the base with a fork and bake the case blind in a moderate oven (180°C, 350°F, Gas Mark 4) for 15–20 minutes. Leave in the tin.

Melt the butter with the condensed milk in a saucepan. Sieve the icing sugar with the cocoa and mix into the saucepan with the coconut. Spread filling over the pastry base and leave it to get quite cold before spreading with chocolate.

Melt the chocolate carefully in a bowl over a pan of hot, not boiling water. Do not stir. Spread the chocolate over the filling, using a palette knife. Mark the top with a fork. When the chocolate is set, cut into slices. *Makes 16*

Ginger Shorties

Illustrated opposite

Metric		Imperial
175 g	**plain flour**	6 oz
	pinch of salt	
125 g	**butter**	4 oz
50 g	**caster sugar**	2 oz
50 g	**Bournville Dark plain chocolate**	50 g
40 g	**crystallised ginger**	1½ oz
	Decoration	
	little caster sugar	
	Icing	
20 ml	**Bournville cocoa**	1 tablespoon
40 ml	**boiling water**	2 tablespoons
15 g	**butter or margarine**	½ oz
125 g	**icing sugar, sieved**	4 oz
5-cm	**pastry cutter**	2-inch
	baking tray	

Sieve the flour and salt together. Rub in the butter until the mixture resembles breadcrumbs. Stir in the sugar. Chop the chocolate and ginger into fairly small pieces and stir in. Knead the dough together, and on a lightly floured surface, roll out to 5 mm/¼ inch thick. Cut out the biscuits with the cutter, rolling the dough again in between. Place the biscuits on a baking tray. Bake in a moderately hot oven (190°C, 375°F, Gas Mark 5) for 10–15 minutes until golden brown. Lift off the tray and dredge with caster sugar.

Sieve the cocoa and mix with the boiling water for the icing. Beat in the butter then the sieved icing sugar to make a smooth and shiny icing. Dip the biscuits into the icing, covering about one-third of the circle. Leave them to set.

Makes about 22

Cherry Clusters (see page 172); Ginger Shorties; Melting Moments (see page 173); Chocolate Biscuits (see page 172); Cottage Cookies (see page 173)

Crackle Snaps

Illustrated on page 163

Metric		Imperial
75 g	**plain flour**	3 oz
25 g	**caster sugar**	1 oz
50 g	**butter**	2 oz
	Topping	
25 g	**butter**	1 oz
20 ml	**golden syrup**	1 tablespoon
25 g	**caster sugar**	1 oz
25 g	**Bournville cocoa**	1 oz
25 g	**'Rice Krispies'**	1 oz
18-cm	**square shallow cake tin**	7-inch

A spoonful of seedless raisins or sultanas can be added to the 'krispie' mixture which can then be heaped into paper cake cases and left to set.

Sieve the flour into a bowl, add the sugar and rub in the butter. When the mixture will stick together, knead slightly then press evenly into the tin. Bake in a moderate oven (180°C, 350°F, Gas Mark 4) for 10–15 minutes. Turn out on to a wire tray.

Measure the butter, syrup, sugar and cocoa into a pan. Heat gently until melted completely. Stir in the 'Rice Krispies' and stir carefully until they are completely covered. Spread over the shortbread base and cut into oblongs.

Makes 10

Topsy-Turvy Bars

Illustrated on page 163

Metric		Imperial
175 g	**Bournville Dark plain chocolate**	6 oz
125 g	**soft margarine**	4 oz
175 g	**caster sugar**	6 oz
2	**eggs**	2
125 g	**sultanas**	4 oz
225 g	**desiccated coconut**	8 oz
125 g	**glacé cherries, chopped**	4 oz
23-cm × 33-cm	**Swiss roll tin**	9-inch × 13-inch
	greaseproof paper	

Grease the tin. Line the base with greaseproof paper and grease this too. Melt the chocolate carefully in a bowl over hot water then spread it evenly on the paper in the tin. Leave the chocolate in a cool place to harden again.

Cream the margarine and sugar together until they are lighter in colour and texture. Beat in the eggs then mix in the sultanas, coconut and chopped cherries. Spread the mixture evenly over the chocolate in the tin and bake in a moderate oven (180°C, 350°F, Gas Mark 4) for 20–30 minutes until golden brown on top. Leave in the tin until it is completely cool then turn out and peel off the paper. The chocolate should be hard. Cut down the centre then into 12 across. Serve the bars with the chocolate upwards. *Makes 24*

Peppermint Squares

Illustrated on page 163

Freeze the squares for up to 3 months. Put waxed paper between the squares and pack carefully. Wrap, seal and label. Defrost at room temperature.

Do not use *soft* margarine in this recipe as the consistency becomes too soft with it.

Metric		Imperial
175 g	**butter or hard margarine**	6 oz
175 g	**soft brown sugar**	6 oz
2	**eggs**	2
150 g	**self-raising flour**	5 oz
25 g	**Bournville cocoa**	1 oz
40 ml	**peppermint cordial**	2 tablespoons
40 ml	**water**	2 tablespoons
125 g	**caster sugar**	4 oz

23-cm × 33-cm	**Swiss roll tin, greased**	9-inch × 13-inch

Soften the butter or margarine slightly to make it easier to beat in the soft brown sugar. Beat well until lighter in colour and texture then beat in the eggs. Sieve the flour and cocoa and stir into the mixture. Turn into the prepared tin and level the surface with a knife. Bake in a moderate oven (180°C, 350°F, Gas Mark 4) for 30–40 minutes. When cooked, the surface should be soft though set.

Mix the peppermint cordial with the water and the sugar. When the cake mixture is cooked, take it out of the oven and immediately spread the paste over the whole of the top surface. This makes a crisp crust when cold. Cut into squares. *Makes 24*

Lollipop Biscuits

Illustrated opposite

Small wooden sticks, but not cocktail sticks, or even clean ice lolly sticks are ideal for these biscuits. Avoid plastic sticks as they will melt in the oven.

To make the biscuits stay on the sticks, push them right in but do not allow the stick to show through the mixture. The baked biscuit will then harden and stay on the stick to be held upright.

Metric		Imperial
	Plain shortbread	
175 g	**plain flour**	6 oz
125 g	**butter**	4 oz
50 g	**caster sugar**	2 oz
	finely grated rind and juice of ½ lemon	
	Chocolate shortbread	
125 g	**plain flour**	4 oz
75 g	**butter**	3 oz
10 ml	**Bournville Cocoa, sifted**	2 teaspoons
50 g	**caster sugar**	2 oz
	vanilla essence	
	a little icing sugar, sifted	
	Decoration	
20 ml	**apricot jam**	1 tablespoon
20 ml	**coloured sugar strands**	1 tablespoon
20	**lollipop sticks**	20
2	**baking trays, greased**	2

Prepare the plain shortbread first. Sift the flour into a bowl and rub in the butter until the mixture resembles fine bread-crumbs. Add the sugar, lemon rind and the strained juice and bind into a firm dough. Chill this dough whilst making the chocolate shortbread in the same way, adding the cocoa, sugar and essence to the rubbed-in ingredients.

Dust the surface lightly with icing sugar. Roll each piece of dough separately into rectangles measuring about 20 × 30 cm/8 × 12 in. Lift the chocolate dough on top of the plain mixture and roll up from the narrow end, like a Swiss roll. Cut into 20 even slices and place slightly apart on baking trays. Press a lollipop stick into each biscuit. Bake in a moderately hot oven (190 c, 375 f, gas 5) for about 20 minutes until golden brown. Leave the biscuits on the baking tray to harden before finally cooling them on a wire tray.

Spread a little jam in the centre of each biscuit and sprinkle with sugar strands. Store in an airtight container. *Makes 20*

Merry-Go-Round (see page 92); Lollipop Biscuits; Jigsaw Roll (see page 73)

Chocolate Biscuits

Illustrated on page 167

Metric		Imperial
125 g	**butter or margarine**	4 oz
50 g	**caster sugar**	2 oz
	few drops of vanilla essence	
125 g	**plain flour, sieved**	4 oz
25 g	**Bournville cocoa, sieved**	1 oz
	pinch of salt	
	Butter icing	
75 g	**butter**	3 oz
175 g	**icing sugar, sieved**	6 oz
40 ml	**hot water**	2 tablespoons
	few drops vanilla essence (optional)	
	Decoration	
	little icing sugar	

baking tray, greased

Cream the butter and sugar together thoroughly. Add the essence and fold in the sieved flour and cocoa with a pinch of salt; it should all mix together quite well. Divide the mixture equally in half then each piece into six. Roll into balls and place them on a greased baking tray, spaced fairly well apart. Flatten each one with a fork, yet leave the mixture quite thick still. Bake in a moderately hot oven (190°C, 375°F, Gas Mark 5) for 12–15 minutes. Lift the biscuits on to a wire tray to cool when they have hardened slightly.

Beat the butter to soften it then beat in the sieved icing sugar and the water. It should be a nice light texture and colour. Vanilla essence can also be added. Sandwich the biscuits together with icing and dust with icing sugar.

Makes 6 complete biscuits

Freeze the biscuits complete, or without the butter icing. Pack, label and seal. They crumble easily when thawed.

Dip the fork in water to prevent it sticking to the biscuit mixture.

Cherry Clusters

Illustrated on page 167

Metric		Imperial
1 quantity	**Chocolate Biscuits mixture**	1 quantity
50 g	**glacé cherries, chopped**	2 oz

Add chopped cherries to the chocolate biscuit mixture. Spoon small heaps on to a greased baking tray and bake as for

Mixed dried fruit or chopped nuts may also be added.

Chocolate Biscuits. They may take a couple of minutes longer as the mixture is thicker. *Makes about 25*

Melting Moments

Illustrated on page 167

Metric		Imperial
1 quantity	**Chocolate Biscuits mixture**	1 quantity
50 g	**porridge oats**	2 oz
6	**glacé cherries, halved**	6

Make up the chocolate biscuit mixture and roll into 12 balls. Roll these in the porridge oats. Place them on a greased baking tray and flatten a little with your fingers. Put half a glacé cherry in the centre of each biscuit. Bake as for Chocolate Biscuits. *Makes 12*

Cottage Cookies

Illustrated on page 167

Freeze the cookies without the marmalade on top. Pack, label and seal.

The cookies can also be rolled in crushed cornflakes, or 'Rice Krispies'.

Metric		Imperial
125 g	**margarine**	4 oz
125 g	**caster sugar**	4 oz
2	**eggs**	2
200 g	**self-raising flour, sieved**	7 oz
25 g	**Cadbury's drinking chocolate**	1 oz
60 ml	**thick marmalade**	2 tablespoons
75 g	**porridge oats**	3 oz
	little extra marmalade peel	

baking tray, greased

Cream the margarine and sugar well together. Beat in the eggs. Fold in the sieved flour and drinking chocolate then the marmalade. Roll small spoonsful of the mixture in the porridge oats and place them on a greased baking tray, allowing room for them to spread. It may be necessary to do two traysful, or bake them in batches. Bake in a fairly hot oven (200°C, 400°F, Gas Mark 6) for about 15 minutes. They should be golden brown but will still be soft. Lift carefully on to a wire tray to cool. Decorate some of the cookies with pieces of marmalade peel. *Makes about 30*

Trefoil Biscuits

Illustrated opposite

Metric		Imperial
150 g	**soft brown sugar**	5 oz
50 g	**Cadbury's Drinking Chocolate**	2 oz
1	**egg**	1
200 g	**self-raising flour, sifted**	7 oz
	finely grated rind of 2 lemons	
75 g	**butter, melted**	3 oz
	Icing	
450 g	**icing sugar, sifted**	1 lb
	juice of 2 lemons	
	yellow food colouring	
2 large packets	**Cadbury's Buttons**	2 large packets
	baking tray, greased	
1	**greaseproof paper piping bag**	1

The undecorated biscuits freeze well.

Polish the Buttons by resting them in the palm of your hand and rubbing them lightly with your finger. This will remove any loose chocolate from the surface of the Buttons and bring them up to a nice shine.

Measure the sugar and drinking chocolate into a bowl, then stir in the egg. Add the flour and lemon rind. Bind to a stiff dough with the butter. Divide the mixture into three even amounts, then roll each one into a sausage shape no more than 2.5 cm/1 in wide – make all three the same length. Wrap separately in greaseproof paper and chill for about 30 minutes.

Cut each roll into thin slices about 0.5 cm/¼ in thick. Overlap three circles on the baking tray, making a trefoil shape. Continue until most of the mixture is used. Roll out a small piece and chop into stalk sized pieces to stick on each biscuit. Bake in a moderate oven (180 c, 350 F, gas 4) for 10–12 minutes. Lift off and cool on a wire tray.

Make a thick coating icing with the icing sugar and strained lemon juice, adding enough food colouring to make a good rich gold colour. Place a good spoonful of the icing in the piping bag. Add a little more liquid to the remaining icing to make it a little thinner. Decorate the biscuits about six at a time, by piping a border of icing round the edge of each biscuit, then filling in the centre with the softer icing. Overlap three Buttons in the centre of each biscuit. Make all the biscuits in the same way and leave to dry. *Makes about 30*

Tracking Cake (see page 68);
Patrol Tents (see page 156);
Trefoil biscuits

Number Biscuits

Illustrated on page 39

Metric		Imperial
125 g	**hard margarine or butter**	4 oz
125 g	**caster sugar**	4 oz
2	**egg yolks**	2
50 g	**ground almonds**	2 oz
125 g	**plain flour, sifted**	4 oz
30 ml	**Bournville Cocoa,** 1 heaped tablespoon	
	sifted	
	almond essence	
4	**thin angelica strips**	4
4	**glacé cherries**	4
	large nylon piping bag	
	large star pipe	
2	**baking trays, greased**	2

It is important to use hard fat for this recipe otherwise the biscuits tend to spread too much during cooking. They keep well in an airtight container, but soften and crumble in the freezer – particularly if kept for a long period.

Cream the margarine and sugar well together; beat in the egg yolks. Mix in the almonds, flour, cocoa and a few drops of essence to taste. Fit the pipe into the piping bag, fill it with the biscuit mixture, then pipe the numbers on to the prepared trays, allowing a little space between each biscuit and making them in batches if necessary. Cut small diamonds of angelica and the cherries into eight, and arrange a few pieces of each in a small decoration on the figures. Refrigerate the biscuits for 10 minutes to allow the mixture to harden before baking in a moderate oven (180 C, 350 F, gas 4) for about 10 minutes. Cool slightly before lifting off the baking trays. *Makes 25–30 biscuits*

Traditional Fare

Black Forest Gâteau and Florentines must surely be two of the most famous recipes in the world. You may have tasted them on holiday abroad or perhaps when eating out. These rich, delicious specialities are rather more expensive to prepare than some of the other recipes in the book but we have simplified them enough for you to try without fear of failure. Treat yourself, your family and your guests to the luxury of a rich chocolate cake or tempting dessert presented in the grand traditional manner.

Florentines

Illustrated on page 179 and back cover

Let the Florentines get completely cold before spreading with melted chocolate. It may be easier to put just a little on first to avoid the chocolate dripping through.

Metric		Imperial
50 g	**butter**	2 oz
50 g	**caster sugar**	2 oz
50 g	**blanched almonds**	2 oz
25 g	**glacé cherries**	1 oz
20 g	**flaked almonds**	$\frac{1}{2}$ oz
25 g	**mixed peel**	1 oz
40 ml	**whipped cream**	1 tablespoon
175 g	**Bourneville Dark plain chocolate**	6 oz
2	**baking trays**	2
	Bakewell paper	

Melt the butter in a pan, stir in the sugar and bring slowly to the boil. Chop the blanched almonds small and the cherries into quarters. Mix the nuts in with the fruit and finally stir in the cream.

Cover the baking trays with Bakewell paper. Put teaspoonsful of the mixture on to the trays, spaced well apart, then flatten them down. Bake in a moderate oven (180°C, 350°F, Gas Mark 4) for 8–10 minutes until they are golden brown. Neaten the edges with a plain pastry cutter or knife. Cool slightly before lifting off the tray with a fish slice. Cook the remaining mixture in the same way.

Melt the chocolate and spread over the smooth side of each Florentine, covering them completely. Stand chocolate side up. When the chocolate begins to set, mark it with a fork to makes swirls on the Florentines. *Makes 15*

Doboz Torte

Illustrated opposite and on back cover

Metric		Imperial
3	**eggs**	3
125 g	**caster sugar**	4 oz
125 g	**plain flour**	4 oz
	pinch of salt	
175 g	**granulated sugar**	6 oz
	Butter icing	
200 g	**Bournville Dark plain chocolate**	7 oz
200 g	**butter**	7 oz
400 g	**icing sugar, sieved**	1 lb

Caramel will not freeze. The cake layers can be assembled with the butter icing. Leave the top one plain and put the caramel on later. Wrap, label and seal. Freeze a little butter icing separately to finish off the cake.

The secret of making caramel successfully is to dissolve the sugar properly. Patience is necessary; wait until the liquid is quite clear.

piping bag and small star vegetable pipe

Make the cake layers the day before they are required. Have ready 5 flat surfaces, such as baking trays or roasting tins that are large enough for 18-cm/7-inch circles. Brush these with oil then dust with flour, shaking off any surplus. Mark a circle on each, using a cake tin or plate as a guide.

Whisk the eggs and caster sugar together in a bowl over hot water, or use an electric mixer. It will take at least 10 minutes to get the mixture thick enough to leave a definite trail. Sieve the flour with a pinch of salt into the mixture and fold in carefully so that the air is not knocked out. Divide the cake mixture evenly between the circles, spread them flat then bake in batches as necessary, in a moderately hot oven (190°C, 375°F, Gas Mark 5) for 6–8 minutes, until cooked through and pale golden brown. Lift off and cool on wire trays. Trim edges so that all the circles are the same size.

Place the granulated sugar in a heavy-based saucepan and just cover it with water. Dissolve the sugar over a very low heat, without stirring, so that the liquid becomes quite clear. Now bring to the boil and cook rapidly until the caramel turns a rich golden brown. Meanwhile lift one cake layer on to a lightly oiled baking tray. Pour the caramel over the cake, completely covering the top. When it is almost hard, mark with a knife into 12 sections. Trim edges if necessary.

Melt the chocolate in a bowl over a pan of hot water. Beat the butter then beat in the sieved icing sugar really well. Mix in the melted chocolate. Sandwich the cake layers together with some of the chocolate butter icing, putting the caramel layer on top. Lift the cake on to a plate or cake board. Attach a small star vegetable pipe to a piping bag and fill it with the remaining butter icing. Pipe zigzags down the side, all round the cake and stars round the top. The cake keeps well in a tin.

Florentines (see page 177);
Doboz Torte

Black Forest Gâteau

Illustrated on title page

Metric		Imperial
	Shortbread base	
50 g	butter	2 oz
25 g	caster sugar	1 oz
75 g	plain flour	3 oz
	Cake mixture	
125 g	soft margarine or butter	4 oz
125 g	caster sugar	4 oz
2	eggs	2
75 g	self-raising flour, sieved	3 oz
25 g	Bournville cocoa, sieved	1 oz
	Filling and decoration	
2 425-g cans	black cherries	2 15-oz cans
30 ml	kirsch or cherry brandy	2 tablespoons
40 ml	red jam	2 tablespoons
250 ml	double cream	$\frac{1}{2}$ pint
125 ml	single cream	$\frac{1}{4}$ pint
75 g	Bournville Dark plain chocolate	3 oz
12	chocolate shapes (see page 10)	12
23-cm	cake tin, greased	9-inch
	greaseproof paper piping bag	
	piping bag and star pipe	

Use fresh cherries when they are in season. Cans of black cherries are sometimes difficult to buy so substitute red cherries, or try a mixture of both.

Make the base first. Cream the butter and sugar together. Mix in the flour and knead lightly to form a dough. Press this evenly into the tin and flatten the surface with a palette knife. Prick with a fork. Bake in a moderately hot oven (190°C, 375°F, Gas Mark 5) for 10–15 minutes until pale brown and cooked. Remove carefully and cool. Wipe the cake tin clean and line it with two circles of greaseproof paper.

For the cake mixture, cream the soft margarine and sugar together. Beat in the eggs one at a time then fold in the sieved flour and cocoa. Spread the mixture evenly in the tin and bake in the moderately hot oven, at the same temperature, for 20–25 minutes until cooked. Turn out and cool on a wire tray.

Drain the juice from the cherries and add the kirsch to the liquid. Remove the cherry stones. Slice the cake through the centre, place the layers on plates and moisten with the cherry juice. Spread the jam on the pastry base. Whip the creams together until the cream holds its shape. Spread one cake layer with cream. Reserve 12 cherries and spread the remainder over the cream. Press the other cake layer on top and lift the whole cake on to the pastry base. Cover the cake with cream, keeping a little for the decoration, spreading it as flat as possible. Grate the chocolate then coat the sides of the cake with it. Melt any remaining in a small bowl over a pan of hot, not boiling water. Fill the paper piping bag. Cut the tip off the end. Mark the cake into 12 sections and pipe a zigzag pattern of chocolate on alternate sections. Place the remaining cream into the piping bag and pipe whirls on each section and one in the centre. Complete the cake by arranging the cherry halves and the chocolate shapes on alternate sections. Carefully lift the cake on to a plate or cake board. *Serves 12*

Brownies

Illustrated on page 183

Metric		Imperial
150 g	**margarine**	5 oz
60 ml	**Bournville cocoa**	2 tablespoons
150 g	**caster or soft brown sugar**	5 oz
2	**eggs**	2
50 g	**self-raising flour, sieved**	2 oz
50 g	**walnuts, chopped**	2 oz
18-cm	**square cake tin,**	7-inch
	greased and base lined	

Melt 50 g/2 oz of the margarine in a pan, stir in the cocoa and set aside. Cream the remaining margarine with the sugar until lighter in colour then gradually beat in the eggs. Fold in the sieved flour then the chopped walnuts and the cocoa mixture. Turn into the prepared tin, smooth the surface and bake in a moderate oven (180°C, 350°F, Gas Mark 4) for about 45 minutes until cooked. Cool in the tin. Later, turn out and cut into squares. *Makes 12 or 16*

Devil's Food Cake

Illustrated opposite

Metric		Imperial
175 g	**plain flour**	6 oz
5 ml	**baking powder**	1 teaspoon
2.5 ml	**bicarbonate of soda**	$\frac{1}{2}$ teaspoon
50 g	**Bournville cocoa**	2 oz
125 g	**butter**	4 oz
225 g	**dark soft brown sugar**	8 oz
2	**eggs**	2
80 ml	**soured cream or plain yogurt**	4 tablespoons
	Frosting	
1	**egg white**	1
45 ml	**cold water**	3 tablespoons
200 g	**granulated sugar**	7 oz
1.25 ml	**cream of tartar**	$\frac{1}{4}$ teaspoon
2.5 ml	**vanilla essence**	$\frac{1}{2}$ teaspoon
2 20-cm	**round shallow cake tins, greased and base lined**	2 8-inch

Freeze the cake complete with the icing. Open freeze then pack later in a rigid container, seal and label.

The frosting has to be made over hot water so that the sugar can melt and give a smooth finish. If you find the cream of tartar difficult to measure, use a couple of good pinches.

Sieve the flour, baking powder and bicarbonate of soda. Mix the cocoa with just enough boiling water to make a smooth paste. Cream the butter and sugar together. Beat in the eggs then the soured cream or yogurt, cocoa and lastly, fold in the sieved dry ingredients. Divide the mixture evenly between the tins, level off the surface and bake in a moderately hot oven (190°C, 375°F, Gas Mark 5) for about 35 minutes. Turn out the cakes and cool on a wire tray, removing the paper lining first.

Place the egg white, water, sugar and cream of tartar into a fairly large bowl and stand this over a pan of hot water. Whisk hard with an electric hand mixer or a rotary whisk for at least 10 minutes, so that the mixture is glossy white, smooth and will stand in peaks. The whisking becomes very stiff to do but the frosting will not harden at all if it does not reach the correct consistency. Add the vanilla essence when the frosting is ready.

Sandwich the cakes together with frosting, lift on to a plate and cover with the remaining frosting, being careful not to get any chocolate cake crumbs into it. Leave the cake for an hour or so as the frosting forms a crust while the inside remains soft. This cake keeps exceptionally well in an airtight tin.

Devil's Food Cake (see above); Brownies (see page 181)

Choux Pastry

Metric		Imperial
125 ml	**water**	$\frac{1}{4}$ pint
50 g	**butter or margarine**	2 oz
2	**eggs**	2
65 g	**plain flour, sieved**	$2\frac{1}{2}$ oz

Measure the water and butter into a saucepan. Melt the butter gently then increase the heat and bring to the boil. Immediately take the pan off the heat and shoot in the flour all at once. Stir the mixture. Beat the eggs together and add a little at a time to the pan, beating hard with a wooden spoon between each addition. If the eggs are very large, the mixture may become too soft so do not add it all. The pastry should come cleanly away from the sides of the pan and have a really glossy appearance. The mixture can be left at this stage.

Éclairs

Metric		Imperial
1 quantity	**choux pastry (see above)**	1 quantity
125 ml	**double cream**	$\frac{1}{4}$ pint
50 g	**Bournville Dark plain chocolate**	50 g
13 g	**butter**	$\frac{1}{2}$ oz
20 ml	**water**	1 tablespoon
25 g	**icing sugar**	1 oz
	piping bag and plain 1.5-cm/$\frac{3}{4}$-inch pipe	
2	**baking trays, greased and lightly floured**	2

Uncooked choux pastry may be kept for 24 hours in the refrigerator, ready to be cooked when required. As an alternative, fill the éclairs with the Cream Puffs filling (see page 152). Omit the chocolate icing but sprinkle with icing sugar.

Make up the choux pastry as described. Fill the piping bag. Pipe the choux pastry into lengths, making 10 to 12, depending on the size. Space them well apart, allowing room for them to rise. Bake in a moderate oven (180°C, 350°F, Gas Mark 4) for 10 minutes then increase the heat to moderately hot (190°C, 375°F, Gas Mark 5) for another 10 minutes. Finally, increase the heat to fairly hot (200°C, 400°F, Gas Mark 6) for another 10 minutes, by which time the éclairs should be well risen, golden brown and firm. Cool on a wire tray, making a small slit in the side of each éclair to let the steam escape.

Whip the cream and fill the éclairs with it. Melt the chocolate and butter with the water in a pan over a gentle heat, stirring continuously. Sieve the icing sugar into a bowl and beat the melted chocolate into it, stirring until smooth. Spread the cold icing on each éclair. Ideally, they should be eaten the same day as choux pastry goes soft after being filled.

Makes 10–12

Profiteroles

To make round buns, rub over the top of each with a wetted finger to smooth the surface.

Metric		Imperial
1 quantity	**choux pastry (see page 184)**	1 quantity
125 ml	**double cream**	¼ pint
20 ml	**caster or icing sugar**	1 tablespoon
	few drops of vanilla essence	
	Sauce	
50 g	**Bournville Dark plain chocolate**	50 g
45 ml	**water**	3 tablespoons
10 ml	**cornflour**	2 teaspoons
10 ml	**sugar**	2 teaspoons
125 ml	**milk**	¼ pint
80 ml	**single cream**	4 tablespoons
	few drops of vanilla essence	

piping bag and 1.5-cm/¾-inch plain vegetable pipe
baking tray, greased and floured

Make up the choux pastry and fill the piping bag. Pipe small mounds of the mixture on to the prepared tray, making about 25 in all. Bake in a moderate oven (180°C, 350°F, Gas Mark 4) for 10 minutes. Increase the heat to moderately hot (190°C, 375°F, Gas Mark 5) for another 10 minutes and finally increase the heat to fairly hot (200°C, 400°F, Gas Mark 6) for about 5 minutes until the choux buns are golden brown and crisp. Make a small slit in the side to let out the steam and cool on a wire tray.

Whip the cream with the sugar and vanilla essence until it will just hold its shape. Fill the piping bag and squeeze cream into each of the buns. Pile them into a dish.

Make the sauce by melting the chocolate in the water, over a gentle heat, in a saucepan. Blend the cornflour and sugar with a little milk, then add the rest of it and empty into the saucepan. Add the chocolate. Stir until the custard comes to the boil and thickens. Cool the sauce a little before adding the cream and vanilla essence. Either have the chocolate sauce hot or cold, poured over the profiteroles. *Serves about 8*

Soufflé

Illustrated on page 190

Metric		Imperial
400 ml	**milk**	¾ pint
30 g	**Bournville cocoa**	1½ oz
75 g	**caster sugar**	3 oz
3	**eggs, separated**	3
275 ml	**double cream**	½ pint
14 g	**gelatine**	½ oz
80 ml	**water**	4 tablespoons
50 g	**Bournville Dark plain chocolate**	50 g
	greaseproof paper	
550-ml	**soufflé dish**	1-pint
	piping bag and star pipe	

Prepare the dish first. Tie a double band of greaseproof paper round the dish, allowing sufficient height for it to come at least 5 cm/2 inches above the rim. Use a double piece of string, put the ends through the loop, separate the pieces and tie up at the other side (see photograph 1, opposite). Grease the dish and paper very lightly.

Bring the milk and the cocoa to the boil, stirring to dissolve the cocoa. Cream the sugar and egg yolks together then stir in the chocolate milk. Return to the pan and heat gently, stirring continuously until the custard thickens. Do not allow the egg custard to boil. Cool a little in the pan.

Whip half the cream and stir into the custard. Dissolve the gelatine in the water and when it is quite clear, pour it into the custard, making sure they are both at the same temperature. Cool the custard fairly quickly by placing the bowl or pan on ice, or in the freezer if you watch it. Avoid getting the custard too thick. When it is just beginning to set, whisk the egg whites until they are at the soft peak stage and fold into the custard (see photograph 2, opposite). Quickly pour the mixture into the prepared soufflé dish and leave to set.

Remove the paper band by pressing a palette knife against the side of the dish and peeling back the paper (see photograph 3, opposite). Whip the remaining cream. Spread cream round the soufflé edge and spoon the remainder into the piping bag. Grate the chocolate, spread it on a large piece of greaseproof paper and stand the dish in the centre. Flick the chocolate up on to the sides, covering them completely (see photograph 4, opposite). Complete the soufflé by piping whirls round the top. *Serves 6*

Do not decorate. Open freeze the soufflé in the paper collar. When firm, wrap in foil then polythene; label and seal. Allow about 4 hours for it to thaw then decorate.

When adding egg whites to soufflés, do not whisk them too hard or they will be difficult to fold in. It is sometimes easier to stir a good spoonful of the chocolate mixture into the egg whites, then fold the egg whites into the chocolate.

The soufflé dish can be lined with Bakewell paper, in which case there will be no need to grease it.

Ideally, a soufflé is better eaten the same day but it can be kept overnight.

1 Tie a double band of greaseproof paper round the dish to make a collar. Secure with string. If desired, lightly grease the dish and paper collar.

2 Fold the beaten egg whites into the chocolate custard, using a metal spoon or spatula.

3 Press a long, flat-bladed knife straight against the side of the dish and carefully peel off the paper, keeping the knife against the soufflé.

4 Spread soufflé edge with whipped cream. Stand the dish in a circle of grated Bournville Dark plain chocolate and flick up on to the cream. Decorate with whipped cream.

187

Orange and Chocolate Soufflé

When making the Soufflé mixture on page 186, add the finely grated rind and the juice of 1 orange to the eggs and sugar.

Hot Chocolate Soufflé

Metric		Imperial
50 g	**butter**	2 oz
50 g	**plain flour**	2 oz
20 ml	**Bournville cocoa**	1 tablespoon
275 ml	**milk**	$\frac{1}{2}$ pint
3	**eggs, separated**	3
50 g	**caster sugar**	2 oz
	Decoration	
	little icing sugar	
	greaseproof paper	
1.2-litre	**soufflé dish, buttered**	2-pint

Depending on the shape of the soufflé dish, it may not always be necessary to tie a paper collar round it. A deeper dish forces the mixture upwards and it will come higher above the rim of the dish, so needs the support of a paper collar.

If the roux is lumpy after the milk has been added, whisk quickly with a rotary whisk and the lumps will disappear.

Line the dish with a paper collar as described in the Soufflé recipe, page 186.

Melt the butter in a saucepan and stir in the flour and cocoa, making a roux. Beat and cook the mixture until it comes away from the sides of the pan. Stir in the milk and continue cooking until the milk is absorbed and is thickened into a sauce. Cool slightly before adding the egg yolks, one at a time, off the heat. Whisk the egg whites to the soft peak stage then whisk in the sugar until it is as stiff again. Fold carefully into the chocolate sauce and turn the mixture into the soufflé dish. Stand the dish in a roasting tin half filled with water. Cook in a fairly hot oven (200°C, 400°F, Gas Mark 6) for about 50 minutes. The soufflé should be well risen with a slight crust on the top. Dust with icing sugar and serve immediately. Single cream is nice with the soufflé but it is not essential. *Serves 4*

Roulade

The roll will probably crack on the top when it is rolled up but this is hidden by the extra icing sugar. The texture is heavier than a Swiss roll so you will need a fork to eat it with.

Metric		Imperial
100 g	**Bournville Dark plain chocolate**	3½ oz
3	**eggs, separated**	3
125 g	**caster sugar**	4 oz
40 ml	**hot water**	2 tablespoons
284 ml	**whipping cream**	½ pint
	icing sugar, sieved	
23-cm × 33-cm	**Swiss roll tin, greased**	9-inch × 13-inch
	greaseproof paper	

Line the Swiss roll tin with greaseproof paper and brush the paper lining well with oil. Melt the chocolate in a bowl over hot water. Whisk the egg yolks and caster sugar together until they are light in colour and texture. Stir the hot water into the melted chocolate then mix this with the egg yolks. Whisk the egg whites stiffly and fold them carefully into the mixture. Pour the mixture into the prepared tin and spread it lightly and evenly into all the corners, so that the surface is as flat as possible, without knocking out the air in the egg whites. Place in the centre of a moderate oven (180°C, 350°F, Gas Mark 4) for 15–20 minutes. Prick a warm skewer into the centre which should come out clean. Leave the mixture in the tin. Cover it with a piece of greaseproof paper and a damp tea towel on top. Leave undisturbed for at least 3 hours, or overnight, keeping the tea towel damp so it will not crisp up.

Whip the cream until it will just hold its shape. Dust a large piece of greaseproof paper with sieved icing sugar and turn out the mixture from the tin on to it. Peel off the paper lining. Spread the cream over the surface and roll up from the short side, like a Swiss roll, using the large piece of greaseproof paper to help. Dust with extra icing sugar. Lift on to a plate and chill the roulade for an hour before eating.

Serves about 6

Chocolate Pots

Illustrated opposite

Metric		Imperial
550 ml	**milk**	1 pint
100 g	**Bournville Dark plain chocolate**	3½ oz
2	**eggs**	2
2	**egg yolks**	2
25 g	**caster sugar**	1 oz
10 ml	**rum or cointreau**	2 teaspoons
80 ml	**whipped cream**	4 tablespoons

Heat the milk in a saucepan, melting all but one of the squares of chocolate in it at the same time. Beat the eggs, egg yolks and sugar in a bowl. When the chocolate is completely melted, pour the hot but not boiling milk on to the eggs, stirring all the time. Add the rum. Strain the chocolate custard back into the clean pan, or into a jug, and divide the custard between 4 or 5 individual ovenproof dishes.

Half fill a roasting tin with warm water. Put the dishes into this, being careful to see that the water cannot come over the top, and bake them in a warm oven (160°C, 325°F, Gas Mark 3) for 40–60 minutes. The custard should be lightly set. Serve the custards hot or cold. Decorate with a spoonful of cream on top and grated chocolate, using the remaining square.

Serves 4 or 5

Chocolate Mousse

Illustrated on page 195

Metric		Imperial
75 g	**Bournville Dark plain chocolate**	3 oz
3	**eggs, separated**	3
	Decoration	
	grated Bournville Dark plain chocolate	

Break the chocolate into a medium-sized bowl and melt it over a pan of hot water. Stir in the egg yolks, off the heat. Whisk the egg whites stiffly and fold into the chocolate, making sure that it is all folded in. Turn the mousse into a glass dish or divide it between individual sundae glasses. Leave in the refrigerator for a couple of hours at least. Sprinkle with a little grated chocolate before serving.

Serves 3–4

To extend the mousse, whip 125 ml/¼ pint double cream and fold into the chocolate and egg yolks, before adding the egg whites. A little rum or brandy may also be added.

The mousse is excellent eaten the day after it is made.

Soufflé (see page 186); Chocolate Pots (see above)

Sacher Torte

Metric		Imperial
175 g	**Bournville Dark plain chocolate**	6 oz
160 g	**butter**	5 oz
150 g	**caster sugar**	5 oz
6	**size 2 eggs, separated**	6
150 g	**plain flour, sieved**	5 oz
	Icing	
75 g	**Bournville Dark plain chocolate**	3 oz
25 g	**butter**	1 oz
80 ml	**water**	4 tablespoons
325 g	**icing sugar**	12 oz
	gravy browning or brown food colouring	
20-cm	**round deep cake tin,**	8-inch
	greased and base lined	

Freeze the cake complete. Pack, label and freeze.

This is an unusual recipe with no raising agent. It is therefore particularly important to whisk the egg whites stiffly and fold them into the mixture, being careful to avoid knocking out the air.

Melt the chocolate for the cake mixture in a bowl standing over a pan of hot water. Cream the butter with half the caster sugar. Beat in the egg yolks and the melted chocolate. Fold in the sieved flour. Whisk all the egg whites together in a large bowl so that they are really stiff. Add the remaining sugar and whisk again very well until they are as stiff. Stir a little into the chocolate mixture to loosen the texture then fold in the remaining egg whites. Turn into the tin and bake in a moderate oven (180°C, 350°F, Gas Mark 4) for 1 hour–1 hour 10 minutes. Test with a warm skewer to see if the cake is cooked through. Turn out and cool on a wire tray.

Make the icing by melting the chocolate with the butter and water in saucepan over gentle heat, stirring continuously. Sieve the icing sugar into a large bowl, make a well in the centre and gradually stir in the liquid chocolate. Beat the icing until smooth and cool so that it is thick enough to spread on the cake. Cover the top and sides of the cake, leaving it quite rough so that the icing swirls attractively. Blend a little gravy browning with the scraps of icing, put it in a paper piping bag and pipe the words 'Sacher Torte' over the top. Lift the cake on to a plate.

Whisked Sponge

The cakes are generally better frozen without the filling but can be completed, packed carefully and frozen for a limited period. Sponges keep well if packed with a piece of greaseproof paper between them.

Whisked sponge mixtures can be difficult to make as the result depends on the amount of air beaten into the mixture. If you repeatedly have difficulty, add 5 ml/1 level teaspoon baking powder, sieved with the flour and cocoa.

To make a quick decoration, lay a pretty paper doily on top of the sponge and dust with icing sugar. Carefully lift off the doily and the pattern will be left on the cake. These cakes should be quite deep and slightly larger tins may be used if less depth is preferred.

Metric		Imperial
3	**eggs**	3
75 g	**caster sugar**	3 oz
75 g	**plain flour**	3 oz
30 ml	**Bournville cocoa**	2 tablespoons
	Filling	
	strawberry or apricot jam	
125 ml	**whipping cream**	$\frac{1}{4}$ pint
	Decoration	
	caster or icing sugar	
2 18-cm	**sandwich cake tins,**	2 7-inch
	greased and base lined	

Place the eggs and sugar in a fairly large bowl, over a pan of hot, not boiling water. An electric mixer is ideal to use here. Whisk until the mixture is really stiff and will leave a good trail; it will take between 10 and 20 minutes by hand. Sieve the flour and cocoa together then sieve it again into the bowl. Fold in carefully so that there are no pockets of flour left. Divide the mixture between the tins and level off the surface by tilting the tins. Do not touch the tops with a knife or spatula as this could knock out some of the air that has been beaten in so carefully. Put the cakes into the centre of a fairly hot oven (200°C, 400°F, Gas Mark 6) for about 15 minutes until they are cooked and spring back when touched. Turn the cakes out on to a wire tray, remove the paper linings and immediately turn them over so that there are no marks on the top. Leave the cakes to cool.

Spread one cake liberally with jam. Whip the cream and spread this on top. Sandwich the two cakes together and dust with caster sugar or sieved icing sugar. Lift on to a plate.

Fondue

Illustrated on page 215

Metric		Imperial
200 g	**Bournville Dark plain chocolate**	7 oz
80 ml	**fresh orange juice**	4 tablespoons
I	**small can evaporated milk, chilled**	I
	grated rind of ½ orange	
	fresh fruit	

Melt the chocolate, broken into squares, with the orange juice and 60 ml/3 tablespoons of the evaporated milk in a fondue dish, or in a bowl over a pan of hot water. Stir occasionally until smooth. Whisk the remaining evaporated milk until it is quite thick then fold into the chocolate mixture. Return to the heat and keep warm. Serve with a selection of prepared fresh fruit and, perhaps, some sponge finger biscuits.

For an even richer fondue, melt the Bournville Dark plain chocolate with 120 ml/6 tablespoons double cream and 40 ml/2 tablespoons of rum.

Use fondue forks or cocktail sticks to dip the fruit in the fondue.

St. Emilion au Chocolat

Illustrated opposite

Metric		Imperial
200 g	**Bournville Dark plain chocolate**	7 oz
125 g	**ratafia biscuits**	4 oz
40 ml	**rum**	2 tablespoons
125 g	**slightly salted butter**	4 oz
125 g	**caster sugar**	4 oz
250 ml	**milk**	½ pint
2	**eggs**	2
40 ml	**whipped cream**	2 tablespoons

Melt the chocolate in a bowl over a pan of hot water. Soak the ratafias in the rum. Cream the butter and sugar together then add the melted chocolate. Put the milk and the eggs into a saucepan and stir over a gentle heat to thicken the custard enough to coat the back of a wooden spoon. Be careful not to boil it. Slowly pour the custard into the chocolate mixture, stirring continuously. Leave in a cold place, preferably a refrigerator, until it is beginning to thicken and set. Spoon half the mixture into a glass dish and cover with a layer of ratafias, leaving out some for the top. Cover the biscuits with the remaining chocolate mixture. Swirl the cream through the centre and arrange the remaining ratafias round the edge. Refrigerate the pudding for several hours until required.

Serves 6–8

Serve a dish of poached fruit or fresh fruit salad with this rich chocolate pudding.

St. Emilion au Chocolat (see above); Chocolate Mousse (see page 190); Bavarian Cream (see page 205)

194

Perfect Puddings

Most of us, I suspect, have a secret hankering for a 'super pud' at the end of a meal. Surely this is the course where appearances count most and can greatly influence our choice. However, it is most disappointing if the taste does not live up to the visual expectations. We often neglect the pudding course as being too much trouble; browse through this chapter and you will find there is no excuse. Here are puddings for the family, Sunday lunch or for that special occasion. Some are cooked in the oven, some prepared in a flash, or even left overnight to leave you free on a busy day. Let your imagination run riot and enjoy a superb chocolate dessert.

Topsy-Turvy Pudding

Metric		Imperial
425-g can	**pears or pineapple rings**	15-oz can
40 ml	**golden syrup**	2 tablespoons
about 8	**glacé cherries**	about 8
125 g	**margarine**	4 oz
125 g	**soft brown sugar**	4 oz
2	**eggs**	2
125 g	**self-raising flour, sieved**	4 oz
50 ml	**Cadbury's chocolate spread**	2 tablespoons
5–10 ml	**arrowroot**	1–2 teaspoons
20-cm	**round cake tin, greased**	8-inch

The pudding may be frozen although it is at its best when eaten fresh.

Make the pudding in a smaller size tin if preferred, when the cooking time should be increased by 5–10 minutes. If made with white sugar the chocolate spread gives a marbled effect, but the flavour of the pudding is better with soft brown sugar.

Drain the juice from the fruit and keep aside. Mix the golden syrup with a spoonful of the juice and pour into the cake tin. Arrange the pear halves or pineapple rings in the tin, with a cherry in the centre of each. Cream the margarine and sugar together. Gradually beat in the eggs and fold in the sieved flour. Mix the chocolate spread with a spoonful of the fruit juice and swirl this through the mixture. Carefully spread over the fruit in the tin and level off the surface. Bake in a moderately hot oven (190°C, 375°F, Gas Mark 5) for about 45 minutes. Turn out the pudding on to a hot plate and serve with the sauce.

Blend the arrowroot with a little of the remaining juice, in a saucepan. Add all the juice and bring the sauce to the boil while stirring continuously. Chocolate spread may be added if a chocolate sauce is preferred with the pudding.

Serves 5

Steamed Chocolate Pudding

Choose a taller basin if you have one so the pudding turns out an attractive shape.

Metric		Imperial
125 g	**margarine**	4 oz
125 g	**caster sugar**	4 oz
2	**eggs**	2
25 g	**Bournville cocoa**	1 oz
150 g	**self-raising flour**	5 oz
750-ml	**pudding basin, greased**	1½-pint
	greaseproof paper or foil	

Cream the margarine and sugar together. Add the eggs, one at a time. Dissolve the cocoa in a very little boiling water and add to the mixture. Fold in the flour. Turn into the pudding basin. Cover with a double layer of greaseproof paper or a piece of foil. Secure. Place in a steamer over a pan of hot water, or into a large saucepan half filled with hot water. Cover and steam for about 1½ hours; the timing is not too crucial as the pudding will wait until you are ready. It may also be cooked in a pressure cooker. Follow the manufacturers instructions but it will normally take about 50 minutes at Low (5-lb) pressure.

Turn out on to a warm plate and serve with custard, single cream or a sweet white sauce. *Serves 4–5*

Orange Ring Pudding

Illustrated on page 199

Metric		Imperial
1 quantity	**Steamed Chocolate Pudding mixture**	1 quantity
2	**oranges**	2

Make up the chocolate pudding mixture. Add the finely grated rind of one orange. (The juice can be used instead of the water, if preferred.) Slice the other orange into circles and line the greased pudding basin with them, placing one on the bottom so that it will look nice when turned out. Cover and steam. *Serves 4–5*

Layered Steamed Pudding

Make up the Steamed Chocolate Pudding mixture on page 197, only adding the Bournville cocoa to half the mixture. Leave the other half plain or add a few drops of orange, vanilla or peppermint essence. Place the mixture in alternate layers in the bowl. Cover and steam as described.

Castle Puddings

Illustrated opposite

Metric		Imperial
125 g	**self-raising flour**	4 oz
2	**eggs**	2
125 g	**soft margarine**	4 oz
125 g	**light soft brown sugar**	4 oz
20 ml	**Bournville cocoa**	1 tablespoon
2.5 ml	**vanilla or orange essence**	½ teaspoon

about 15 dariole moulds, well greased

Sieve the flour into a bowl. Add the eggs, margarine and sugar. Beat the ingredients well together until they are completely blended. Divide the mixture in half. Mix the cocoa with a very little boiling water and add this to one amount. Stir the essence into the other. Drop alternate spoonsful of the mixtures into the moulds so that they are just over half full. Depending on the size, there will be between 12 and 15. Cover each one with a small piece of foil. Put them into a steamer placed over a pan of hot water and cook for about 30 minutes. The water should bubble gently and must not be allowed to run dry. Alternatively, the puddings may be cooked in the oven, in the same way as the Owl Madeleines (see page 154) when they can be cooked in batches. Serve with thin custard. *Makes about 15*

The puddings can be frozen but will take some time to reheat, so it is only worth it if there is extra cake mixture to be used up perhaps.

Dariole moulds are sometimes called castle pudding tins. Larger individual tins may be used but the cooking time must be increased correspondingly.

Orange Ring Pudding (see page 197); Castle Puddings (see above); Chocolate Bakewell Tart (see page 200)

Chocolate Bakewell Tart

Illustrated on page 199

Metric		Imperial
	Pastry case	
50 g	**margarine**	2 oz
25 g	**white fat**	1 oz
150 g	**plain flour**	5 oz
	Filling	
75 g	**jam**	3 tablespoons
50 g	**self-raising flour**	2 oz
30 ml	**Bournville cocoa**	1 tablespoon
50 g	**margarine**	2 oz
50 g	**caster sugar**	2 oz
1	**egg**	1
25 g	**ground almonds**	1 oz
2.5 ml	**almond essence**	$\frac{1}{2}$ teaspoon
	finely grated rind of $\frac{1}{2}$ lemon	

18-cm	**flan ring, on a baking tray**	7-inch

Make up the pastry by rubbing the fats into the flour, until the mixture resembles breadcrumbs. Add just enough cold water to bind the mixture together. Knead lightly and roll out the pastry on a floured board. Line the flan ring, being careful not to stretch the pastry or it will shrink. Keep the scraps for the trellis. Spread the jam in the base.

Sieve the flour and cocoa. Cream the margarine and sugar together and slowly beat in the egg. Fold in the sieved flour and cocoa and stir in the ground almonds, essence and the grated lemon rind. Spread the mixture evenly in the pastry case. Roll out the scraps of pastry, cut strips and arrange them in a trellis across the top. Stick the ends on to the flan with a little water. Bake in a fairly hot oven (200°C, 400°F, Gas Mark 6) for 15 minutes then reduce the heat to moderate (180°C, 350°F, Gas Mark 4) for a further 15 minutes or until cooked. Serve hot or cold. *Serves 6*

Wrap, label, seal and freeze the flan.

It is often handy to have pastry ready to use quickly. Measure out two or three times the basic recipe, rub the fats into the flour but do not add the water. Keep the rubbed-in mixture in a closed plastic container in the refrigerator, to use when required. It will keep for 2 months.

Veiled Apple Maidens

Illustrated on page 202

Fresh raspberries in season are particularly good in this recipe. Decorate with raspberries on top and mix some with the apples, or stew the raspberries lightly and use on their own.

Metric		Imperial
425-g can	**raspberries**	15-oz can
450 g	**cooking apples**	1 lb
25 g	**butter**	1 oz
30 ml	**sugar**	1 heaped tablespoon
175 g	**fresh brown breadcrumbs**	6 oz
75 g	**demerara sugar**	3 oz
20 ml	**Bournvita**	1 tablespoon
75 g	**Bournville Dark plain chocolate**	3 oz
125 ml	**double cream**	$\frac{1}{4}$ pint
80 ml	**top of the milk**	4 tablespoons
	or single cream	
6	**individual sundae glasses or a**	6
20-cm	**flan ring**	8-inch

This recipe can be served in individual glasses or as one ring.

Drain the raspberries and put about 60 ml/3 tablespoons of the juice into a saucepan. Peel, core and slice the apples. Add the apple slices to the pan with the butter and sugar. Stew carefully then purée the apple and cool. Mix the breadcrumbs, demerara sugar and Bournvita together. Grate the chocolate coarsely and add two-thirds. Whip the cream and top of the milk together. Spoon some of the breadcrumb mixture into each of the glasses. Add the raspberries to the apple purée and divide this between the glasses. Spread a thin layer of cream in each. Finish off with another layer of breadcrumbs. Leave the puddings at this stage until they are required.

Decorate with a spoonful of cream on each glass and the remaining chocolate.

If making one dish only, place the greased flan dish on a suitable sized serving plate. Press half the breadcrumb mixture on to the base then add the fruit. Spread a thin layer of cream over the top. Repeat the breadcrumb layer. Finish off by masking the top with all the remaining cream. Leave the pudding in the flan ring until it is required. Decorate with the grated chocolate.

This pudding is better made well in advance so that the fruit can soak into the breadcrumb mixture. *Serves 6*

Chocolate Queen of Puddings

Illustrated opposite

Metric		Imperial
550 ml	**milk**	1 pint
50 g	**butter**	2 oz
50 g	**Cadbury's drinking chocolate**	2 oz
125 g	**fresh breadcrumbs**	4 oz
3	**eggs, separated**	3
about 60 ml	**lemon curd**	2 rounded tablespoons
150 g	**caster sugar**	6 oz
750-ml	**pie dish, greased with butter**	1½-pint

Heat the milk with the butter and drinking chocolate. Place the breadcrumbs in the dish. Beat the egg yolks into the milk then pour over the breadcrumbs. Leave to stand for about 30 minutes if possible. Bake in a moderate oven (180°C, 350°F, Gas Mark 4) for about 40 minutes until set.

Spread the top with the lemon curd, or jam may be used. Whisk the egg whites really stiffly, fold in half the sugar and whisk again. Fold in the remaining sugar and pile the meringue on top of the base. Increase oven to very hot (230°C, 450°F, Gas Mark 8). Cook for about 5 minutes.

Serves 4

Bread Fingers

Illustrated opposite

Metric		Imperial
250 ml	**milk**	½ pint
25 g	**Cadbury's drinking chocolate**	1 oz
1	**egg**	1
6	**thick, large slices of bread**	6
	oil for frying	
50 g	**caster sugar**	2 oz
	assorted jam	

Mix a little ground cinnamon with the caster sugar.

Whisk the milk and drinking chocolate together in a saucepan while warming it. Off the heat, whisk in the egg. Cut the crusts off the bread slices then cut each slice into three finger shapes. Dip the bread fingers into the chocolate custard. Fry them on both sides in hot shallow oil, in a frying pan. Drain on kitchen paper. Dust with caster sugar and place a spoon of jam in the centre of each finger. Serve hot.

Makes 18

Chocolate Queen of Puddings (see above); Veiled Apple Maidens (see page 201); Bread Fingers (see above)

Hungarian Chocolate Mousse

Metric		Imperial
100 g	**Bournville Dark plain chocolate**	$3\frac{1}{2}$ oz
15 ml	**instant coffee**	3 teaspoons
30 ml	**water**	2 tablespoons
4	**egg whites**	4
100 g	**caster sugar**	4 oz

The mousse can be made several hours in advance and kept in a refrigerator until required.

Grate the chocolate and keep a little on one side for the decoration. Put the remaining chocolate, coffee and water into a bowl standing over a pan of hot, not boiling water. Stir occasionally until the chocolate is melted and the mixture is smooth. Whisk the egg whites until they stand in peaks. Whisk in half the sugar and continue whisking until it is just as stiff again. Fold in the remaining sugar and the chocolate mixture, using a figure of eight movement so that the minimum amount of air is knocked out of the egg whites. Make quite sure that all the egg white is folded in and does not show. Carefully divide between 4–6 glasses and sprinkle over the grated chocolate. *Serves 4–6*

Masked Coffee Cups

Illustrated on page 207

Metric		Imperial
500 ml	**milk**	1 pint
50 g	**semolina**	2 oz
15 ml	**instant coffee**	1 tablespoon
125 g	**caster sugar**	4 oz
	Sauce	
50 g	**soft brown sugar**	2 oz
25 g	**Bournville cocoa**	1 oz
125 ml	**milk**	$\frac{1}{4}$ pint
5 125-ml capacity	**moulds, rinsed with cold water**	5 $\frac{1}{4}$-pint capacity

If suitable moulds are not available, cups may be substituted. Use old cups, or the oven-to-table ware ones are ideal. Cool the mixture a little before putting it in, to avoid breaking the cold pottery.

Warm the milk in a saucepan then sprinkle in the semolina, coffee and sugar. Bring to the boil, stirring continuously. Reduce the heat and continue stirring and cooking for a few minutes to thicken the semolina. Divide between the prepared moulds and leave to cool and set.

Measure all the sauce ingredients into a pan. Stir over a low heat to dissolve the sugar then boil for a couple of minutes until the sauce is as thick as you require. Serve the sauce hot or cold over the turned out Coffee Cups. *Serves 5*

Bavarian Cream

Illustrated on page 195

If a plate or dish is sprinkled with a very little cold water before a pudding is turned out on to it, this makes the surface slippery and the pudding can be moved easily.

Metric		Imperial
2	**eggs, separated**	2
25 g	**caster sugar**	1 oz
100 g	**Bournville Dark plain chocolate**	$3\frac{1}{2}$ oz
250 ml	**milk**	$\frac{1}{2}$ pint
2.5 ml	**vanilla essence**	$\frac{1}{2}$ teaspoon
14 g	**gelatine**	$\frac{1}{2}$ oz
60 ml	**water**	3 tablespoons
125 ml	**whipping cream**	$\frac{1}{4}$ pint
2	**crystallised violets**	2
750-ml	**jelly mould, rinsed out with cold water**	$1\frac{1}{2}$-pint
	piping bag and star pipe	

Cream the egg yolks with the sugar until they are lighter in colour. Break up the chocolate and place it in a saucepan with the milk and vanilla essence. Whisk over a gentle heat until the chocolate has dissolved, without letting it boil. Whisk the milk into the egg yolks then return to the pan. Stir the custard over a gentle heat when the mixture should thicken enough to coat the back of the wooden spoon.

Dissolve the gelatine in the water and when quite liquid and clear, pour it into the chocolate custard. Leave in a cool place until the mixture begins to thicken. Whisk the egg whites stiffly and whip the cream. Fold one good spoonful of whipped cream and the egg whites into the mixture. Pour into the prepared mould and leave to set for several hours. Later turn the mould out on to a plate and decorate with remaining cream, piped in stars round the edge and on top. Finish with two crystallised violets — or use pieces of glacé cherry. *Serves 6*

Dreamy Mocha Dessert

Illustrated opposite

Metric		Imperial
75 g	soft margarine	3 oz
75 g	caster sugar	3 oz
25 g	Bournville cocoa, sieved	1 oz
50 g	hazelnuts or mixed nuts, chopped	2 oz
1	egg	1
20 ml	sherry	1 tablespoon
20 ml	top of the milk	1 tablespoon
200 ml	strong black coffee	7 fl oz
	1 packet (8) trifle sponges	
	Decoration	
75 g	soft margarine	3 oz
175 g	icing sugar, sieved	6 oz
	vanilla essence	
25 g	Bournville Dark plain chocolate, grated	1 oz
12	hazelnuts, blanched	12
	greaseproof paper	
1-kg	loaf tin, greased	2-lb
	piping bag and star pipe	

Fold a piece of greaseproof paper to fit the length of the tin, with the ends hanging out at either end. Grease the paper too. Cream the margarine and sugar until lighter in colour and texture. Beat in the sieved cocoa, chopped nuts and the egg. Keep the mixture on one side.

Mix the sherry and milk into the strong coffee. Dip 4 of the sponges into the coffee and lay them side by side on the base of the tin. Spread the cocoa mixture on top and to the sides. Dip the remaining sponges in coffee and press them level on top. Chill overnight.

To make the decoration, cream together the margarine, sieved icing sugar and a few drops of vanilla essence, adding a little milk if necessary to make it a spreading consistency. Dip the tin in warm water and invert the dessert on to a suitable plate. Spread the icing on top. Fill the piping bag with the star pipe attached and pipe stars round the top and bottom of the loaf shape. Decorate with 3 lines of grated chocolate, hazelnuts down the centre and at each corner.

Serves 8

Paradise Ring (see page 213); Dreamy Mocha Dessert (see above); Masked Coffee Cups (see page 204)

Banana Cream

Illustrated on page 227

Metric		Imperial
100 g	**Bournville Dark plain chocolate**	4 oz
125 ml	**double cream**	$\frac{1}{4}$ pint
125 ml	**natural yogurt**	$\frac{1}{4}$ pint
2	**large, very ripe bananas**	2

For a dinner party dessert, add 30 ml/2 tablespoons sherry.

Reserve two squares of chocolate. Melt the remainder in a bowl over a pan of hot water. Take off the heat and allow the melted chocolate to cool a bit. Whisk the cream and yogurt together until it will just hold its shape. Be careful not to over-whip the cream. Mash the bananas on a plate then fold them with the chocolate into the cream. Divide the cream between the glasses. Grate the remaining chocolate on top, covering the cream with quite a thick layer. Serve chilled.

Serves 4–5

Golden Crunch Layer

Illustrated on page 211

Metric		Imperial
75 g	**Bournville Dark plain chocolate**	3 oz
125 g	**butter**	4 oz
60 ml	**golden syrup**	3 tablespoons
125 g	**icing sugar, sieved**	4 oz
1	**small orange**	1
175 g	**cornflakes**	6 oz
125 ml	**double cream**	$\frac{1}{4}$ pint
125 ml	**single cream**	$\frac{1}{4}$ pint
410-g can	**peach slices**	$14\frac{1}{2}$-oz can
2 18-cm	**round shallow cake tins, well greased**	2 7-inch
	piping bag and star pipe	

Break the chocolate into pieces and melt it with the butter and syrup in a large pan. Stir in the sieved icing sugar and the finely grated rind of the orange. Crush the cornflakes slightly before adding them too. Stir well so that they are completely coated in chocolate. Divide the mixture evenly between the tins, flattening it a little with a palette knife; avoid crushing it too much. Leave in a cold place for a couple of hours, or overnight. Segment the orange for the decoration.

Whip the double and single cream together until it will hold its shape. Warm the bases of the cake tins quickly to loosen the chocolate mixture. Turn out one layer on to a clean surface and the other on to the dish from which it will be served. Pipe whirls of cream at intervals round the chocolate layer on the table. Spread the remaining cream on to the other layer. Divide the peach slices and orange segments between the two layers. Lift the decorated layer on top of the other and eat within an hour. *Serves 6*

Pears and Chocolate Sauce

Illustrated on page 211

For an easy and quick dessert, canned pear halves may be used. There is no comparison in the taste, especially when fresh pears are in season.

Metric		Imperial
225 g	**light soft brown or**	8 oz
	granulated sugar	
550 ml	**water**	1 pint
	juice of $\frac{1}{2}$ orange or lemon	
5-cm	**piece of cinnamon stick**	2-inch
6	**dessert pears**	6
	Sauce	
100 g	**Bournville Dark plain chocolate**	$3\frac{1}{2}$ oz
25 g	**butter**	1 oz
15 ml	**rum**	1 tablespoon
25 g	**soft brown sugar**	1 oz
15 ml	**lemon juice**	1 tablespoon
15–30 ml	**pear juice**	1–2 tablespoons
1	**large block vanilla ice cream**	1

Dissolve the sugar in the water in a deep pan then boil for about 2 minutes with the fruit juice and cinnamon stick added. Thinly peel the pears, leaving the stalks on where possible. Stand the pears upright in the syrup and poach them gently for about 15 minutes until they are tender. Tilt the lid on the pan to prevent all the water evaporating but do not allow it to boil over. Turn the pears occasionally so that they are cooked on all sides. Leave them to cool in the syrup.

To make the sauce, break the chocolate into a saucepan. Stir in the butter, rum, sugar, lemon juice and the pear juice. Heat gently until the chocolate has melted then, stirring continuously, bring the sauce to the boil and simmer for a minute. Put spoonsful of ice cream round the pears in individual dishes and pour the chocolate sauce over the top.

Serves 6

Snowy Chocolate Ring

Illustrated opposite

Metric		Imperial
25 g	**Bournville cocoa**	1 oz
125 g	**soft margarine**	4 oz
225 g	**caster sugar**	8 oz
	few drops of vanilla essence	
3	**eggs**	3
125 g	**self-raising flour, sieved**	4 oz
425-g can	**black cherries**	15-oz can
80 ml	**kirsch**	4 tablespoons
142 ml	**whipping cream**	$\frac{1}{4}$ pint
750-ml	**ring mould tin, well greased**	$1\frac{1}{2}$ pint

Blend the cocoa with just enough boiling water to make it into a thick paste. Cream the margarine with half the sugar until they are lighter in colour and texture. Add the vanilla essence. Beat in one whole egg and two egg yolks, reserving the whites for the meringue topping. Add the cocoa, then fold in the sieved flour. Turn into the prepared tin, level off the surface and bake in a moderately hot oven (190°C, 375°F, Gas Mark 5) for about 35 minutes. Leave the cake in the tin for a few minutes then loosen the edges and turn out on to a wire tray.

Drain the cherries but keep the juice. Stone the fruit. Place the cake upside down on an ovenproof plate that is big enough to allow the meringue as well. Soak the cake with kirsch and the cherry juice, pricking it with a skewer to allow the liquid to be absorbed properly. Leave for about an hour if possible. Whip the cream, fold in the stoned cherries and chill.

Fill the cake with the cream and spread the rest on top. Whisk the egg whites to the stiffness of meringue, fold in half the remaining sugar and whisk again until it will stand in peaks. Fold in all the sugar. Completely cover the cake with meringue, leaving no gaps at all. Bake in a very hot oven (230°C, 450°F, Gas Mark 8) for about 5 minutes until tinged with brown. Alternatively the dessert may be popped under a hot grill but the sides will not brown evenly. Serve immediately. *Serves 6*

The cake should be frozen without the cream filling or meringue topping. Wrap, label and seal. Defrost the cake before filling and covering.

To make this a more traditional Baked Alaska, fill the centre with scoops of ice cream and pile the cherries on top before covering with meringue. The cake may crack on top when baking but this does not matter.

Snowy Chocolate Ring (see above); Golden Crunch Layer (see page 208); Cherry Cascade (see page 212); Pears and Chocolate Sauce (see page 209)

Cherry Cascade

Illustrated on page 211

Metric		Imperial
1 packet	**sponge fingers**	1 packet
425-g can	**red cherries**	15-oz can
20 ml	**cherry brandy**	1 tablespoon
375 ml	**milk**	$\frac{3}{4}$ pint
30 g	**Bournville cocoa**	1 oz
50 g	**caster sugar**	2 oz
2	**eggs, separated**	2
14 g	**gelatine**	$\frac{1}{2}$ oz
40 ml	**water**	2 tablespoons
	angelica pieces	
1-kg	**loaf tin**	2-lb

If the custard does curdle, blend 10 ml/2 teaspoons of custard powder with a little milk. Add the curdled custard, return to the pan and bring to the boil, stirring continuously. If it is very bad, it may be necessary to whisk the mixture too.

Arrange the sponge fingers, sugar side downwards, in the base of the tin. You will need about 10, depending on the actual size of your tin. Drain the cherries and pour 125 ml/$\frac{1}{4}$ pint of the juice, mixed with the cherry brandy, over the fingers. Warm the milk, cocoa and sugar together then beat in the egg yolks. Stir with a wooden spoon and cook the custard gently until it thickens enough to coat the back of the spoon. Do not allow it to boil or it may curdle. Cool the custard. Meanwhile stone the cherries.

Dissolve the gelatine in the water and when it is quite clear, stir into the custard. Ideally the custard and gelatine should be at the same warm temperature. As the custard cools, it should thicken and when it does, fold in the stoned cherries, reserving some for the decoration. Whisk the egg whites stiffly and fold in so that there are no patches of white left, then pour the mixture into the tin. Chill until firm. Later turn the dessert on to an oblong plate and decorate with cherries in the shape of a flower, using angelica pieces for the stalks and leaves. Extra cherries may be arranged round the dessert if liked. Serve with single cream. *Serves 6–8*

Paradise Ring

Illustrated on page 207

The sponge fingers and cake may be frozen but not the assembled pudding.

This can be made with plain bought sponge fingers but the softer texture of home-made ones complement the chocolate mousse better. Gelatine mixtures tend to toughen in the refrigerator and are therefore better left to set in some other cool place.

Metric		Imperial
20	home-made Chocolate Sponge Fingers (see page 141)	20
1 18-cm	round sponge cake (see Whisked Sponge, page 193)	1 7-inch
175 g	Bournville Dark plain chocolate	6 oz
4	eggs, separated	4
15 ml	instant coffee	2 teaspoons
14 g	gelatine	$\frac{1}{2}$ oz
80 ml	water	4 tablespoons
125 ml	double cream	$\frac{1}{4}$ pint
80 ml	single cream or top of the milk	4 tablespoons
25 g	Bournville Dark plain chocolate	1 oz
20-cm	round loose-based cake tin	8-inch
at least 1 metre	pretty ribbon	at least $1\frac{1}{4}$ yards
	piping bag and star pipe	

Oil the cake tin lightly. Cut the ends off the sponge fingers so that they are all more or less the same size. Place the sponge cake in the centre of the tin then pack the sponge fingers in the gap round the edge, flat side on the tin. Melt the chocolate in a fairly large bowl over a pan of hot water then stir in the egg yolks and the instant coffee. Dissolve the gelatine in the water without boiling and when it is quite clear, pour into the chocolate mixture. Leave to cool slightly. Whisk the egg whites stiffly and fold into the chocolate mixture. Turn the mixture into the prepared tin and leave for several hours to set, not in a refrigerator.

Lightly whip the creams or top of the milk together until it will just hold its shape. Melt the small amount of chocolate. Spread cream over the chocolate mousse in the tin and drop in the chocolate, swirling it with a skewer to give a marbled effect. Carefully push up the base of the tin then slide the pudding on to a plate. Tie the ribbon round the sponge fingers which will help to keep them in place. Pipe any remaining cream round the base. *Serves 6–8*

Chocolate Ice Cream and Sauce

Illustrated opposite

Metric		Imperial
4	**egg yolks**	4
125 g	**caster sugar**	4 oz
550 ml	**milk**	1 pint
75 g	**Bournville Dark plain chocolate**	3 oz
5 ml	**vanilla essence**	1 teaspoon
125 ml	**double cream**	$\frac{1}{4}$ pint
	Sauce	
50 g	**Bournville Dark plain chocolate**	50 g
80 ml	**golden syrup**	4 tablespoons
	knob of butter	
	ice cream wafer biscuits	

If the sauce gets cold, it will thicken. Heat to melt it again.

Make the custard in a double boiler if possible. Otherwise, it must be cooked over a very slow heat so that the eggs do not curdle.

Beat the eggs and sugar together in the top of a double boiler. Add the milk and cook until the custard thickens, stirring occasionally. Grate the chocolate into the custard, add the vanilla essence and whisk until smooth. Cool the custard. Whip the cream, fold into the cold egg custard and pour into an ice cube tray, or a metal container. Place in a food freezer or the freezing compartment of the refrigerator. Beat the mixture two or three times before it hardens, to remove large ice crystals and make a smooth consistency. An ice cream maker used in the freezer avoids the necessity for any beating. Serve the ice cream with the chocolate sauce and ice cream wafers.

To make the sauce, break the chocolate into squares and heat with the syrup and butter. Leave until smooth then beat quickly. Serve over the scoops of ice cream. *Serves 6–8*

Chocolate Chip Ice Cream

Metric		Imperial
1 quantity	**Chocolate Ice Cream**	1 quantity
100 g	**Bournville Dark plain chocolate**	$3\frac{1}{2}$ oz
4	**Cadbury's Flakes from the Family Pack**	4

Make up the chocolate ice cream. Add the chocolate, chopped into small pieces before freezing. Serve with a Flake.

Chocolate Ice Cream and Sauce (see above); Nutty Chocolate Ice Cream (see page 216); Orange and Chocolate Ice Cream (see page 216); Ice Cream Pyramid (see page 216)

Nutty Chocolate Ice Cream

Illustrated on page 215

Metric		Imperial
1 quantity	**Chocolate Ice Cream**	1 quantity
125 g	**walnuts, halved**	4 oz

Make up the chocolate ice cream. Reserve a few of the best walnut halves for the top, chop the remainder and add to the ice cream before freezing. Serve with an ice cream wafer.

Ice Cream Pyramid

Illustrated on page 215

Metric		Imperial
1 quantity	**Chocolate Ice Cream and Sauce**	1 quantity
	sponge flan case	
6–8	**meringue halves**	6–8

Fill the sponge flan case with scoops of ice cream. Dot meringue halves over the top and pour on the chocolate sauce. For an easy alternative sauce melt 40 ml/2 tablespoons Cadbury's chocolate spread with 10 ml/2 teaspoons water.

Serves 6–8

Orange and Chocolate Ice Cream

Illustrated on page 215

Metric		Imperial
3	**egg yolks**	3
75 g	**caster sugar**	3 oz
275 ml	**milk**	$\frac{1}{2}$ pint
3	**oranges**	3
75 g	**Bournville Dark plain chocolate**	3 oz
5 ml	**vanilla essence**	1 teaspoon
125 ml	**double cream**	$\frac{1}{4}$ pint

Stir the egg yolks and sugar together in the top of a double boiler, or cook in a pan over an extremely slow heat. Add the milk and cook the custard, stirring gently until it thickens enough to coat the back of a wooden spoon. Do not let the custard get too hot or it will curdle.

Choose oranges with good skins. Carefully squeeze out the juice; there should be about 275 ml/$\frac{1}{2}$ pint. If not, make it up with concentrated orange drink. Retain the orange shells. Melt the chocolate in the orange juice and vanilla essence over a gentle heat. Do not let it get too hot. Pour the liquid into the egg custard and cool. Later, whip the cream and fold in. Pour into an ice cube tray or metal container and freeze. Beat several times before it hardens.

Scoop the ice cream into the orange shells—it can also be served on its own. Return to the freezer until required. Decorate with a chocolate leaf or perhaps a scented geranium leaf. *Serves about 6*

Sunbathing Penguins

Illustrated on page 127

Metric		Imperial
6	**bananas**	6
6	**Cadbury's Flake from the Family Pack**	6
25 g	**chopped nuts**	1 oz
2	**small egg whites**	2
100 g	**caster sugar**	$3\frac{1}{2}$ oz
	baking tray	
	nylon piping bag	
	medium star pipe	

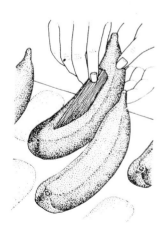

Select curved bananas with pointed stalk ends, to represent beaks. A tray of éclair tins, if available, are ideal to stand the bananas on to keep them upright. Crumpled foil can also be used to support the bananas.

Stand the bananas on the baking tray so that they curve upwards. Bake in a moderate oven (180 c, 350 f, gas 4) for 20–30 minutes until the bananas are black. Make a slit in the skin along the top edge of each banana then push in a Flake. Sprinkle over the nuts. Whisk the egg whites stiffly, add half the sugar and whisk again until just as stiff. Fold in remaining sugar. Fit the pipe into the piping bag and fill with the meringue. Pipe a close zig-zag over the top of each banana, using all the meringue, and stand them on the baking tray again. Increase the oven heat to hot (220 c, 425 f, gas 7) and bake the bananas for about 5 minutes to set the meringue. Serve immediately. *Makes 6*

Mont Blanc Nests

Illustrated opposite

Metric		Imperial
	Meringue nests	
2	**egg whites**	2
125 g	**caster sugar**	4 oz
	Filling	
100 g	**Bournville Dark plain chocolate**	3½ oz
2	**medium oranges**	2
225 g	**sweetened chestnut purée**	8 oz
125 ml	**double cream**	¼ pint
80 ml	**single cream or**	4 tablespoons
	top of the milk	
	baking tray covered with	
	Bakewell paper	
	piping bag and star vegetable pipe	
	plain icing pipe	

A dry pastry brush is useful for brushing off the orange rind from the grater. If you want to use one orange only, peel the grated orange half that has not been squeezed and decorate the nests with half a slice each.

Draw six or seven circles measuring about 6 cm/2½ inches in diameter on the back of the paper, leaving some space between them. Use a felt tipped pen so the lines will show through.

Whisk the egg whites really stiffly. Fold in half the sugar and whisk again until they are as stiff. Fold in the remaining sugar. Fill the piping bag, with the star pipe attached, with meringue and pipe a spiral inside each marked circle, working from the centre towards the outside. Pipe round the outside edge twice more, making an edge for the nest. There will be either six or seven, depending on the size of the egg whites. Dry out the nests in a very cool oven (110°C, 225°F, Gas Mark ¼) for at least 4 hours. When the top has quite set and is firm enough to handle, the nests may be lifted carefully and turned over to dry on the other side.

Break the chocolate into squares and melt it in a basin over a pan of hot water. Grate one orange finely and add the rind to the chocolate, with about 40 ml/2 tablespoons of the orange juice. Mash the chestnut purée into the mixture, making a smooth consistency. Fill the piping bag again, this time with a small plain pipe attached, then pipe the mixture unevenly into the meringue cases. Alternatively, use a spoon. Whip the creams together and pile a spoonful on top of each meringue nest. Decorate with a thin slice of orange curled on top. *Makes 6 or 7 nests*

Cherry and Chocolate Meringue (see page 221); Meringue Cascade (see page 224); Mont Blanc Nests (see above); Chocolate Meringues (see page 222)

Baked Marbled Cheesecake

Metric		Imperial
	Base	
125 g	**plain flour**	4 oz
	pinch of salt	
50 g	**caster sugar**	2 oz
50 g	**margarine**	2 oz
	Filling	
100 g	**Bournville Dark plain chocolate**	$3\frac{1}{2}$ oz
300 g	**cream cheese**	12 oz
175 g	**caster sugar**	6 oz
50 g	**plain flour**	2 oz
5 ml	**vanilla essence**	1 teaspoon
4	**eggs**	4
142-ml carton	**natural yogurt**	5-fl oz carton
20-cm	**round loose-based cake tin, greased**	8-inch

This cheesecake freezes well. Wrap in foil or waxed paper and a polythene bag. Seal, label and freeze.

The top may crack but this often happens with baked cheesecakes.

Sieve the flour with a pinch of salt. Stir in the sugar and rub in the margarine. Press the mixture together then press it on to the base of the tin. Bake in a fairly hot oven (200°C, 400°F, Gas Mark 6) for 10 minutes.

Melt the chocolate in a small bowl over a pan of hot water. Beat the cream cheese with the sugar in a large bowl then blend in the flour and vanilla essence. Beat in the eggs one at a time and finally add the yogurt. Pour half the filling over the base. Mix the melted chocolate into the remainder and drop in spoonsful over the vanilla filling. Lightly swirl the two colours together to give a marbled effect. Lower the oven temperature and bake in a warm oven (160°C, 325°F, Gas Mark 3) for 1 hour. Turn off the oven and leave the cheesecake in it for a further hour. Take out of the tin when cold. *Serves 6–8*

Cherry and Chocolate Meringue

Illustrated on page 219

Illustrated on page 219

The meringue shell will store well in a large airtight container.

Granulated sugar can easily be ground down in a blender to use as caster sugar for this type of recipe.

Metric		Imperial
	Meringue case	
3	**egg whites**	3
75 g	**caster sugar**	3 oz
75 g	**icing sugar**	3 oz
40 ml	**Bournville cocoa**	2 tablespoons
	Filling	
100 g	**Bournville Dark plain chocolate**	3½ oz
75 g	**cake crumbs**	3 oz
50 g	**ground almonds**	2 oz
425-g can	**black cherries**	15-oz can
60 ml	**cherry brandy or**	4 tablespoons
	cherry juice	
275 ml	**double cream**	½ pint

large baking tray covered
with Bakewell paper
piping bag and star pipe

Mark a 26-cm/10½-inch circle on the covered baking tray. Whisk the egg whites really stiffly then add the caster sugar and whisk again until it is as stiff. Fold in the icing sugar and cocoa sieved together. Fill the piping bag and pipe a continuous spiral to fill the space inside the marked circle. Pipe a second layer of overlapping·loops round the outer edge, to make a raised edge. Bake the meringue case in the lowest possible oven (110°C, 225°F, Gas Mark ¼) for about 5 hours, or overnight so that the meringue sets. It may be slightly soft in the middle but this does not really matter.

Grate the chocolate coarsely. Mix half of it with the cake crumbs and ground almonds. Melt the remaining grated chocolate and spread it inside the meringue case. Drain the cherries, reserve 8 or 9 cherries for the top and stone the remainder. Place the stoned cherries on top of the chocolate. Pile the cake crumb mixture on top and moisten it with the cherry brandy, or use cherry juice. Press it down slightly to make a fairly firm and flat top. Whip the cream until it will just hold its shape. Spread most of the cream over the top. Pipe a border round the edge and rosettes in the meringue loops. Arrange a whole cherry on top of each. Cut into about 10 pieces. *Serves 10*

Chocolate Meringues

Illustrated on page 219

Metric		Imperial
3	**egg whites**	3
75 g	**caster sugar**	3 oz
75 g	**icing sugar**	3 oz
25 g	**Bournville cocoa**	1 oz
	Decoration	
125 ml	**double cream**	$\frac{1}{4}$ pint
3	**Cadbury's Flakes**	3
4	**glacé cherries**	4
12	**paper cake cases**	12

	large piping bag and star	
	vegetable pipe	
	baking tray covered with	
	Bakewell paper	

Using a mixture of caster and icing sugar produces a really smooth and crumbly meringue.

Whisk the egg whites really stiffly (see photograph 1, opposite). An electric mixer is ideal to use as it aerates the egg whites well and therefore gives a larger volume. Add the caster sugar and continue whisking so that the meringue is as stiff again. Sieve the icing sugar and cocoa together and fold in (see photograph 2, opposite). At this stage, the mixture becomes rather dry but it will all mix in. Fill the piping bag and pipe rosettes on the prepared tray (see photograph 3, opposite). Make between 20 and 24; the exact number depends on the size of the eggs. Cook the meringues in a very cool oven (130°C, 250°F, Gas Mark $\frac{1}{2}$) for about 1 hour then lower the heat to the lowest possible temperature for another 4 or 5 hours to dry out the meringues. Lift them off the paper and store in an airtight tin until required.

Whip the cream with a little top of the milk if preferred, until it will just hold its shape. Place a pair of meringues into a paper case then pipe or spread cream in between (see photograph 4, opposite). Decorate with a piece of Flake, cutting each one into three pieces, and small pieces of cherry. Pair all the meringues in the same way.

Makes 10–12 meringue pairs

1 Whisk the egg whites as stiffly as possible until standing in peaks and almost dry in consistency.

2 With a metal spoon, fold in the Bournville cocoa and icing sugar, sieved together, using a figure-of-eight movement.

3 Hold the filled piping bag upright and pipe even-sized rosettes on the prepared baking tray.

4 Pair the meringues, place the pairs in the paper cases and pipe cream between them.

Meringue Cascade

Illustrated on page 219

Metric		Imperial
3	**egg whites**	3
75 g	**caster sugar**	3 oz
75 g	**icing sugar, sieved**	3 oz
10 ml	**instant coffee powder**	2 teaspoons
	Crème au beurre	
175 g	**unsalted butter**	6 oz
175 g	**granulated sugar**	6 oz
75 ml	**water**	2 fl oz
3	**egg yolks**	3
175 g	**Bournville Dark plain chocolate**	6 oz

**large baking tray covered
with Bakewell paper**

piping bag and star pipe

To make Gâteau Diane: divide the meringue mixture between three 15-cm/6-inch circles. Layer them up with the crème au beurre and decorate with stars piped round the top. 50 g/2 oz of finely ground roasted hazelnuts may also be added to the uncooked meringue.

Always use fresh egg whites to make meringues. If they have been kept in the refrigerator, allow them to come to room temperature before using.

Whisk the egg whites really stiffly. Mix the caster sugar and the sieved icing sugar together. Add half the sugar and continue whisking until the mixture is as stiff again. Fold in the remaining sugar. Fill the piping bag with half the meringue and pipe whirls on to the prepared tray. Fold the coffee powder in to the remaining meringue and pipe on to the baking tray too. They spread slightly more than the plain meringues. Dry out the meringues in a very cool oven (110°C, 225°F, Gas Mark ¼) for about 4 hours until they are firm and will lift off easily. Store the meringues in an airtight container until they are required.

Make the special chocolate butter cream by softening the butter and beating it in a bowl. Dissolve the sugar in the water over gentle heat, in a saucepan. When all the granules have disappeared, boil rapidly until the short thread stage is reached. To test this, oil your first finger and thumb, dip a spoon in to the boiling syrup and touch it. When it is ready, you should be able to draw out a short thread before it breaks. It is important that this stage is reached otherwise the crème au beurre will not thicken enough.

Beat the egg yolks together using an electric mixer if available. Pour on the sugar syrup very slowly and continue beating as the mixture thickens and becomes much paler in colour. When all the syrup has been added, beat in the butter a spoonful at a time. Melt all but 50 g/2 oz of the chocolate in a bowl over hot water and add this too. The crème au beurre may now be left in the refrigerator for several days if necessary.

To assemble the dessert, spread the meringues with the chocolate crème au beurre which should not be too cold or it will be difficult to handle. Pile them up on an attractive dish, mixing the plain and coffee meringues. Grate the remaining chocolate and sprinkle it liberally over the top. The dessert may be assembled the day ahead and is nice to eat when it is slightly softer. *Serves at least 8*

Silky Crunch Pie

Substitute Cadbury's Dairy milk chocolate for the Bournville Dark plain chocolate if a milk chocolate flavour is preferred.

Metric		Imperial
	Biscuit crust base	
175 g	digestive biscuits	6 oz
50 g	butter	2 oz
25 g	caster sugar	1 oz
	Filling	
25 g	butter	1 oz
25 g	cornflour	1 oz
25 g	caster sugar	1 oz
375 ml	milk	$\frac{3}{4}$ pint
75 g	Bournville Dark plain chocolate	3 oz
	Decoration	
125 ml	double cream	$\frac{1}{4}$ pint
	small packet Cadbury's Buttons	
18-cm	shallow dish	7-inch
	piping bag and star pipe	

Crush the biscuits but do not make them too fine as this makes the crust rather dense and heavy. Melt the butter in a saucepan. Stir in the crushed biscuits and the sugar. Press the mixture on to the base and up the sides of the dish.

Melt the butter for the filling, in a saucepan. Blend in the cornflour with the sugar then gradually add the milk. Stir continuously while bringing the sauce to the boil and cook for a couple of minutes to thicken. Take the pan off the heat. Break up the chocolate and stir it into the hot sauce until melted. Pour the filling into the biscuit crust and leave it to set.

Whip the cream until it will hold its shape. Pipe rosettes round the edge of the pudding and decorate with the Buttons. *Serves 5–6*

Ice Mountain

Illustrated opposite

Metric		Imperial
200 g	**Bournville Dark plain chocolate**	7 oz
40 ml	**sugar**	2 tablespoons
60 ml	**lime juice cordial**	3 tablespoons
12	**trifle sponges, or**	12
250 g	**sponge cake**	9 oz
2	**eggs, separated**	2
125 ml	**double cream**	$\frac{1}{4}$ pint
125 ml	**single cream**	$\frac{1}{4}$ pint
1.5-litre	**pudding basin**	$2\frac{1}{2}$-pint

Reserve two squares of chocolate. Melt the remainder in a basin over a pan of hot water, with the sugar and lime juice. Meanwhile split all the trifle sponges in half to make thin pieces. Line the basin with the soft spongy side of the cake on the outside. Fill in the gaps with pieces of cake cut to fit. When the chocolate has melted, add the egg yolks, making sure the mixture is not too hot. Whisk the egg whites stiffly. In a separate bowl, whip half the amount of both creams together quite stiffly. Add the chocolate to the cream then fold in the whisked egg whites. Spoon some of the mixture into the basin covering the sponge in the bottom. Arrange a layer of sponge on top, again filling in the gaps. Repeat these processes, ending with sponge. All the chocolate mixture should be used up. Put a plate on top, the same size as the top of the bowl. Press it down with weights. Leave in the refrigerator for a day.

Ease a knife down the sides of the bowl then turn out the pudding on to a plate. Whip the remaining cream and spread it quite thinly over the pudding. Cover with grated chocolate. Cut into about 6 wedges. *Serves 6–7*

Fondue (see page 194); Chocolate Sponge Fingers (see page 141); Ice Mountain (see above); Banana Cream (see page 208)

Pirates' Puddings

Illustrated on page 78

Metric		Imperial
50 g	sponge cake	2 oz
1 (411-g)	can fruit cocktail	1 (14½-oz)
1	strawberry flavour jelly	1
1 (150-g)	carton strawberry yogurt	1 (5-oz)
50 g	Bournville Dark plain chocolate, grated	50 g
16	seedless raisins	16
8	small walnut pieces	8
3	glacé cherries, sliced	3
8	ring biscuits from Cadbury's	8
	Bournville Assorted	
8	waxed paper trifle cases	8

If it is easier, the jelly can be left in a cold place until almost set before pouring over the cake and fruit, in which case it can all be added at once. These novel trifles are popular with younger children who like the tanginess of the jelly.

Divide the cake between the trifle cases. Drain the fruit, reserving the syrup to make up the jelly. Add enough water to the syrup to give just over 275 ml/½ pint. Pour this liquid into a saucepan. Add the broken up jelly tablet and stir over low heat until dissolved. Do not allow the jelly to boil. Remove from the heat and allow to cool. Whisk in the yogurt. Spoon the fruit over the cake and pour half the jelly on top. Leave in the refrigerator to thicken so that the fruit does not rise, but do not put the reserved jelly in the refrigerator. Later, pour the remaining jelly on top and leave to set completely.

Sprinkle the chocolate on for hair, arrange raisins as eyes, a piece of walnut for a nose and a slice of cherry for a mouth. Cut the biscuits in half and stick in on either side of the faces. Make them all in the same way. Chill the puddings until ready to eat. *Makes 8*

Frogland

Illustrated on page 127

Depending on the size of the bowl or the number of children to feed, double the amount of jelly and increase the frogs and marshmallow flowers so that there is one of each for each person.

Metric		Imperial
1	**lime flavour jelly**	1
	blue food colouring	
125 g	**plain butter icing (page 21)**	4 oz
10 ml	**Bournville Cocoa**	2 teaspoons
	yellow food colouring	
1 packet	**Cadbury's Buttons**	1 packet
5	**Cadbury's Creme Eggs**	5
5	**glacé cherries**	5
1	**chocolate bun (page 21)**	1
5 or 6	**marshmallows**	5 or 6
14 g	**angelica**	$\frac{1}{2}$ oz
	large shallow glass bowl	
2	**star pipes**	2
2 or 3	**greaseproof paper piping bags**	2 or 3

Make up the jelly as directed on the packet, using slightly less water to give a firm set. Add a little blue food colouring to represent a pond colour, then pour the jelly into the bowl and leave to set.

Have the butter icing ready. Blend the cocoa with enough boiling water to make a thick paste and cool before mixing into one-third of the butter icing. Add yellow food colouring to the remaining amount, making some darker if liked. Cut the tips off the piping bags, drop in the pipes and fill with the different coloured icings. Pipe a chocolate star on ten Buttons, arrange them next to each other in pairs with the butter icing on top, then stand a Creme Egg on top. Complete each 'frog' by piping a line of pale butter icing at one end for the mouth and placing two cherry halves, secured with a little butter icing, above for the protruding eyes. Arrange the frogs on the set jelly, standing one on the cake.

Snip the marshmallows into flowers and pipe a star in the centre of each. Stick them on to the jelly with butter icing and arrange in clusters. Decorate with angelica diamonds and longer pieces of angelica to represent reeds sticking out of the jelly. Additional stars of butter icing and halved Buttons may be put round the edge of the jelly. *Serves 5*

Sweets and Candies

Sweet making has become rather a specialised hobby and there are several complete books devoted to the subject. We are lucky enough to have a very high standard of confectionery and sugar products available from manufacturers, and Cadbury's is one of the largest. The high degree of technology and skill involved in tempering chocolate or getting the sugar boil right, takes years to perfect. Coating fondants smoothly with chocolate, pulling sugar and making Easter eggs are better left to the experts. We have therefore not tried to compete with commercial confectionery and have given recipes here that can easily be made at home, without any special equipment.

Scrumptious Squares

Illustrated opposite

Metric		Imperial
	Base	
25 g	**caster sugar**	1 oz
150 g	**plain flour**	5 oz
125 g	**butter**	4 oz
	Filling	
125 g	**butter or margarine**	4 oz
125 g	**light soft brown sugar**	4 oz
40 ml	**golden syrup**	2 tablespoons
1	**small can condensed milk**	1
2.5 ml	**vanilla essence**	$\frac{1}{2}$ teaspoon
175 g	**Bournville Dark plain chocolate**	6 oz

18-cm	**square shallow cake tin, greased**	7-inch

Add the sugar to the flour then rub in the butter until it resembles breadcrumbs. Knead slightly then press the shortbread mixture into the tin. Bake in a moderate oven (180°C, 350°F, Gas Mark 4) for 25 minutes. Cool in the tin.

Stir the butter, brown sugar, syrup and condensed milk together in a heavy based pan over a gentle heat, until dissolved. Now boil for 7 minutes but keep stirring to prevent the fudge catching on the bottom. Add the vanilla essence then beat with a wooden spoon, off the heat, until cool and shiny. Pour over the base in the tin. When cold, melt the chocolate in a bowl over hot water and spread over the fudge. When cool, cut into squares. *Makes 49*

Quick Chocolate Fudge (see page 236); Coconut Ice (see page 233); Surprise Bites (see page 232); Truffles (see page 232); Mallow Cherry Cushions (see page 237); Scrumptious Squares (see above)

230

Surprise Bites

Illustrated on page 231

Metric		Imperial
50 g	**butter**	1½ oz
30 ml	**Bournville cocoa**	2 tablespoons
90 ml	**condensed milk**	3 tablespoons
50 g	**soft brown sugar**	2 oz
175 g	**desiccated coconut**	6 oz
123-g packet	**marshmallows**	4.34-oz packet

This is a recipe which children will enjoy making and find fairly easy to do.

Melt the butter in a saucepan. Add the cocoa, condensed milk and sugar and heat until melted, stirring continuously. Off the heat, add all but 25 g/1 oz of the coconut. Divide mixture equally into 15 and flatten the pieces between your hands. Mould this round the marshmallows, forming balls. Toss in the remaining coconut. Allow to harden slightly before they are eaten. Keep in an airtight container until required.

Makes 15

Truffles

Illustrated on page 231

Metric		Imperial
175 g	**Bournville Dark plain chocolate**	6 oz
40 ml	**brandy or fruit squash**	2 tablespoons
30 g	**unsalted butter**	1½ oz
50 g	**icing sugar, sieved**	2 oz
50 g	**ground almonds**	2 oz
8	**glacé cherries, halved**	8
16	**small sweet paper cases**	16

Truffles may be frozen without the cherries but this is not usually necessary as they keep well in a cool place. The liquor taste and smell disappears in the freezer. Pack carefully, seal and label.

For a different effect, roll some of the truffles in Cadbury's drinking chocolate or Bournville cocoa.

Break up two-thirds of the chocolate into a bowl and place this over a pan of hot water. Add the brandy and leave to melt. Take off the heat and stir in the butter, which should not be too hard. Mix in the sieved icing sugar and the almonds so that it is well blended. Leave in a cool place if necessary until the mixture is firm enough to handle. Divide into about 16 even-sized pieces and roll into balls. Grate the remaining chocolate, place on a piece of greaseproof paper and roll the truffles in it. Pop each one into a paper case and press half a cherry into the top. *Makes 16*

Ruffled Robins

Metric		Imperial
1 quantity	**Truffles mixture**	1 quantity
5	**glacé cherries, halved**	5
25 g	**flaked almonds**	1 oz
	angelica pieces	

Divide the truffle mixture into 10 slightly larger balls. Roll them in grated Bournville plain chocolate. Stick half a glacé cherry on one side of each ball, with 2 flaked almonds just above for the 'beak'. Make 'tails' from the angelica.

Makes 10

Coconut Ice

Illustrated on page 231

The coconut ice is not too stiff. If a harder texture is preferred, add extra coconut or cocoa.

Metric		Imperial
200 ml	**condensed milk**	8 tablespoons
350 g	**icing sugar**	12 oz
175 g	**desiccated coconut**	6 oz
	few drops of cochineal food colouring	
20 ml	**Bournville cocoa**	1 tablespoon

18-cm	**square cake tin, greased**	7-inch

Mix the condensed milk and the icing sugar together in a bowl. Stir in the coconut. Divide the mixture in half. Add a few drops of the colouring slowly to one amount, making it pink. Spread this in the tin. Sieve the cocoa into the remaining mixture and stir in well. Spread on top of the pink coconut ice in the tin, levelling the surface. Leave overnight to set. Cut into squares. *Makes 36 pieces*

Mallow Fudge

Illustrated opposite

You do not need a sugar thermometer to make this recipe. Have a saucer of *cold* water near and every so often, drop a little mixture into the water. When ready, the fudge will set quite firmly as it drops in the water. If in doubt boil for a couple of minutes longer. Beat fudge really hard to get the correct shine and silky texture.
For plain chocolate fudge omit marshmallows.

Metric		Imperial
450 g	**granulated sugar**	1 lb
50 g	**butter**	2 oz
25 g	**Bournville Cocoa**	1 oz
40 ml	**honey**	2 tablespoons
200 g	**condensed milk**	7 oz
80 ml	**water**	4 tablespoons
125 g	**marshmallows**	4 oz
18-cm	**square shallow cake tin, greased**	7-in

Measure all the ingredients, except the marshmallows, into quite a large saucepan. Using a wooden spoon, stir continuously over a very low heat until *all* the sugar granules have dissolved. Slowly bring to the boil, then cook steadily, but do not burn, until the soft ball stage is reached: that is, 114 c/238 f on a sugar thermometer. Stir the mixture only occasionally. Take the pan off the heat and immediately beat really hard with the wooden spoon until the fudge thickens, is smooth and not at all grainy.

Whilst still hot, add the marshmallows to the pan, then pour the fudge into the prepared tin. The marshmallows will melt slightly, swirl them through a couple of times. Leave to set overnight, then cut into squares. *Makes 36 pieces*

Praline Swirls

Illustrated opposite

For a special occasion, stir in a spoonful of brandy, rum or liqueur.

Metric		Imperial
100 g	**Bournville Dark plain chocolate**	3½ oz
50 g	**butter**	2 oz
1.25 ml	**vanilla essence**	¼ teaspoon
75 g	**icing sugar, sifted**	3 oz
25 g	**hazelnuts, finely ground**	1 oz
18	**crystallised violets**	18
18	**paper sweet cases**	18
	nylon piping bag	
	medium star pipe	

Cadbury's Chocolate Box (see page 88); Mallow Fudge; Praline Swirls

Break up the chocolate and melt it, with the butter, in a pan over a low heat. Off the heat, stir in the essence, then the icing sugar and hazelnuts. Beat well to thoroughly mix. Fill the piping bag with this mixture, then pipe a good whirl into each of the cases placed on a tray. Place a violet on each and refrigerate for at least 30 minutes. *Makes 18*

Flake Envelopes

Illustrated on page 78

Metric		Imperial
225 g	**marzipan**	8 oz
	red and green food colouring	
	caster sugar	
1	**Cadbury's Flake Family Pack**	1

Knead the marzipan until soft, then roll out quite thinly on a sugared surface. Cut into 6.5-cm/2½-in squares, working the scraps together to roll and cut out again in between, making 18 squares in all. Colour a small amount of the remaining marzipan bright red and a slightly larger piece green. Roll very small amounts of the red marzipan into holly berries then coat them in sugar. Roll out the green marzipan into a flat sheet and cut into narrow strips, as illustrated, to make the leaves. Pinch out the edges of the leaves to represent holly.

Lay a Flake diagonally across each marzipan square and fold up the corners, pressing them together over the Flake. Press a marzipan holly leaf and berries on to each as shown in the picture. Sprinkle with sugar. *Makes 18*

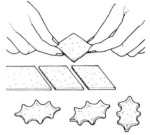

Make fairly thick flat strips of green marzipan, then cut out diamond shapes about 2.5 cm/1 in. in length. Pinch the ends and edges for the holly leaf points and twist them so that they curl up realistically. Leave the leaves to dry for a short time.

Quick Chocolate Fudge

Illustrated on page 231

Metric		Imperial
100 g	**Bournville Dark plain chocolate**	3½ oz
50 g	**butter**	2 oz
30 ml	**milk**	2 tablespoons
5 ml	**vanilla essence**	1 teaspoon
425 g	**icing sugar**	1 lb
18-cm	**square shallow tin,**	7-inch
	lightly greased	

Break up the chocolate and melt it with the butter in a bowl placed over a pan of hot water. Stir occasionally to help the chocolate to soften. Take the bowl off the heat. Stir in the milk and vanilla essence then gradually beat in the icing sugar, sieving it as you do so. Blend thoroughly before turning the fudge into the prepared tin. Level the surface with a knife. Leave the fudge to get cold then cut into squares. *Makes 36 pieces*

Mallow Cherry Cushions

Illustrated on page 231

Sprinkle the surface with icing sugar when rolling out the sweets.

Metric		Imperial
	Centre	
50 g	**butter**	2 oz
40 ml	**Bournville cocoa**	2 tablespoons
50 g	**icing sugar, sieved**	2 oz
25 g	**ground almonds**	1 oz
15 ml	**brandy or sherry**	1 tablespoon
	Outer layer	
50 g	**granulated sugar**	2 oz
50 g	**butter**	2 oz
30 ml	**water**	2 tablespoons
123-g packet	**marshmallows**	4.34-oz packet
125 g	**icing sugar, sieved**	4 oz
25 g	**walnuts, chopped**	1 oz
25 g	**glacé cherries, chopped**	1 oz

Make the centre first. Melt the butter in a saucepan and cook the cocoa in it. Take the pan off the heat and stir in the sieved icing sugar, ground almonds and the brandy. Chill the mixture so that it can harden.

Dissolve the granulated sugar in the butter and water over low heat and when it is quite clear, boil for about 5 minutes. Take the pan off the heat. Stir in the marshmallows and when they have melted, add the sieved icing sugar and the chopped walnuts and cherries, mixed together. Cool this mixture too. When it is cold and firm enough to handle, divide the mixture in half and roll into two strips, each measuring about 33 cm × 7.5 cm/13 inches × 3 inches. Halve the mixture for the centre too and form into two rolls the same length. Wrap the flat strips round the chocolate rolls, joining the edges by rolling them slightly. Cut each of the rolls in half, making four shorter ones. Wrap these individually in waxed or greaseproof paper and leave in the refrigerator to harden. Later cut into slices. *Makes 24*

Index

Cadbury's